# Protecting Trade Secrets

# Protecting Trade Secrets

**Seth C. Oranburg**

PROFESSOR OF LAW
UNIVERSITY OF NEW HAMPSHIRE
FRANKLIN PIERCE SCHOOL OF LAW

DIRECTOR, PROGRAM ON ORGANIZATIONS,
BUSINESS, AND MARKETS
NYU LAW'S CLASSICAL LIBERAL INSTITUTE

CAROLINA ACADEMIC PRESS
Durham, North Carolina

ISBN: 978-1-5310-3437-5
eISBN: 978-1-5310-3438-2
LCCN: 2025950107

Carolina Academic Press
700 Kent Street
Durham, North Carolina 27701
(919) 489-7486
www.cap-press.com

Printed in the United States of America

# Contents

# Acknowledgments

Thanks to Ryan Vacca. Ryan is now the John D. Lawson Professor of Law and Associate Dean for Academic Affairs at the University of Missouri School of Law. More importantly (to me), he was my cherished colleague at the University of New Hampshire Franklin Pierce School of Law. When a curricular need for me to teach Trade Secrets thrust me into the intellectual property world, Ryan generously shared his materials and coached me on teaching effectively. Ryan's confidence in my abilities and his passion for the subject sparked my love for the trade secret-contract connection. Over time, I reshaped the course to reflect my transactional focus, distinct from Ryan's litigation-centered approach, as you will see in this book. And while our teaching styles diverged, Ryan still provided a thorough review of this book on its own terms, offering invaluable comments that greatly improved this work while preserving my vision. A great mentor and true leader helps others shine in their unique way. Ryan, through his kindness and humility, inspires countless students and colleagues. I'm grateful to be numbered among them. And thank you, Ryan, for the salsa—perhaps we'll keep that our own trade secret.

Thanks also to my UNH FP Hybrid JD students who reviewed this manuscript. I feel deeply honored by the opportunity not only to teach but also to learn from this diverse and talented "non-traditional" cohort. In particular I thank Vinh Nguyen and Eric Lee for thoughtful and constructive comments.

## Why This Book

This book offers a practice-forward complement to the traditional casebook. It is built around a single, organizing insight: the best way to understand trade secret law is to design a plan that applies it. Rather than starting with abstract theory and hoping students can extrapolate practice, this book begins with a practical challenge—how to protect a company's trade secrets—and develops deeper understanding along the way. The result is a clear, concrete, and rigorous guide to one of the most complex and consequential areas of modern intellectual property law.

Each chapter scaffolds learning around a specific output: identifying secrets, developing policies, allocating responsibilities, and responding to legal and ethical challenges. This approach helps students grasp not only what the law says but also what it demands in real-world settings. The book draws on leading scholarship, doctrinal sources, and business strategy literature to integrate theory with application.

It is especially well-suited for experiential courses, where students learn by doing, but its modular structure and doctrinal foundations also make it adaptable for seminars or advanced classes in intellectual property or business law. It supports a range of assessment methods, from traditional exams to simulation-based deliverables, and culminates in a comprehensive capstone: a polished, portfolio-ready Trade Secret Protection Plan for a simulated client.

## How This Book Works

This book is structured to support flexible, experiential, and simulation-friendly instruction while remaining grounded in core legal doctrine. It prepares students to practice trade secret law by building a trade secret protection plan, step-by-step, applying legal principles in context, and producing professional-grade work product by course's end.

The company-side transactional planning lens offers students a coherent introduction to trade secret law through the perspective of safeguarding a business's proprietary knowledge. Although it acknowledges that practitioners may also represent employees, license trade secrets, or litigate disputes, the book deliberately focuses on one core aspect of IP practice to support a learn-by-doing method and build confidence before branching into adjacent domains.

Each chapter integrates concise doctrinal explanations, real-world examples, and application-oriented prompts. Key terms and legal tests are introduced clearly, with references to foundational cases, statutes, and scholarly debates. Case excerpts provide optional depth for students who want to explore precedent without interrupting the flow of applied learning.

Assignments, reflection prompts, and workshop exercises are interwoven throughout, enabling instructors to use the book in flipped, hybrid, or traditional classroom formats. Chapters are both modular and cumulative, allowing instructors to follow the full sequence or select only those that align with specific course objectives. By preparing students not just to understand trade secret law but also to implement it with clarity, creativity, and strategic judgment, the book serves as a bridge between classroom and practice.

Trade secret law is one of the most vital pillars of modern intellectual property law. By anchoring doctrine in concrete outputs, this book invites students to treat trade secret protection not as a compliance task but rather as a deliberate strategy for long-term value creation.

# Protecting Trade Secrets

# Chapter 1
# Understanding Trade Secret Law

Trade secrets are perhaps the most powerful—and the most precarious—form of intellectual property. They offer protection without registration, without formal procedures, and without expiration. A trade secret can remain exclusive for decades, but only if its owner keeps it that way. The law does not create trade secrets; it recognizes and enforces them after the fact. This makes trade secret law both deceptively simple and intensely practical. It is a body of law that rewards vigilance, structure, and foresight.

The modern definition of "trade secret" is found in the Uniform Trade Secrets Act (UTSA), which has been adopted by 48 states.

> **DEFINITION OF "TRADE SECRET"**
>
> UTSA § 1(4)
>
> "Trade secret" means information, including a formula, pattern, compilation, program, device, method, technique, or process, that:
>
> (a) Derives independent economic value, actual or potential, from not being generally known to, and not being readily ascertainable by proper means by, other persons who can obtain economic value from its disclosure or use; and
>
> (b) Is the subject of efforts that are reasonable under the circumstances to maintain its secrecy.

New York relies on common law principles, as reflected in the Restatement (First) of Torts § 757, which similarly defines a trade secret as any formula, pattern, device, or compilation of information used in one's business that provides a competitive advantage and requires reasonable efforts to maintain its secrecy. North Carolina has not formally adopted the UTSA, but many practitioners believe its state laws are effectively similar to the UTSA is most respects.

A core concept in how law defines trade secrets is "reasonable" efforts. Trade secret law does not demand absolute secrecy or perfect protection. Rather, it requires safeguards that are appropriate and proportionate to the context. But how much effort is enough to earn legal protection? As with many legal standards, the answer is: it depends. Depends on what? That is the question this book aims to answer by showing what businesses must do to build, maintain, and defend their trade secrets in practice.

Unlike patents or trademarks, trade secrets do not depend on public notice or overt use. Their value comes from being kept quiet. A process for manufacturing composite materials, a pricing algorithm, a customer list, or a proprietary training manual can qualify as a trade secret so long as it meets the legal definition and is subject to reasonable efforts to maintain its secrecy. That is where the real challenge lies: protecting that which is unseen, often across departments, locations, vendors, and even borders.

While patent law gives patent holders broad rights to exclude others from independent development or reverse engineering on patented inventions, trade secret law gives trade secret holders the narrow right to sue for "misappropriation," which is also defined in the UTSA.

## DEFINITION OF "MISAPPROPRIATION"

UTSA § 1(2)

"Misappropriation" means:

(a) Acquisition of a trade secret of another by a person who knows or has reason to know that the trade secret was acquired by improper means; or

(b) Disclosure or use of a trade secret of another without express or implied consent by a person who:

(1) Used improper means to acquire knowledge of the trade secret; or

(2) At the time of disclosure or use, knew or had reason to know that his knowledge of the trade secret was derived from or through a person who had utilized improper means to acquire it; or acquired under circumstances giving rise to a duty to maintain its secrecy or limit its use; or derived from or through a person who owed a duty to the person seeking relief to maintain its secrecy or limit its use; or

(3) Before a material change of his position, knew or had reason to know that it was a trade secret and that knowledge of it had been acquired by accident or mistake.

The key word in the misappropriation definition is "improper." There are proper means of acquiring, using, and disclosing others' trade secrets, which are not prohibited by trade secret law. However, upon a showing that some information is a trade secret that has been misappropriated by improper acquisition, improper use, or improper disclosure, the court will award remedies. A common remedy for misappropriation is an injunction that stops or prevents misappropriation.

**INJUNCTIVE RELIEF**

UTSA § 2

Actual or threatened misappropriation may be enjoined.

Alternatively, or additionally, courts can order a misappropriator to pay money damages for the harm.

**DAMAGES**

UTSA § 3(1)

. . . Damages can include both the actual loss caused by misappropriation and the unjust enrichment caused by misappropriation . . . [or] a reasonable royalty for a misappropriator's unauthorized disclosure or use of a trade secret.

In cases of "willful and malicious" misappropriation, courts may award "exemplary" damages of up to twice the amount of actual damages in addition to the compensatory award, effectively allowing treble damages in total. Courts may also award attorneys' fees to the prevailing party where a misappropriation claim or defense was brought in bad faith.

The Defend Trade Secrets Act (DTSA) creates a federal civil cause of action for trade secret misappropriation and largely mirrors the substantive provisions of the UTSA as adopted by most states. The DTSA also includes two notable features absent from most state laws. First, it authorizes "ex parte civil seizure," an extraordinary remedy that allows a court to order the seizure of property without advance notice to the accused party, but only in exceptional circumstances where standard injunctions would be inadequate to prevent the immediate and irreparable dissemination of a trade secret.

Second, the DTSA expressly provides for extraterritorial application, permitting claims against acts of misappropriation occurring outside the United States so long as the offender is a US person (which has a broad meaning, including any natural person, corporation, business trust, estate, trust, partnership, association, joint venture, government, governmental subdivision or agency, or any other legal or commercial entity) or the misappropriation has a sufficient nexus to US commerce.

**EXTRATERRITORIALITY**

18 USC § 1837

This chapter [18 USCS §§ 1831 et seq.] also applies to conduct occurring outside the United States if—

(1) the offender is a natural person who is a citizen or permanent resident alien of the United States, or an organization organized under the laws of the United States or a State or political subdivision thereof; or

(2) an act in furtherance of the offense was committed in the United States.

Two deceptively complex and essential questions lie within this relatively straightforward statutory framework. First, what counts as improper means of acquiring, using, or disclosing a trade secret? This *ex post* inquiry (litigated after the fact) often turns on business norms, industry expectations, and case-specific judgments about fairness and intent. Second, what qualifies as reasonable efforts to protect a secret in the first place? This *ex ante* question (regarding steps taken before any misappropriation occurs) demands proactive safeguards: legal, operational, and cultural. The chapters that follow will equip you to navigate both dimensions with practical insight and strategic clarity.

This opening chapter lays the foundation for understanding trade secrets as both a legal and business concept. It begins with the historical origins of trade secret doctrine and then defines what qualifies for protection. From there, it examines the meaning of misappropriation and surveys the remedies available when secrecy is lost. Along the way, it introduces key cases and legal standards that form the backbone of modern trade secret practice.

Above all, this chapter establishes the central premise of the book: trade secret protection is not a passive entitlement. It is an active process. Everything that follows will build on this insight.

# 1.1. Introduction to Trade Secret Law

Trade secrets are perhaps the least known of the major intellectual property forms. They depend entirely on secrecy. Owners must protect their confidential business information from public view rather than relying on government registration. If the secret leaks out, the law usually cannot restore its exclusivity. Yet, when properly guarded, trade secrets can preserve a significant competitive edge for as long as the information remains hidden. Examples include manufacturing methods, specialized formulas, customer lists, or other commercially valuable data that is not generally known in the industry.

Historically, societies recognized that exclusive knowledge fosters innovation. Medieval guilds protected recipes, formulas, and skills to secure their economic positions. Early American courts likewise enforced agreements and duties not to misuse confidential information, well before modern statutes described "trade secrets" by name. Two 19th-century Massachusetts cases—*Peabody v. Norfolk* and *Vickery v. Welch*—are among the most influential of these early decisions. They show how courts began treating secret commercial knowledge as an asset worthy of legal protection, even without a patent.

### LEGAL PROTECTION OF SECRET PROCESSES

*Peabody v. Norfolk*
98 Mass. 452 (1868)

Peabody invented a proprietary jute-manufacturing process and disclosed it to Norfolk under an agreement forbidding further disclosure or use. Norfolk later attempted to exploit that process himself. The court granted Peabody an injunction, ruling that keeping a process hidden (rather than patenting it) did not forfeit its protection. The court called such hidden know-how "property" that equity would protect, and it highlighted that employees or associates who gain knowledge under a duty of confidence cannot lawfully disclose it or profit from it in breach of trust.

By the time *Peabody* was decided, courts had already grappled with business transactions that hinged on secret knowledge. Sometimes, parties tried to buy or sell exclusive processes or recipes. If a seller refused to share the full details, the buyer might sue, claiming they paid for something they never received. In these disputes, judges had to decide whether a secret method could be treated like any other piece of property. They generally concluded that it could be, as long as both parties recognized its confidential nature.

### LEGAL TRANSFER OF A SECRET METHOD

*Vickery v. Welch*
36 Mass. (19 Pick.) 523 (1837)

Welch agreed to sell a chocolate-making process—plus his mills—to Vickery, who believed he was purchasing the exclusive right to Welch's secret. After the sale, Welch withheld part of the process and argued that the contract should not bar him from reusing or reselling it. The court sided with Vickery. It held that a secret business method can be sold as a valuable asset, and once sold, the former owner cannot continue exercising the same secret in a way that nullifies the buyer's exclusive rights. The decision foreshadowed modern contract-based trade secret cases by confirming that an owner may convey a hidden method as if it were property, subject to conditions preserving confidentiality.

These 19th-century cases offered a legal foundation: a person who develops secret knowledge can share it selectively and expect others to keep it concealed. If a recipient violates that trust, courts may enforce the original agreement or implied duty. In the early 20th century, judges extended these principles. They recognized that limited disclosure, under appropriate safeguards, often helps a business grow without destroying secrecy. For example, a famous Supreme Court ruling in 1905 upheld the Board of Trade's practice of restricting its grain price quotations to paying subscribers who promised not to circulate them further.

### CONTROLLED DISTRIBUTION PROTECTS SECRET INFORMATION

*Board of Trade of City of Chicago v. Christie Grain & Stock Co.*
198 U.S. 236 (1905)

The Chicago Board of Trade compiled real-time grain price data. It provided that data to specific subscribers under confidentiality conditions. A competitor obtained the information indirectly and published it. The Supreme Court held that the Board had not lost its property rights by sharing its data under strict limitations. This early decision showed how a secret could remain protected if the owner maintained firm rules on who gets access and under what terms.

Over time, courts clarified that is the manner of acquisition—rather than the mere fact of possession—often determines liability. People who independently discover or reverse engineer an unpatented formula are free to use it, no matter how much the original inventor wants to keep it hidden. But employees, partners, or outsiders who obtain the same information through breach of confidence face potential liability. In 1917, the Supreme Court famously underscored that "the breach of trust" lay at the heart of trade secret law.

**TRADE SECRET LAW FOCUSES ON TRUST**

*E. I. du Pont de Nemours Powder Co. v. Masland*
244 U.S. 100 (1917)

Justice Holmes declined to label the misappropriated manufacturing information as "property" in a strict sense. Instead, he stressed that disclosing or using data given in confidence is a wrong in itself. Once a business shares valuable secrets under conditions of trust, the recipient must not exploit them to the owner's detriment. This emphasis on a breach of confidence rather than on technical definitions of property still guides trade secret disputes today.

In the mid-1900s, the UTSA codified many of these common law rules. Most states have adopted some version of the UTSA, ensuring that secrecy, competitive value, and reasonable efforts at concealment remain the threshold elements. Then in 2016, Congress enacted the DTSA, establishing a federal civil cause of action. A key Supreme Court case addressed whether opting for secrecy conflicts with patent law.

**PATENT LAW AND TRADE SECRECY COEXIST**

*Kewanee Oil Co. v. Bicron Corp.*
416 U.S. 470 (1974)

Kewanee Oil maintained industrial processes as secrets rather than seeking patents. When ex-employees took that know-how to a competitor, the competitor argued that state trade secret law was incompatible with federal patent policy. The Supreme Court disagreed. It ruled that trade secret protection does not undermine the patent system's goals because patents demand disclosure, whereas trade secrets do not. Both routes can advance innovation, and each developer decides which path to follow.

Hence, the modern body of trade secret law began taking shape well before the 20th century, propelled by cases like *Peabody*, *Vickery*, *Board of Trade*, and *Masland*, and later refined by *Kewanee* and statutory reforms. Together, these authorities confirm that secret information can be protected if

(1) it is kept confidential with reasonable diligence,
(2) it has value precisely because it is not generally known, and
(3) others acquire it improperly or in breach of a duty of trust when disputes arise.

Modern technology and remote collaboration make secrecy both more challenging and more critical. The next sections will situate trade secrets within the larger intellectual property landscape (Section 1.2) and explain how courts define and safeguard this oldest-yet-ever-evolving form of IP.

# 1.2. Trade Secrets Within the Intellectual Property Framework

Trade secrets occupy one corner of a larger intellectual property landscape that also includes patents, copyrights, and trademarks. These other forms of IP typically rely on some measure of public disclosure or visible use to secure rights. Patents require public disclosure of an invention in exchange for a time-limited monopoly. Copyrights protect original expressions and often assume wide distribution of those works. Trademarks focus on public identification and distinctiveness in commerce. By contrast, trade secrets demand silence. They require no registration or government filing. Their protection continues for as long as the information remains confidential and yields economic value to its owner. This section compares and contrasts trade secrets with each of the other IP types, highlighting why some businesses choose secrecy while others lean on patents, copyrights, or trademarks—or a mixture of them all.

## 1.2.1. Trade Secret vs. Patent

Patents and trade secrets both shield innovation but adopt opposing approaches. A patent discloses the technology behind an invention so the public can learn from it, in exchange for an exclusive right—generally lasting 20 years—to block others from making, using, selling, or importing that invention. Trade secrets, on the other hand, demand that you hide the critical details. If the innovation is discovered independently or reverse engineered, you cannot stop the new user by citing trade secret law. If someone simply figures out the recipe, you are out of luck. By contrast, a patent can block even innocent third parties who arrive at the same invention on their own.

Whether to disclose information in pursuit of a patent, or to keep a process hidden as a trade secret, is a strategic choice. If an invention is easy to reverse engineer, secrecy may not protect it because competitors can unlock the idea by studying the final product. In that scenario, a patent might be better—disclosure is forced, but it stops copycats for a limited term. Conversely, if the invention can feasibly stay hidden (like a factory process or an internal algorithm) and has potential value beyond 20 years, secrecy could be advantageous. Owners then skip the cost and lengthy procedure of patent prosecution and avoid revealing details to the public. However, they do face the downside risk that if someone else discovers the same method independently, there is no recourse under trade secret law.

A practical compromise involves patenting certain core aspects of a technology while still treating refinements, negative data, or unpatentable features as trade secrets. This approach ensures some exclusive rights via patent law while other knowledge stays confidential within the firm. However, care is needed when drafting patent applications or marketing materials so that you do not accidentally disclose too much and destroy your secrecy.

## 1.2.2. Trade Secret vs. Copyright

Copyright law safeguards original create expressions that are fixed in a tangible medium, such as novels, music, films, computer code, or even a painting's specific arrangement of lines and shapes. It arises immediately upon creation and does not require any degree of secrecy. In fact, copyrighted works are often widely published and distributed to reach an audience. The copyright owner can sue anyone who makes unauthorized copies or adaptations of the expression.

Trade secrets revolve around maintaining confidentiality. They protect what lies behind the visible expression, such as the undisclosed logic in a software algorithm or the exact combination and settings of equalizers and compressors that a producer uses to shape the sound of a song via a music studio production. Once you release a copyrighted work to the public, you cannot claim that its core contents remain hidden—even if the public faces license restrictions, the expression itself is "out there." For trade secret status to endure, you must show that you took real steps to keep the relevant details from becoming general knowledge.

Even so, you can combine both systems. A developer might copyright a finished program's user interface and compiled object code, then keep the source code a secret. If a competitor obtains that source code via improper means—say, by hacking or by betrayal of a non-disclosure agreement (NDA)—both copyright infringement (if they literally copied the text) and trade secret misappropriation (if they exploited the hidden logic) could apply. But if a rival writes its own functionally similar code that uses the same ideas but not the same expression, copyright might not help at all, while trade secret law could still address whether those ideas were gained improperly.

## 1.2.3. Trade Secret vs. Trademark

Trademarks help consumers identify a product or service. Their entire value flows from public visibility: a brand name, a logo, or a slogan must be "out in the open" so customers see it and distinguish it from competing marks. Trade secrets thrive in concealment. Yet, in practice, trademarks and trade secrets often coexist: a famous trademark can rest on a well-promoted brand name while the process that creates that brand's distinctive product remains hidden. One iconic example is Coca-Cola: the name and logo are trademarks known worldwide, while the secret formula is protected only by corporate silence.

**TRADEMARK AND TRADE SECRET FORMULA TOGETHER**

*Coca-Cola Bottling Co. v. The Coca-Cola Co.*
269 F. 796 (D. Del. 1920)

In this early dispute, independent bottlers challenged The Coca-Cola Company's trademark and exclusive control of its secret syrup formula. The court recognized that Coca-Cola's name and logo functioned as a famous trademark, even while the syrup's exact recipe remained a protected secret. Coca-Cola had never publicly disclosed the precise blend of flavoring oils and other ingredients. By keeping the formula hidden and requiring strict confidentiality among bottlers, Coca-Cola preserved a trade secret that complemented its strong brand identity. The ruling emphasized that trademark law protects the public-facing symbol of a product, whereas trade secret law shields the behind-the-scenes method or recipe. As a result, Coca-Cola could leverage both forms of intellectual property: the trademark drew consumers to a recognizable beverage, while the undisclosed formula kept rivals from duplicating the drink's taste. This combination of secrecy and branding became a foundational model for other companies seeking dual protection.

Sometimes, a company keeps an upcoming brand identity a secret until a product's launch. That pre-launch name or logo might function as a "trade secret" to prevent early leaks. But once the trademark is revealed publicly, any secrecy behind it ends. Meanwhile, the brand might represent a product whose special features remain locked away from the competition. In that sense, trademarks and trade secrets work side by side: one is broadcast to the marketplace, and the other is guarded within the organization.

## 1.2.4. Trade Secrets in the IP Landscape

Patents, copyrights, trademarks, and trade secrets each protect different kinds of value. Patents reward inventors for disclosing new inventions. Copyrights grant exclusive rights in creative works. Trademarks enhance brand recognition and consumer trust. Trade secrets preserve hidden methods or data that yield an advantage by virtue of not being generally known.

Some businesses patent or trademark the public-facing aspects of their products while keeping behind-the-scenes practices secret. Others forgo the patent system entirely if they believe they can maintain secrecy longer than a 20-year patent term. Still others rely on copyrights for original expression but retain trade secret protection for the knowledge behind that expression. The choice depends on many factors, including how easily competitors might reverse engineer a product, whether the invention meets patentability standards, and whether disclosure could spur unwanted competition.

In the following sections, we will examine exactly how law defines a trade secret (Section 1.3), how misappropriation arises (Section 1.4), and how businesses can fortify their confidential information against improper exposure. Understanding trade secrets in this broader IP framework lets you see why companies might choose silence as part of their innovation strategy—and why that silence must be accompanied by consistent, carefully managed efforts to keep the secret from escaping.

# 1.3. Defining a Trade Secret: The Three Essential Elements

Trade secret law hinges on three essential requirements. First, the subject matter must qualify as "information." Second, that information must hold independent economic value precisely because it is not generally known and not readily ascertainable by proper means. Third, the business that seeks protection must undertake reasonable efforts to keep the information confidential. Although these elements appear straightforward, courts weigh them carefully. Each factor plays a crucial part in determining whether knowledge genuinely deserves legal safeguards as a trade secret.

This section explores these requirements step by step, examining what kinds of "information" can receive protection, how businesses can prove that their information remains unknown and offers a competitive edge, and why only those who actively guard their secrets can invoke the protections of trade secret law. Understanding these criteria illuminates the careful balancing that courts perform between promoting fair competition and punishing dishonest acts of theft or breach of confidence.

## 1.3.1. Information

A trade secret claim begins with the assertion that specific content qualifies as "information." Statutes such as the UTSA and the federal DTSA define this term in broad, inclusive language encompassing formulas, patterns, compilations, programs, devices, methods, techniques, processes, and similar intangible knowledge. Consequently, "information" may refer to anything from chemical formulas or advanced algorithms to marketing plans or specialized data sets. The key point is that courts focus on the intangible content, not on a physical object or an employee's personal skill.

Many companies rely on technical trade secrets, such as manufacturing processes, recipes, or engineering designs. A company might also have business trade secrets, including strategic plans, sales tactics, or curated customer lists. Often, a single enterprise relies on multiple types of confidential knowledge to stay ahead of rivals. For example, a pharmaceutical firm might keep one set of secrets tied to a production process, another set related to the identity of specialized suppliers, and a third set involving results from negative research. All of these might qualify as protected "information," provided they are both novel to outsiders and deliberately hidden from general circulation.

Trade secret law does not treat broad, nebulous concepts as "information." If the alleged secret is merely an idea that any skilled person in the field would conceive, courts will reject it as too abstract. The owner must show that the knowledge is sufficiently concrete and detailed. In some cases, a single concept or notion might straddle the line between a protectable method and an unprotectable idea. Courts will look to see whether the claimant can articulate precise steps, formulas, or data that differentiate the secret from everyday industry knowledge.

### SEPARATING CONCEPTS FROM CONCRETE DATA

*Altavion, Inc. v. Konica Minolta Systems Laboratory, Inc.*
226 Cal. App. 4th 26 (2014)

Altavion alleged that a general idea for embedding secure barcodes in documents was a trade secret. The court distinguished between broad conceptual statements (such as "use barcodes for authentication") and the specific underlying algorithms, designs, and implementations that Altavion kept confidential. The general concept alone was deemed too vague for protection. However, the court found that once Altavion provided detail on how exactly it coded and integrated the barcodes, that narrower, concrete content qualified as information. This ruling shows that courts demand definable facts or methods, not merely a creative notion or aspiration.

A second point of emphasis is that employees' general know-how or skill is not "information" in the sense of a trade secret. Over time, workers accumulate expertise, develop professional judgment, and learn standard techniques. Courts will not prevent employees from using their accumulated competencies, even if they sharpened them while working for one employer. What counts as a secret must go beyond typical skill or routine knowledge. If a departing worker takes a confidential formula or proprietary blueprint, that crosses the line. But if they merely recall and use typical design principles known throughout the industry, courts treat it as part of their general skillset.

Finally, trade secret law does not require the alleged secret to be recorded on paper or stored in a database. An individual might hold the knowledge purely in memory, and as long as the method or formula remains genuinely undisclosed, it can still be protectable. Many older precedents reference trade secrets passed verbally between employees under an implicit or explicit expectation of confidentiality. Today's world mostly uses digital repositories, but the principle remains that intangible substance—the actual data, design, or process—matters more than the medium. What remains crucial is that the owner can later define and describe it with enough specificity for a court to see how it differs from everyday skill and unprotected knowledge.

## 1.3.2. Independent Economic Value from Not Being Generally Known and Not Readily Ascertainable

The second prong captures two closely connected requirements. The secret must possess value because it is not generally known, and it must not be so easily discoverable by lawful means that secrecy confers no real advantage. Courts usually group these concepts by asking whether the owner truly gains a meaningful competitive edge by keeping others in the dark or whether a rival could lawfully replicate the information with trivial effort. If the secrecy does not matter to the information's economic utility or if a competitor can reverse engineer the solution with minimal trouble, the law sees no cause for trade secret protection.

### *1.3.2.1. Independent Economic Value*

Trade secret law requires that the information at issue derive independent economic value from remaining confidential. This means the information must be valuable precisely because other potential users do not know it. If everyone in the field already understands or can freely access the same content, secrecy cannot add anything to its economic worth. Thus, many businesses highlight how exclusive knowledge saves costs, enables better products, or opens new markets. They might show how a trade secret shortens development time, yields superior performance, or protects pricing strategies, all of which translate to a head start or competitive advantage. Conversely, if the knowledge does not meaningfully advance the owner's efficiency or revenue, or if it is trivial, the law sees no strong reason to treat it as a protectable secret.

Owners typically demonstrate "independent economic value" by explaining how competitors would gain a significant benefit if they learned the secret or how the owner would suffer losses if the information leaked. Courts often accept direct testimony supported by some factual demonstration, like development costs, special production methods, or time saved by skipping trial-and-error phases, that the secrecy grants a real business edge.

**ECONOMIC VALUE IN NONPROFIT CONTEXTS**

*Religious Tech. Ctr. v. Lerma*
908 F. Supp. 1362 (E.D. Va. 1995)

The Church of Scientology sued over internet postings of its "Operating Thetan" materials, claiming that they were valuable trade secrets. The court noted that the Church sold the esoteric teachings only to qualified adherents who paid fees and pledged confidentiality. By limiting access, the Church maintained that these texts derived monetary worth from remaining undisclosed. Critics argued that the spiritual nature of the content made it ill-suited for commercial protection. The court, however, evaluated the alleged "independent economic value" by examining the Church's business model of licensing and fees, indicating that intangible or non-technical material can still qualify if it confers a tangible benefit from secrecy. Although the ultimate dispute involved constitutional and fair-use arguments, the case underscored how an organization's careful restriction of potentially "religious" content can fall under the umbrella of trade secret law if it demonstrates economic importance linked to confidentiality.

In short, the heart of "independent economic value" is the link between secrecy and commercial benefit. A company may show that the secret knowledge is expensive or time-intensive to replicate, that only a few insiders have it, and that disclosing it would hand rivals a shortcut. As soon as other players can obtain and use the same information, its exclusivity—and thus its competitive worth—evaporates. This prong ensures that only meaningful secrets of genuine commercial significance, rather than general or incidental knowledge, earn the shield of trade secret protection.

### *1.3.2.2. Not Generally Known*

"Not generally known" means the information is not widely recognized or published in the relevant field. Courts do not require absolute invisibility. A small circle of people might be aware of the data, yet it can still be a secret if they learn it under confidentiality obligations or if the group remains too small to nullify the owner's advantage. However, if many competitors independently use the same approach or if the technique appears in readily accessible industry references, the knowledge ceases to be a secret.

This focus on "not generally known" underlies the principle that trade secret law rewards businesses that keep a competitive insight to themselves. If the insight is already spreading freely, secrecy is not what makes it valuable. In practice, the lines can blur. One enterprise might share certain details selectively with partners under strict NDAs or present partial glimpses to potential investors. These controlled disclosures do not automatically destroy secrecy if they preserve confidentiality. But if the information appears widely—for instance, in a patent filing or a public regulatory submission—the law deems it general knowledge.

Courts also ask whether a competitor, upon hearing vague references, could locate the same data in public sources. If the answer is yes, the material is effectively known. Some owners attempt to hide an innovation behind licensing or restricted distribution. But if the product is widely sold and includes enough clues or is accompanied by manuals that detail the innovation, a court might conclude that the knowledge is functionally public. The key consideration is whether the secrecy effectively keeps the knowledge restricted to a small, controlled circle that cannot freely pass it along.

**VALUE FROM LIMITED CIRCULATION**

*Board of Trade of City of Chicago v. Christie Grain & Stock Co.*
198 U.S. 236 (1905)

In the early 1900s, the Board of Trade compiled grain price quotations and shared them only with paying subscribers under confidentiality-like conditions. A competitor tried to publish these quotes, arguing they were not truly secret. The Supreme Court disagreed, emphasizing that the Board's practice of limiting the data to authorized users preserved secrecy and value. Although some subscribers possessed the information, it was not "generally known" because the Board never released it into a fully open forum. The Board's careful control sustained the advantage arising from restricted access, which supported the conclusion that the data was protectable.

To show that the information is not generally known, owners often present evidence of their internal security policies, limited distribution, and explicit instructions to recipients about confidentiality. This helps persuade courts that the knowledge remains in a defined circle rather than having spilled across the entire industry. Equally important is demonstrating that no legitimate publication or public discussion has surfaced which might defeat a secrecy claim.

### *1.3.2.3. Not Readily Ascertainable*

Closely related to being "not generally known" is the question of whether the information is "not readily ascertainable." If a competitor can lawfully discover the secret with minimal effort, the secrecy advantage collapses. Common lawful methods include independent creation, reverse engineering, or research using public data. Trade secret law is built around the idea that no one can be prevented from stumbling on the same insight if they do so honestly. It only punishes theft, deception, or breaches of confidence.

Reverse engineering has become a central focal point in technology-driven industries. Purchasing a competitor's widget, disassembling it, and analyzing its components are considered fair game. If doing so reveals the competitor's once-hidden design, that design is not a protected secret in the eyes of the law. The same logic applies to software decompilation or cryptanalysis, though license agreements may place additional contractual restrictions. Courts generally hold that if the average skilled competitor could replicate the process or outcome through public channels and standard investigative methods, it is readily ascertainable and does not qualify for trade secret protection.

Yet if the relevant method remains buried so deeply that an adversary would need extraordinary guesswork or a major research project to replicate it, the secrecy stands. A manufacturing technique that requires specialized knowledge or extremely involved trial and error may remain secure for years, even if the final product is sold openly. This situation often arises with intangible "know-how" embedded in processes that do not manifest on the product's surface.

### NOVEL COMBINATIONS CAN BE TRADE SECRETS

*Hertz v. Luzenac Group*
576 F.3d 1103 (10th Cir. 2009)

Luzenac produced a talc product using common steps in a specific sequence that yielded superior performance. Former employees took that knowledge to a rival. At first, the court dismissed the claim, reasoning that each individual step was known in the industry. On appeal, the Tenth Circuit concluded that combining these steps in that particular way was not readily ascertainable. Since no competitor had successfully pieced the steps together on their own, the synergy of steps held legitimate secrecy value. This highlights that even if the pieces are public, the unique assembly can remain protected if it is not easy for outsiders to deduce.

In effect, "not readily ascertainable" means that the secret-owner does not rely on broad ignorance alone but also on the fact that legitimate channels of discovery would be significantly challenging. A rival's inability to replicate the knowledge, short of unethical or illegal conduct, supports the notion that secrecy has real worth. Conversely, if an opponent can replicate the information with a minimal investment of time or capital, secrecy cannot be said to drive the knowledge's economic value.

When evaluating this prong, courts consider the cost, complexity, and typical capabilities of industry players. They do not require that a secret be absolutely impossible to figure out. Rather, the standard is that acquiring the secret fairly would require unusual or burdensome effort beyond what is considered routine or trivial. If acquiring it is so easy that a competitor merely needs to buy the product and do a simple test, the owner cannot claim trade secret status for that data or design.

### 1.3.3. Subject to Reasonable Efforts to Maintain Secrecy

The final requirement embodies a fundamental principle: to deserve legal protection, an owner must treat the information as secret. Courts do not automatically guard knowledge that a business fails to secure. Rather, the law expects the claimant to adopt consistent, practical measures to ensure the information stays hidden. Failing to do so signals that the business itself did not regard the data as confidential, so the public policy interest in protecting it diminishes.

One common example is the use of nondisclosure agreements (NDAs) for anyone who might gain access to the knowledge. While NDAs alone are not a panacea, they reflect a recognition that the information is special and must be shielded. Other frequent methods are labeling documents or files as "confidential"; restricting physical access to sensitive areas; implementing digital controls, like password-protected servers; and keeping distribution on a "need-to-know" basis. The specific steps vary widely depending on industry, scale, and the nature of the secret. A small family restaurant might keep one copy of its sauce recipe in a locked drawer, while a global tech company invests in advanced cybersecurity.

Nevertheless, courts want a consistent story. If an owner brandishes NDAs but then freely distributes the purported secret in brochures or marketing materials, that owner undermines the argument for secrecy. Judges examine whether the business's internal culture, training, and policy enforcement align with the concept of confidentiality. When a leak occurs, the owner's swift and decisive response can prove to the court that secrecy truly matters to the organization.

**AN NDA IS NOT ENOUGH**

*nClosures Inc. v. Block & Co.*
770 F.3d 598 (7th Cir. 2014)

nClosures developed a metal iPad case and had a nondisclosure agreement with a manufacturer. Despite this paperwork, the company publicly showcased designs and shared them widely without additional security measures. The court refused to recognize trade secret status, explaining that simply having an NDA is not enough when the owner's actual conduct does not reinforce secrecy. By failing to consistently limit access or label materials as confidential, nClosures effectively treated its design as public information, so the law declined to treat it as protected.

Reasonable efforts also must adapt over time. A data security approach that sufficed years ago might be woefully inadequate today, especially in fields prone to hacking or digital espionage. Companies that rely heavily on trade secrets often update security protocols, run internal audits, and ensure that employees remain mindful of confidentiality obligations. Courts look favorably on periodic training sessions that educate staff on how to avoid accidental disclosures and on clear policies for employees who depart the company. If a large firm fails to maintain even basic cybersecurity, it is more likely that a court will conclude the firm did not truly act to keep the data secret.

Some owners worry that excessive secrecy can hamper collaboration or marketing efforts. Yet the law's requirement is not total lockdown but rather reasonableness. Limited disclosures to potential investors or licensees do not kill a trade secret so long as those disclosures are controlled by NDAs and explicit confidentiality rules. Distribution within the firm is acceptable if the recipients need the information for legitimate tasks and if internal controls prevent casual sharing. The overarching question is whether the business systematically indicates that the information is private and invests proportionate resources in keeping it out of unauthorized hands.

When a trade secret lawsuit arises, defendants often argue that the alleged secret was not "reasonably" protected. They may point to large numbers of employees with unlimited access, a lack of confidentiality markings on documents, or anecdotal evidence that managers openly discussed the knowledge in public forums. Plaintiffs counter by documenting the steps they took, such as locked offices, restricted server permissions, mandatory NDAs, and immediate action against suspicious behavior. This factual clash often decides whether the court deems the secrecy claim genuine or perfunctory.

The bottom line is that trade secret law rewards diligence. Owners who use NDAs, restrict access, mark documents, and swiftly respond to potential leaks can demonstrate that they truly rely on secrecy. This approach, in combination with the other two elements, establishes the strong foundation needed to seek injunctions and damages if the secret is later stolen or misappropriated. Without these measures, a court is likely to hold that the business did not do its part and thus cannot invoke legal protection.

## 1.3.4. Synthesizing the Three Elements

Information deserving trade secret status must meet all three criteria simultaneously. It must be detailed enough to qualify as "information," not a broad or obvious idea. It must carry genuine economic weight arising from its obscurity, meaning it is not generally known or readily discoverable through lawful methods. Finally, the owner must actively preserve that obscurity through steady and reasonable efforts rather than merely proclaiming secrecy after the fact. Only when these factors align does the law step in to penalize thieves, deter unethical ex-employees, and safeguard honest competition based on properly acquired knowledge.

Trade secrets can last indefinitely—far longer than patents—precisely because the law does not fix an expiration date. That unique advantage goes hand in hand with the owner's ongoing obligation. A single misstep, such as a public disclosure, can instantly destroy the secrecy. Once the information becomes freely available, the advantage dissolves. Additionally, a competitor who stumbles on the same method independently or reverse engineers it through diligence commits no misappropriation. Thus, the entire mechanism of trade secret law revolves around preventing wrongful acquisition or betrayal, not halting legitimate research.

By insisting on these three elements, courts balance competing policy goals. They encourage businesses to develop valuable but hard-to-patent insights while preserving the freedom of others to discover knowledge on their own. They also require owners to show genuine responsibility: if a business invests in secrecy, the law invests in protecting it. This relationship fosters a culture in which companies carefully classify and handle critical data and cultivate strategies to manage risk. Once a secret is recognized under these principles, the next question is how the law defines and polices misappropriation. That topic will be explored in the next section, where the focus shifts to the line between fair competition—such as open-market reverse engineering—and illicit acts that breach a duty of confidentiality or rely on deceit. Understanding these elements is essential background for seeing where courts set the boundaries and how trade secret disputes pivot on issues of trust, wrongdoing, and commercial fairness.

## 1.4. Misappropriation of Trade Secrets

Misappropriation is the critical fault line where trade secret rights meet real-world wrongdoing. Even if information qualifies as a valid trade secret, there is no legal violation unless an individual or entity acquires, uses, or discloses the secret in an improper way. This emphasis on unfair conduct preserves legitimate competition by allowing parties to discover the same knowledge independently or reverse engineer a publicly available product. The law steps in, however, when someone crosses boundaries of trust or deception. This section explores how the statutes define misappropriation, details the main categories of improper behavior, explains how "use" and "disclosure" can become actionable, and concludes with the notion of "proper means," most notably reverse engineering and independent discovery.

## 1.4.1. Statutory Foundations and Wrongful Conduct

Modern US trade secret statutes, including the UTSA and the DTSA, define "misappropriation" in ways that revolve around wrongdoing. These laws focus on whether the trade secret was obtained by "improper means" or whether a party who had lawful access to the secret went on to breach a duty in using or disclosing it. Courts label misappropriation as unethical, dishonest, or unfair conduct, in contrast to harmless or authorized ways of discovering the same information.

Typically, a trade secret owner alleges misappropriation by showing that the defendant either stole or spied on the information (improper acquisition) or exceeded the scope of authorized access (improper use or disclosure). In each instance, courts look for the crossing of a line—some element of trickery, breach of contract, or knowing violation of the rightful owner's expectations. If the defendant's discovery is entirely independent or arises from a product openly sold, liability usually cannot attach.

Trade secret law's equitable origins are crucial here. A party who knowingly subverts commercial morality (the common law's equitable norm of fair competition and honest dealing in commerce) by deceiving or betraying trust will likely face liability. This principle underpins the entire framework. It ensures that employees can gain specialized knowledge on the job and still move within the industry, provided they do not exploit or reveal actual secrets in direct violation of a legal or ethical duty.

## 1.4.2. Improper Acquisition

Improper acquisition may be the most blatant form of misappropriation. It encompasses actions such as theft, trespass, hacking, bribery, or espionage—any deliberate method of bypassing the trade secret owner's safeguards. Whether the secret was stored physically or digitally, the question is whether the defendant achieved access through deceptive or unauthorized means.

### AERIAL ESPIONAGE AS IMPROPER ACQUISITION

*E. I. du Pont de Nemours & Co. v. Christopher*
431 F.2d 1012 (5th Cir. 1970)

In this frequently cited case, du Pont was constructing a chemical plant with a partially open roof. Christopher took aerial photographs of the facility to discover its manufacturing process. The Fifth Circuit condemned this conduct as industrial espionage, concluding that flying overhead to circumvent du Pont's reasonable security measures was an improper means of acquiring the trade secret. The court's decision underscores how even clever yet lawful tactics—like renting a spy plane—can become actionable when they effectively subvert the owner's secrecy efforts.

Bribery or inducement to breach a nondisclosure agreement also qualifies as improper acquisition. For example, a competitor might pay a current employee to leak confidential documents. The competitor's knowledge that the insider is violating a duty suffices to prove wrongdoing. A more subtle scenario might involve posing as a potential partner or investor under false pretenses just to extract valuable information. Once the facade is exposed, a court can hold that the defendant's actions were illegitimate.

Significantly, courts look beyond the direct thief. If another person knowingly receives the stolen information and exploits it, that person commits misappropriation. A person who exploits a stolen trade secret cannot claim ignorance if the circumstances raise red flags, such as a suspiciously low "sale" price for the data or the presence of obvious confidentiality markings. By extending liability, the law deters conspiracies and after-the-fact profiteers.

## 1.4.3. Improper Use

Even when acquisition was initially authorized, misappropriation can arise through "improper use." Here, the person in possession of the trade secret goes beyond the scope of any permitted purpose. Perhaps they acquired the information under a confidentiality agreement or in the context of limited research. If they then deploy the secret in ways the owner never agreed to, the law regards it as misappropriation.

For instance, a technician might be hired to refine a manufacturing method under strict nondisclosure terms. If that technician later forms a rival startup and employs the exact method for personal gain, it counts as improper use. Courts typically scrutinize the original context of the relationship—particularly written agreements that define how far the authorized use extends. A nondisclosure agreement (NDA) or license might say, "You may use this secret only to produce X for us, no other uses are permitted." Any usage outside that clause can become grounds for litigation.

**IMPROPER USE OF PROPERLY ACQUIRED INFORMATION**

*3M Co. v. Pribyl*
259 F.3d 587 (7th Cir. 2001)

In this case, several former employees left 3M to form a rival venture called Accu-Tech Plastics. While at 3M, they had legitimate access to its technical manuals and operating procedures, which detailed resin formulations and precise methods for producing specialized plastics. However, once they started Accu-Tech, they directly incorporated these confidential processes into their new enterprise. The Seventh Circuit found that although the employees obtained 3M's procedures lawfully in their prior roles, their subsequent application of the same proprietary steps to build a competing business was an unauthorized use of trade secrets.

Because the employees knew 3M's processes were secret and had signed confidentiality obligations, the court emphasized that their actions clearly went beyond permissible use. That knowledge belonged to 3M for its own production advantage and was not to be repurposed at a new company without permission. In ruling for 3M, the court enjoined Accu-Tech's continued exploitation of the procedures and awarded damages reflecting the head start gained by circumventing the normal learning curve. *3M Co. v. Pribyl* illustrates that even when acquisition is initially legitimate, reusing secret knowledge in an unapproved venture can constitute misappropriation.

Measuring damages or injunction scope in improper use cases can be complicated, as the defendant likely had partial or temporary rights. Courts may restrict them from further use for a set "head start" period or until the advantage gained from the breach dissipates. They might also assess monetary relief—lost profits, unjust enrichment, or a reasonable royalty—for the unauthorized benefit the defendant derived. The key remains that the defendant's usage exceeded whatever was originally authorized, and they knew or should have known that it violated the owner's expectations.

## 1.4.4. Improper Disclosure

A similarly damaging variant of misappropriation arises when a party who knows the secret reveals it to others without license to do so. Even a single disclosure to a competitor can unravel years of investment if that competitor can immediately exploit the knowledge. When disclosure reaches the public domain, the secret's entire advantage typically vanishes. By imposing liability for unauthorized disclosure, the law encourages anyone entrusted with confidential knowledge to preserve it carefully.

Wrongful disclosure often appears in employee departure scenarios. An employee may email key documents to a personal account or keep a USB drive of strategic files. If they share these files with their new employer or upload them online, they breach their duty not to reveal them. The severity of misappropriation can be even higher when distribution is so broad that re-sealing the knowledge is impossible. Courts react strongly, often ordering injunctions, awarding damages, and punishing malicious intent with enhanced remedies.

## WRONGFUL INDUCEMENT TO DISCLOSE CONFIDENTIAL INFORMATION

*Board of Trade of City of Chicago v. Christie Grain & Stock Co.*
198 U.S. 236 (1905)

In this early Supreme Court decision, the Chicago Board of Trade provided grain price quotations exclusively to a limited group of paying subscribers under strict confidentiality terms. A competitor induced insiders to disclose this information, thereby making the data publicly accessible. The Court focused on the act of disclosure itself as the critical wrongdoing rather than on how the information was acquired or used subsequently. This case set a precedent by holding that deliberately breaching a confidentiality arrangement through unauthorized disclosure is sufficient to trigger liability under trade secret law.

Disclosure can also be negligent or reckless rather than intentional. An organization might post sensitive source code online by mistake or might neglect to redact trade secret details from a regulatory filing. While an errant slip might not always reflect malicious conduct, courts often treat it as destructive to secrecy if the code or data truly become public. The question is whether the defendant had a clear duty (contractual or ethical) to avoid exposing the information but disregarded that obligation. If so, liability likely follows, although the remedy may vary depending on intent and consequences.

## IMPROPER DISCLOSURE OF PROPERLY ACQUIRED INFORMATION

*MicroStrategy, Inc. v. Business Objects, S.A.*
331 F. Supp. 2d 396 (E.D. Va. 2004)

In this case, MicroStrategy asserted that its former employees, who were bound by confidentiality agreements, improperly disclosed sensitive internal documents to Business Objects. The documents at issue included MicroStrategy's "Business Objects Competitive Recipe" and a volume discount schedule. MicroStrategy had taken extensive measures to keep both secret. The court found that these materials were not publicly available and could only have been obtained through a breach of the employees' duty of confidentiality. As a result, Business Objects was enjoined from possessing, disclosing, or using the misappropriated documents. This case illustrates that even when information is acquired properly or indirectly (for example, via former employees), any unauthorized further disclosure that undermines the owner's efforts to maintain secrecy constitutes misappropriation.

Unauthorized disclosure is particularly damaging when it renders a secret no longer secret. Once confidential information is disseminated widely, the owner's exclusive advantage evaporates. Courts are therefore quick to enjoin further disclosures and, in many cases, award damages that reflect the loss of the secret's economic value.

## 1.4.5. Proper Means: Reverse Engineering and Independent Discovery

Trade secret law does not create a monopoly over knowledge. Competitors remain free to discover or replicate a secret if they do so by honest methods—commonly by reverse engineering a purchased product or conducting original R&D. Owners who choose secrecy over patenting accept the risk that, once a product is sold openly, skilled rivals might analyze and deduce the hidden aspects.

### *1.4.5.1. Reverse Engineering*

Reverse engineering refers to examining and dismantling a legitimate copy of an item to understand its workings. As long as it was obtained lawfully on the market, trade secret law deems this approach permissible. If the original owner wanted to keep the details hidden, they might have used physical security (potting compound in electronics, for instance) or contractual limits (shrink-wrap or labeling disclaimers that bar reverse engineering). These restrictive covenants ultimately depend on contract-law principles of assent and enforceability. A shrink-wrap or click-through license may validly bar reverse engineering, but a unilateral label typically does not, and even a valid agreement can be void if it conflicts with public policy. Where no such measure or contract precludes analysis, the competitor may replicate the design.

**THE RIGHT TO REVERSE ENGINEER**

*Bonito Boats, Inc. v. Thunder Craft Boats, Inc.*
489 U.S. 141 (1989)

In invalidating a Florida statute that prohibited copying boat hull designs, the Supreme Court reaffirmed the policy that absent patent protection, a product released publicly is fair game for reverse engineering. The Court reasoned that states cannot grant a de facto perpetual monopoly by banning lawful investigative methods. Trade secret owners must adopt their own safeguards if they wish to keep knowledge hidden.

Any attempt to label normal analysis or testing as "improper acquisition" typically fails unless the owner can show a breach of contract or an extraordinary infiltration tactic, for example, aerial espionage used to photograph a plant under construction to glean process details. Courts encourage reverse engineering as a driver of innovation and competition, balancing the secrecy-based regime. Once the competitor obtains the data from the product itself, no misappropriation claim can stand, provided no NDAs or license restrictions exist.

### *1.4.5.2. Independent Discovery*

A similarly valid avenue is independently creating or discovering the same knowledge. Nothing in trade secret law grants the first developer an automatic monopoly if a second developer invests time and skill to reach the same solution. The second developer need not pay royalties or face litigation if they never accessed the first company's data. Plaintiffs trying to prove misappropriation must show the defendant's knowledge was tainted by improper means or a breach of duty, not merely that both parties ended up with alike results.

**INDEPENDENT DISCOVERY AS A LAWFUL PATH**

*Winston Research Corp. v. Minnesota Mining & Mfg. Co.*
350 F.2d 134 (9th Cir. 1965)

In this historical dispute, Winston Research created a product resembling a design by 3M. 3M alleged theft of confidential information. Winston, however, showed documentation of its own engineering progress that paralleled 3M's developments without tapping into 3M's proprietary data. The Ninth Circuit ruled that honest independent discovery does not constitute misappropriation. Because Winston's approach did not rely on secret disclosures, 3M's claim failed.

By preserving reverse engineering and independent discovery as "proper means," trade secret law encourages a dynamic marketplace. Businesses cannot rely on secrecy alone if their product is easy to replicate once sold. Instead, they must weigh the pros and cons: either reveal the invention for patent coverage or invest in robust internal measures that deter reverse engineering. In either case, the law ensures that fair competition is not stifled and that cunning espionage or breach of confidence is the real target of enforcement.

Courts often examine evidence such as lab notebooks, timelines, or internal emails to confirm that the second entity truly did the work themselves rather than piggybacking on the original secret.

Because misappropriation depends on the defendant's knowledge that it is acting improperly—a bona fide second inventor who stumbles on the same method has no liability—this feature of trade secret law also supports the choice some businesses make to patent their inventions if they fear easy duplication. If the trade secret is likely to be discovered independently or is embedded in a publicly sold product, relying solely on secrecy might be a gamble.

### 1.4.6. Balancing Ethics and Competition

Trade secret misappropriation law attempts to strike a delicate balance. On one side, owners should be able to share confidential knowledge internally (or with partners) without surrendering their competitive advantage. On the other, competition demands that no single firm can lock down knowledge that rivals develop or discern through legitimate methods. The line thus runs between ethical and unethical actions: theft, breaches of contract, and secret betrayals are punished, while open research and honest observation are allowed.

By focusing on improper acquisition, use, or disclosure, courts preserve the rightful balance between encouraging investment in undisclosed knowledge and preventing undue hindrance to independent or reverse-engineered discoveries. This ethic is deeply rooted in older cases and persists in modern statutes. Under the UTSA and the DTSA, plaintiffs must show both that they possess a valid trade secret and that the defendant's means or motive was wrongful. Where these elements coincide, the law steps in.

Next, we examine the remedies available when a trade secret holder proves misappropriation. These remedies range from injunctions to damage awards and sometimes to punitive measures for willful and malicious wrongdoing. These remedies reinforce the system by helping to restore the owner's position, punish unscrupulous tactics, and deter others from similarly breaching commercial morality.

## 1.5. Remedies for Trade Secret Misappropriation

Trade secret law delivers protection through a set of remedies that both deter wrongdoing and compensate owners for the harm caused by misappropriation. When a court confirms that a party has wrongfully acquired, used, or disclosed a protected secret, it can invoke a blend of injunctions, damages, fee awards, and other equitable measures. This section explores how these remedies operate under the

UTSA and the DTSA. It also highlights ways in which judges tailor relief to fit the facts, from halting production lines that rely on stolen knowledge to imposing royalties on further usage.

## 1.5.1. Remedial Goals

The overriding purpose of trade secret remedies is threefold:

1. Stop further wrongdoing by enjoining ongoing or imminent misappropriation.
2. Restore the owner's position by awarding damages that approximate lost profits or the defendant's unjust gains.
3. Deter malicious acts by allowing punitive damages and attorneys' fee awards in severe cases.

Trade secret owners need swift action if an opposing party threatens to disseminate or continues profiting from the misappropriated data. At the same time, courts seek to avoid crippling legitimate competition. They therefore calibrate remedies to neutralize unfair advantages while respecting good-faith market activities.

## 1.5.2. Injunctive Relief

An injunction is often the most urgent form of relief because trade secrets lose value quickly once exposed. Preliminary injunctions stop defendants from exploiting or disclosing a secret while litigation unfolds. A court may later enter a permanent injunction if it finds liability proven at trial.

Under both the UTSA and the DTSA, plaintiffs can request to enjoin "actual or threatened misappropriation." This language enables courts to intervene even without proof that the defendant has already disclosed or used the secret, provided there is a serious risk they soon will.

### *1.5.2.1. Preliminary Injunctions*

To obtain a preliminary injunction in a civil lawsuit, a plaintiff generally must establish the four factors required by *Winter v. Natural Resources Defense Council, Inc.*, 555 U.S. 7 (2008):

(1) a likelihood of success on the merits,

(2) irreparable harm if not granted,

(3) the balance of hardships favors the plaintiff, and

(4) alignment with the public interest. Trade secret claimants often meet the irreparable harm standard by demonstrating that once the secret is out, no monetary sum can fully restore exclusivity.

**PRELIMINARY INJUNCTION TO PREVENT INEVITABLE DISCLOSURE**

*Bimbo Bakeries USA, Inc. v. Botticella*
613 F.3d 102 (3d Cir. 2010)

A high-level baking executive had intimate knowledge of Bimbo's secret recipes. He accepted employment with a direct competitor, but the court recognized a risk that he could "inevitably" disclose key data in his new role. The Third Circuit upheld a preliminary injunction blocking him from starting the new job. This outcome underscores how courts can step in even before disclosure occurs, provided the facts suggest a genuine threat of misuse.

A preliminary injunction grants the plaintiff valuable breathing room. It ensures that the defendant cannot commercialize or further spread the secret, which might otherwise undermine the entire reason for litigating. If the defendant has begun production, the injunction may freeze operations, impose a special monitor, or require immediate return of confidential files.

### *1.5.2.2. Permanent and Tailored Injunctions*

If the plaintiff establishes liability at trial, a permanent injunction may issue to prohibit continued misappropriation. However, courts sometimes must balance fairness. A defendant who merged the misappropriated knowledge into a complex product might not be able to "unlearn" it. Judges occasionally craft "head start" injunctions, preventing usage for the period it would have taken the defendant to develop the secret lawfully.

**PERMANENT INJUNCTION TO PREVENT FURTHER MISAPPROPRIATION**

*American Can Co. v. Mansukhani*
742 F.2d 314 (7th Cir. 1984)

In this landmark case, American Can Company brought suit against its former executive, Mansukhani, for misappropriating proprietary ink formulas and using them to manufacture competing products. The court found that Mansukhani had violated his duty of confidentiality by exploiting the secret formulas to gain a competitive advantage. As a remedy, the court granted a permanent injunction that barred Mansukhani from using or disclosing the stolen formulas in any further business activities. The decision underscored the critical role of injunctive relief in trade secret cases, emphasizing that once confidential information is misappropriated, preventing further use is essential to protect the owner's market position and safeguard its investment in secrecy.

In exceptional circumstances, the UTSA permits courts to transform a strict ban into a reasonable royalty arrangement—particularly where enforcing a complete prohibition might inflict disproportionate hardship. This approach recognizes that some projects, once deeply dependent on the stolen secret, cannot be easily dismantled. The defendant must pay ongoing royalties instead, effectively licensing what they wrongfully obtained, but at a court-imposed rate rather than a negotiated one.

## 1.5.3. Damages: Lost Profits, Unjust Enrichment, and Royalties

In addition to—or instead of—an injunction, owners can seek damages for the economic harm misappropriation caused. Courts applying the UTSA or the DTSA generally allow three primary calculations:

(1) actual loss,

(2) unjust enrichment, or

(3) a reasonable royalty.

Courts may adopt any measure that best captures the harm or ill-gotten gains.

### *1.5.3.1 Actual Loss*

Actual loss focuses on how the plaintiff's own business suffered. If the defendant used the secret to undercut prices, the owner may present sales or profit records showing that but for the misappropriation, the plaintiff's business would have captured more revenue. Calculating such damages often demands expert analysis and modeling of what the owner's position would have been without the wrongful conduct. Another angle is the cost of extra R&D or marketing needed to recover from the competitor's sudden leap forward.

However, actual loss can be challenging to prove if the plaintiff's revenue drop stems from multiple market factors or if the timeline for the competitor's product launch is uncertain. Defendants typically argue that their success or the plaintiff's slump was due to external market conditions, not the stolen data.

### 1.5.3.2. *Unjust Enrichment*

Where the defendant's actions yield measurable profits, courts may award those gains as damages. This avoids letting a misappropriator retain benefits from cheating. The logic is that if the defendant saved R&D time or otherwise reaped windfall revenue, that advantage should revert to the rightful owner. Plaintiffs might show that the defendant slashed development costs or reached customers faster, thereby securing profits it could not have earned but for the secret.

**MONEY DAMAGES FOR UNJUST ENRICHMENT**

*3M v. Pribyl*
259 F.3d 587 (7th Cir. 2001)

In this case, ex-employees used 3M's specialized manuals and manufacturing know-how to start a competitor business. The court affirmed that the defendant's swift market entry and profit signaled unjust enrichment from the secret knowledge. 3M's internal procedures, though partly known in the industry, gained protectable status from their unique combination, and damages reflected the competitor's windfall.

This measure can overlap with actual loss, but sometimes one measure is easier to demonstrate. If the defendant's product soared in sales while the plaintiff's market share held steady, actual loss might appear minimal, yet the defendant's enrichment is substantial. Courts can pick whichever approach ensures equitable relief.

### 1.5.3.3. *Reasonable Royalty*

Courts sometimes turn to a "reasonable royalty" measure—essentially, imagining a hypothetical negotiation between the owner and the misappropriator for licensed use of the secret. This approach is useful when actual loss or unjust enrichment is too speculative or cannot be fully proven. However, the royalty must be supported by evidence, not mere speculation. The judge or jury must base the estimate on relevant facts—such as comparable licenses, expert testimony, or market conditions—to determine what fee the defendant would likely have paid if it had acted lawfully.

**REASONABLE ROYALTY AWARD FOR MISAPPROPRIATION**

*Altavion, Inc. v. Konica Minolta Systems Laboratory, Inc.*
226 Cal. App. 4th 26 (2014)

In this case, Altavion, a small technology company specializing in digital stamping methods, brought suit after Konica Minolta Systems Laboratory secretly filed patent applications covering Altavion's confidential digital stamping technology. Although Altavion had not patented its technology, it had disclosed detailed information under a nondisclosure agreement, thereby establishing that its methods had substantial economic value derived from their secrecy. The court rejected Konica Minolta's argument that confidential information could not yield a royalty-based award, and it instead calculated damages using a reasonable royalty framework. This approach involved a hypothetical negotiation to determine what Konica Minolta would have paid for a license to legally use Altavion's technology. The award underscored that even unpatented, economically valuable confidential information merits compensation when misappropriated, thereby reinforcing the principle that a trade secret's value is intrinsically linked to its restricted availability.

A royalty measure can apply where the defendant's product only partially relies on the secret, or where the product has not yet hit the market but the theft is established. It also suits cases where equitable relief alone does not suffice and the court wants to ensure the plaintiff is compensated for any advantage the defendant retains.

## 1.5.4. Enhanced Damages and Attorneys' Fees

For egregious, willful behavior, both the UTSA and the DTSA permit punitive or exemplary damages, often capped at double the compensatory sum. If a court finds that the defendant acted maliciously or engaged in knowing conspiracy, such heightened awards punish wrongdoing and discourage future acts.

**PUNITIVE DAMAGES FOR DELIBERATE CONSPIRACY**

*Cognis Corp. v. Chemcentral Corp.*
430 F. Supp. 2d 806 (N.D. Ill. 2006)

In a scenario where employees conspired to pass a chemical formula to a competitor, the court concluded that their systematic cover-up and refusal to cease exploitation warranted exemplary damages. Such an award signaled that trade secret theft accompanied by subterfuge requires measures beyond compensatory remedies.

Attorneys' fees are the costs a party pays to its lawyers for litigating a case. Under the American Rule, each side ordinarily bears its own fees unless a statute, contract, or court order provides otherwise.

Both the Uniform Trade Secrets Act (UTSA) and the federal Defend Trade Secrets Act (DTSA) create limited exceptions to this rule. Each authorizes fee shifting in three defined circumstances:

(1) when a claim of misappropriation is made in bad faith, allowing the defendant to recover fees;
(2) when a motion to terminate an injunction is made or resisted in bad faith, allowing either party to recover; and
(3) when willful and malicious misappropriation is proven, allowing the prevailing plaintiff to recover.

These statutory mechanisms reflect trade secret law's equitable heritage and operate as reciprocal deterrents against bad-faith litigation tactics on both sides.

The DTSA further conditions recovery on prevailing-party status, a requirement that some federal courts have interpreted more narrowly than comparable provisions under the UTSA, particularly when a case is dismissed without prejudice.

## 1.5.5. Additional Equitable Remedies

Not every case of misappropriation fits neatly into a standard remedy like damages or a blanket injunction. Sometimes, courts must craft creative or flexible equitable relief to fit the nuances of the wrongdoing and the harm. These "additional equitable remedies" respond to the challenges of unwinding entangled uses of secret information, mitigating reputational damage, or restoring a semblance of pre-disclosure secrecy. The goal is to eliminate any lingering unfair advantage gained through misappropriation, even when monetary compensation or basic injunctive orders fall short.

One example arises when a defendant has built a new technology, process, or business model that is inseparably based on misappropriated information. In such situations, courts may impose what is called a production injunction—not merely barring further use of a secret but also blocking the defendant from manufacturing or selling any resulting products derived from it. These injunctions are designed to prevent misappropriators from enjoying the fruits of their misconduct, even if they have since made technical modifications. If the core advantage remains rooted in stolen knowledge, the court may treat any downstream product as tainted and off-limits.

### INJUNCTION TO NEUTRALIZE AN UNFAIR HEAD START

*General Electric Co. v. Sung*
843 F. Supp. 776 (D. Mass. 1994)

GE sued its former employee, Dr. Chien-Min Sung, who took proprietary diamond-manufacturing documents and transferred the technology to Iljin Diamond Manufacturing. The court found that Iljin's entire industrial process for saw-grade diamonds was "substantially derived" from GE's confidential documents. Recognizing that a simple use injunction would not suffice—because Iljin could not realistically "unlearn" the trade secrets—the court imposed a seven-year production injunction. This barred Iljin from manufacturing the product itself during the estimated time it would have taken to independently develop the technology. The ruling reinforced that when a secret is tightly woven into a product's core, courts may go beyond use-based restrictions and freeze commercial activity altogether to neutralize the misappropriator's advantage.

Other cases may call for even broader structural or organizational remedies. For instance, courts have ordered internal audits, the appointment of monitors, destruction of contaminated code, or even the transfer of licensing rights back to the victim. These forms of relief are typically tailored to ensure the defendant cannot continue benefiting from any knowledge improperly gained, even if it was only used in part.

### MANDATING CODE DESTRUCTION TO REMEDY MISAPPROPRIATION

*Syntel Sterling Best Shores Mauritius Limited v. The TriZetto Group, Inc.*
68 F.4th 792 (2d Cir. 2023)

In this recent case, Syntel was found to have deliberately misappropriated Trizetto's confidential software architecture and code during the course of a failed outsourcing relationship. The jury awarded damages, but the court went further. It ordered the destruction of Syntel's infringing code and enjoined

Syntel from using or disclosing any of Trizetto's trade secrets, including in derivative products or services. This remedy recognized that once trade secrets infect a rival's development process, the only way to restore fairness may be to purge all resulting outputs. By combining permanent injunction with mandatory deletion of source materials, the court signaled that equitable relief can directly address the structural damage caused by trade secret theft.

These cases exemplify a broader truth: courts have wide discretion in crafting remedies that ensure fairness and restore competitive balance. When a defendant's entire operation or product line becomes tainted by stolen secrets, monetary damages may be inadequate or difficult to measure. Equitable tools—production bans, code destruction, licensing transfers, monitoring, and even dissolution of partnerships—offer the flexibility needed to unwind misuse and neutralize the misappropriator's ill-gotten advantage.

Additional equitable remedies also highlight how seriously courts take the duty of secrecy. These rulings reinforce that misuse of confidential information is not a mere contract breach or commercial inconvenience. It is a breach of trust that can reshape entire industries, and courts stand ready to issue sweeping and lasting orders to rebalance the playing field.

### 1.5.6. The Importance of Prompt Action and Thorough Evidence

A trade secret owner may possess strong legal rights, but enforcement depends heavily on timing and preparation. Courts do not automatically protect trade secrets. They reward vigilance. Plaintiffs who act quickly and substantiate their claims with detailed records are far more likely to secure strong remedies. By contrast, delay or disorganization can render even the most valuable trade secrets unprotectable in practice.

When a company discovers possible misappropriation, time is of the essence. A trade secret that has not yet been used or disclosed may still be contained. But if a plaintiff hesitates, the knowledge may spread, be embedded into a rival product, or even reach the public domain. At that point, the core requirement of secrecy can be irreversibly lost. Courts recognize this danger, which is why they often issue preliminary injunctions when the plaintiff shows immediate and irreparable harm. But they will only act swiftly if the plaintiff does.

**PROMPT ACTION LEADS TO INJUNCTION GRANTED**

*IBM v. Papermaster*
No. 08-CV-9078 (S.D.N.Y. 2008)

IBM moved quickly to enjoin its former executive, Mark Papermaster, from joining Apple, arguing that the risk of trade secret disclosure was imminent. Although Papermaster had not yet revealed any confidential information, IBM convinced the court that his deep knowledge of its microprocessor technology—and the similarity of his role at Apple—posed a serious threat. The court granted a preliminary injunction, noting that IBM had acted promptly and supported its claim with clear evidence of both the confidential nature of the information and the competitive risk. This case exemplifies how timeliness strengthens a plaintiff's credibility and allows courts to intervene before the damage is done.

Equally important is the ability to clearly define the trade secret and demonstrate the measures taken to protect it. Courts do not accept vague references to "proprietary knowledge" or "confidential methods." They require specificity—what the secret is, how it was secured, and how its disclosure or use caused harm. Plaintiffs must show that the secret was treated as such: labeled confidential, shared only under nondisclosure agreements, and protected through physical, digital, or procedural barriers.

Injunctions and damages are not awarded based on moral indignation alone. They depend on the plaintiff's own diligence. Courts ask: Did the company take secrecy seriously before the misappropriation occurred? Did it monitor access, enforce policies, and follow up on violations? These background facts shape the court's perception of whether the trade secret was real and worth protecting.

**CULTURE OF SECRECY SUPPORTS ENFORCEMENT OF TRADE SECRET RIGHTS**

*Data General Corp. v. Digital Computer Controls, Inc.*
357 A.2d 105 (Del. Ch. 1975)

Data General alleged that a competitor had acquired confidential engineering drawings through former employees. The court credited Data General's consistent enforcement of confidentiality practices: it marked documents as proprietary, used employee agreements with nondisclosure clauses, and limited internal access on a need-to-know basis. Because the company demonstrated a longstanding commitment to secrecy, the court found that the drawings qualified as trade secrets. This case shows that courts look not only at the misappropriation but also at the plaintiff's prior behavior in safeguarding its information.

Taken together, these decisions illustrate a simple but powerful lesson: a trade secret is only as strong as the company's willingness to treat it as one. Courts will intervene to protect secrecy, but only when plaintiffs can prove

(1) that they acted promptly upon discovering a threat and,

(2) that they consistently treated the information as confidential.

The best way to prepare for litigation is not after a breach but well before it, by building a record of reasonable, diligent, and consistent secrecy practices.

### 1.5.7. Powerful and Nuanced Relief

Remedies represent the mechanism by which trade secret law defends confidentiality. They balance the need for prompt, often drastic measures—like halting production lines or awarding significant damages—against the principle that competition should remain free for independent or reverse-engineering innovators. Hence, a plaintiff who proves wrongful acquisition, use, or disclosure can expect an array of tools: immediate injunctions, monetary relief pegged to losses or ill-gotten gains, attorneys' fees if malice is evident, and possibly an ongoing royalty arrangement if banning usage entirely seems inequitable.

These outcomes show that trade secret protection can be powerful for a business that invests in properly designating and securing its knowledge. Yet the law does not automatically reward lax secrecy or block legitimate discovery methods. By understanding these remedial principles, owners can gauge the practical benefits and limits of trade secrets as an intellectual property strategy, while potential defendants can see how high the stakes are if they encroach on proprietary data through unethical or unauthorized methods.

## 1.6. International Comparisons

The US approach to trade secrets, exemplified by the UTSA and the federal DTSA, has shaped modern discourse on protecting undisclosed commercial knowledge. However, American courts and laws do not operate in a vacuum. As companies increasingly function across borders, they must consider how other jurisdictions define and enforce trade secrets. While many legal systems share core ideas—requiring secrecy, economic value, and efforts to protect it—they sometimes differ significantly in scope, procedural mechanisms, or available remedies. This section examines the UTSA and the DTSA alongside international frameworks: the Agreement on Trade-Related Aspects of Intellectual Property Rights (TRIPS), the European Union's Trade Secrets Directive, and prominent regimes in China, Canada, Mexico, and Israel.

The TRIPS framework did not emerge in a vacuum. It grew out of geopolitical pressure that was catalyzed by a coordinated campaign by the United States pharmaceutical industry to globalize patent and data protections. That mobilization quickly shaped American trade policy. The United States used §301 trade sanctions and Generalized System of Preferences conditionality to pressure Brazil, Thailand, India, and several Caribbean Basin states to accept intellectual property norms that they had resisted in WIPO forums.

For most of the twentieth century, trade secret protection remained fragmented. Brazil primarily addressed trade secrets through criminal unfair competition provisions, and comprehensive treatment arrived only with the Industrial Property Law of 1996. Within Europe, member states relied on inconsistent frameworks that ranged from Dutch tort law to Maltese contract principles to limited or nonspecific statutory coverage. Earlier international efforts, including the 1967 Stockholm revision of the Paris Convention and the 1996 WIPO Model Provisions on Protection Against Unfair Competition, offered soft law guidance that urged states to curb acts contrary to honest practices but did not impose binding obligations. Building on the domestic Uniform Trade Secrets Act of 1979, amended in 1985, the United States championed inclusion of trade secret standards in the Uruguay Round negotiations.

When the World Trade Organization's Agreement on Trade Related Aspects of Intellectual Property Rights entered into force in 1995, it became the first multilateral treaty to mandate explicit legal protection for undisclosed information under Article 39. That provision incorporates by reference Article 10bis of the Paris Convention and its standard of preventing unfair commercial use. The ambiguity surrounding Article 39.3, particularly whether it compels data exclusivity for pharmaceutical test data, has been interpreted by most commentators and by state practice as not mandating exclusivity. WTO dispute settlement has largely focused on other provisions of TRIPS, for example the Canada–Patent Protection of Pharmaceutical Products dispute on patent exceptions rather than data protection.

Article 39 established a contested global baseline for trade secret protection. That baseline has been reinforced through TRIPS plus bilateral agreements and, in the United States, by the Defend Trade Secrets Act of 2016, which federalized misappropriation claims and confirmed substantial extraterritorial reach when an act in furtherance occurs within the United States. For practitioners, the history shows that TRIPS set a floor for protecting undisclosed information and that the operative standards continue to evolve through national legislation, trade agreements, and WTO interpretation.

### 1.6.1. TRIPS: A Global Baseline for Trade Secret Protections

The World Trade Organization (WTO) Agreement on TRIPS lays the foundation for how member countries treat undisclosed information.

Article 39 of TRIPS insists that member states must protect commercially valuable secrets against unfair competition, echoing the general premise of American trade secret law. TRIPS differs from the UTSA in that it is not a uniform model law but an international agreement. TRIPS does not prescribe a detailed procedural code; it sets minimum substantive standards for protecting undisclosed information, requiring members to protect commercially valuable information kept secret through reasonable measures against disclosure, acquisition, or use contrary to honest commercial practices. It calls for preventing information from being disclosed, acquired, or used by third parties "in a manner contrary to honest commercial practices," especially when that data is valuable and subject to reasonable steps to remain confidential.

This high-level alignment with the UTSA and the DTSA underscores the broad global consensus on punishing industrial espionage, deception, or breaches of trust. Still, each WTO member retains flexibility in how it translates TRIPS obligations into domestic statutes. Enforcement provisions, damage calculations, and injunctive relief vary widely. Some countries accord trade secret disputes specialized treatment in specialized courts, while others handle them under more general civil or commercial codes. As long as they uphold the basic TRIPS principles of protecting undisclosed knowledge, states satisfy their treaty obligations.

The result is a baseline that resembles American doctrine, even though the details can diverge. A firm that experiences misappropriation abroad cannot directly invoke TRIPS against a foreign actor. Instead, enforcement of TRIPS obligations occurs through the WTO's Dispute Settlement Body and must be initiated by a member state, not a private party. As a result, companies often depend on their home governments to press trade secret concerns through diplomatic or trade channels rather than direct legal action. In practice, this means that the effectiveness of TRIPS often turns on local procedural norms, national implementation, and the political will to enforce.

Nonetheless, TRIPS serves as a crucial benchmark: it establishes minimum standards and reflects international consensus that unethical methods of extracting undisclosed commercial information (often referred to as confidential know-how) should be penalized. In many cases, stronger protections arise through "TRIPS-plus" provisions negotiated in bilateral or regional trade agreements, which go beyond the baseline obligations of TRIPS. The United States, in particular, has used trade leverage—including §301 investigations and bilateral agreements—to encourage stricter enforcement of trade secret norms. At the same time, the Doha Declaration, which clarified that TRIPSdoes not and should not prevent members from taking measures to protect public health, and related debates highlight ongoing tensions between intellectual property enforcement and access to knowledge, particularly in fields like health and technology.

## 1.6.2. The EU Trade Secrets Directive

Historically, EU member states had varied approaches to trade secret enforcement. Some, such as Germany, possessed robust protections, while others relied on less-defined unfair competition principles. In 2016, the EU approved the Trade Secrets Directive (Directive 2016/943) to harmonize these differences and ensure consistent standards. The Directive defines a trade secret similarly to the UTSA and the DTSA, focusing on secrecy, commercial value, and reasonable measures for protection. It also lists specific acts of unlawful acquisition, use, or disclosure, mirroring the "misappropriation" language found in American statutes.

The EU Directive instructs member states to ensure that courts can grant injunctions, damage awards, and orders to preserve confidentiality during litigation. By emphasizing that owners must prove actual or potential economic value from secrecy, the Directive aligns closely with American doctrines. Yet procedural aspects still vary from one member state to another. The Directive sets minimum requirements, but the actual enforcement environment can reflect local judicial practices. In certain EU countries, the courts might provide swifter preliminary injunctions, while in others, the threshold for proving irreparable harm may be higher or the measure of damages more conservative.

Another distinctive factor is that EU law generally upholds employee mobility and requires balancing the interests of workers and employers. Courts aim to protect trade secrets while allowing workers to change jobs freely. They also work to prevent employees from acting disloyally or misusing confidential information. This balance is important because it safeguards business interests while respecting employee rights to career mobility.

Like the DTSA, the EU framework invalidates nondisclosure obligations if the knowledge has become generally known or can be deduced through fair means. However, divergences in civil procedure, evidentiary rules, and local cultural attitudes about competition can subtly shape outcomes. For international businesses operating in multiple EU jurisdictions, it remains vital to monitor local court trends and national statutes that implement the Directive in nuanced ways.

## 1.6.3. China: Evolving Enforcement Under Anti-Unfair Competition Law

China's stance toward trade secret law has evolved dramatically. It was once perceived as a high-risk environment for foreign companies, given the country's lax enforcement and the difficulties in gathering evidence of misappropriation. But amendments to the Anti-Unfair Competition Law and complementary regulations over the past decade have strengthened legal recourse for trade secret owners. Chinese courts are now more willing to grant civil or even criminal remedies, especially for large-scale theft or conspiratorial behavior.

These reforms align Chinese doctrine more closely with UTSA and DTSA principles. Chinese law requires that the information be unknown to the public, confer commercial value because of that secrecy, and be guarded by appropriate measures. Employees, contractors, and business partners bear a duty to uphold confidentiality obligations. If they commit fraud, theft, or inducement to obtain the secret, courts can issue injunctions and award damages.

Enforcement challenges persist in areas such as evidence gathering. Plaintiffs may struggle to prove misappropriation without robust discovery procedures. Still, recent cases demonstrate that high-profile disputes—particularly those involving sensitive technology or major foreign investment—can result in significant judgments or criminal charges. Foreign firms often buttress their trade secret posture in China by combining strict internal controls with local partnerships that mitigate risk. They also sometimes keep key aspects of secret processes outside the country. Such strategies do not guarantee immunity from theft, but they reflect an awareness that Chinese law, while improved, may not always respond in the same manner as American courts. Yet as China's commercial ambitions continue to grow, trade secret enforcement remains a crucial and intensifying field of legal reform.

### 1.6.4. Canada: Blend of Statutory and Common Law Principles

Canada's provincial legal frameworks generally parallel the American approach. Although there is no single nationwide statute mirroring the UTSA, Canadian courts rely on common law rules against breaches of confidence, plus various provincial legislation targeting unfair competition. A plaintiff must show that the information was secret, valuable because of secrecy, and shared in an environment implying confidentiality. Wrongful acquisition or disclosure will then give rise to potential injunctions and monetary remedies.

Canadian courts often cite English case law in addition to looking to American precedent. They share the general principles that legitimate reverse engineering is permissible and that employee mobility should not be unreasonably constrained. Some provinces have rules reminiscent of the UTSA in style, if not in codified detail. Damages can be calculated through lost profits or unjust enrichment, but large punitive awards are less common than in the United States. Canada also recognizes that some nondisclosure obligations can overlap with non-competition or non-solicitation clauses, and those must not exceed the reasonable scope needed to protect genuine secrets.

Because Canada is a party to the USMCA (formerly NAFTA), cross-border firms dealing with trade secrets may find streamlined enforcement under certain circumstances. They remain mindful, however, that provincial differences exist, especially in Quebec's civil law system, which takes guidance from French legal traditions. Generally, if a company carefully demonstrates secrecy and invests in appropriate protective measures, Canadian courts can be counted on to uphold the essence of the UTSA/DTSA approach.

### 1.6.5. Mexico: Recent Reforms and Distinct Procedural Hurdles

Mexico's Federal Law for the Protection of Industrial Property, which replaced earlier legislation, governs trade secrets alongside patents, trademarks, and other IP rights. The law defines a trade secret as information kept confidential by reasonable means, possessing real or potential economic value, and not generally known. In that sense, it overlaps significantly with UTSA/DTSA standards. Unauthorized acquisition through deceit, breach of contract, or other disloyal acts is considered an infringement, and the law provides for injunctions and damages.

Despite this similarity on paper, enforcement in Mexico can involve unique procedural challenges. Civil litigation may progress slowly, and collecting evidence of misappropriation is not always straightforward. Some cases also can shift into criminal domains if the theft is grave, but that route entails higher burdens of proof. Trade secrets intersect with Mexico's broader competition policies, meaning that certain NDAs must not be drafted so broadly that they become anticompetitive or infringe labor rights.

Many international companies that enter Mexico adopt parallel measures: they create robust internal compliance (requiring NDAs and limiting disclosure), keep certain key processes abroad, and closely monitor potential local partners or subcontractors. Although Mexico's statutory language mirrors that of more mature systems, the reality can vary from region to region. Nevertheless, Mexico's efforts to modernize its IP and trade secret laws under the USMCA framework continue to reduce discrepancies with US practice, offering more reliable protection for foreign and domestic businesses alike.

### 1.6.6. Israel: Balancing Innovation with Confidentiality Obligations

Israel's trade secret regime draws largely from the Commercial Torts Law of 1999, buttressed by case law that resembles common law unfair competition doctrines. The statutory framework bars the use or disclosure of a trade secret without the owner's consent if it was obtained in bad faith, through breach of confidence, or by other unethical means. Israeli courts also embrace the notion that genuine secrecy must exist and must be guarded actively by the owner. If a secret becomes publicly available, or if a competitor discovers it independently, protection dissolves.

In addition, Israeli courts can impose injunctions and grant damages. They emphasize the significance of employee mobility and the public interest in fostering entrepreneurship, so they tend to confirm that only "truly secret" processes deserve sweeping NDAs or post-employment restrictive covenants. This stance aligns with that of many EU countries, where an employer's interest in secrecy must be balanced against a professional's freedom to use their general skills.

Enforcement in Israel can be quite proactive for technology-based businesses, given the country's status as a leading tech innovator. Organizations that demonstrate thorough internal controls and make immediate responses to suspected leaks typically find the courts to be supportive. On the other hand, if a firm attempts to rely on trade secret rhetoric without consistent security measures or it tries to stifle normal employee transitions, the judicial response will be measured. Overall, Israel's system incorporates core UTSA/DTSA elements—secrecy, value, and wrongdoing—while sustaining a policy backdrop that encourages open innovation under controlled conditions.

## 1.6.7. Convergence and Divergence in Global Trade Secret Regimes

International legal regimes have largely converged on the substantive definitions of a "trade secret" and its "misappropriation." But rights and responsibilities that flow from that definition diverge significantly.

The UTSA (promulgated in 1979 and amended in 1985), the DTSA (enacted May 11, 2016), the World Trade Organization's Agreement on Trade-Related Aspects on Intellectual Property (entered on Jan. 1, 1995), the EU Trade Secrets Directive (adopted on June 8, 2016), China's anti-unfair competition law reforms (2018/19), Israel's Commercial Torts Law (1999), the Canada–United States–Mexico Agreement Implementation Act (entered on July 1, 2020), and Mexico's Federal Law for the Protection of Industrial Property (entered on Nov. 5, 2020) have all nudged global practices toward broadly similar criteria:

**A trade secret is information that remains confidential, holds commercial value specifically because of that secrecy, and is actively protected by its owner. Acquiring or using the knowledge through deception or breach of confidence triggers liability.**

Nevertheless, important differences persist in procedural rules, discovery powers, and cultural attitudes toward competition. While American courts can award expansive damages or punitive relief, some other systems limit recoveries or treat litigation as less adversarial. In certain jurisdictions, it may be harder to secure a swift injunction or to gather the evidence needed to prove misappropriation. Where US law might promptly issue a preliminary injunction to maintain the status quo, foreign courts may require a more stringent standard of proof or a detailed showing of irreparable harm.

Another area of divergence arises in how vigorously courts uphold employee mobility. In the United States, many states disfavor overly broad noncompetition clauses but do enforce reasonable NDAs. The EU, Canada, Israel, and other jurisdictions similarly respect employees' freedom to move between jobs, yet they often scrutinize confidentiality agreements to ensure they do not hamper legitimate transitions. China's approach remains fluid, balancing a growing recognition of trade secret rights against the reality of robust local competition. The bottom line is that while the UTSA and the DTSA are not global law, their emphasis on secrecy, value, and wrongdoing forms an international template that local lawmakers have borrowed and adapted.

Ultimately, companies with multinational footprints must harmonize their secrecy strategies. They must implement consistent internal controls, from NDAs to segmented access to sensitive data, to ensure compliance with both American frameworks and foreign statutes. By treating secrecy as a global discipline—limiting who sees the information, training employees in multiple jurisdictions, and quickly enforcing rights when leaks emerge—owners maximize their odds of securing remedies in varied legal arenas. Understanding the parallels and distinctions among trade secret regimes around the world enables businesses to navigate cross-border challenges and remain vigilant against misappropriation, whether in a US district court action under the DTSA or a specialized proceeding in a far-flung jurisdiction.

# 1.7 Frictions and Trade-Offs

Trade secret law is not only about locking up knowledge; it is about steering innovation, labor, and competition. Courts judge "reasonable efforts," but what counts as reasonable reflects deeper policy choices about what to protect, how strongly, and against whom. As you move toward building your own Trade Secret Protection Plan (TSPP), keep an eye on four recurring tensions that shape both legal outcomes and business practices.

## 1.7.1. Secrecy vs. Mobility

Employers often seek to stop departing engineers from carrying know-how (which can be even more general than what trade secret law defines as protectable information) to rivals. Some use NDAs, noncompetes, or "inevitable disclosure" claims to limit risk. But states like California treat post-employment mobility as a public good and prohibit most noncompetes on policy grounds. Courts in mobility-friendly jurisdictions will scrutinize overbroad restrictions and may deny injunctive relief that looks like a restraint on ordinary career moves.

## 1.7.2. Confidentiality vs. Competition

NDAs are essential—but when drafted too broadly, they can suppress ordinary commercial competition. For example, a vendor asked to sign an NDA may worry that it prevents future work with other customers. Recent empirical studies suggest that many NDAs now function as de facto noncompetes, thus triggering scrutiny under antitrust law and FTC policy. Enforcement hinges not only on content but also on context and proportionality.

### 1.7.3. Security vs. Transparency

Some trade secret claims intersect with employee obligations to report misconduct, raise product-safety concerns, or alert regulators. While secrecy is critical to commercial integrity, it must sometimes yield to whistle-blower protections and public-interest disclosures. Courts and legislatures increasingly carve out exceptions for "good faith" disclosure, especially where health, safety, or illegality is at stake.

### 1.7.4. Protection vs. Innovation

Firms must often choose between the secrecy of trade secret law and the disclosure required for patent protection. This decision reflects a broader policy trade-off between static control (holding onto exclusive rights) and dynamic spillovers (allowing others to build and improve). Patent law offers time-limited monopolies with full disclosure; trade secrets offer longer potential duration, but only if secrecy is maintained and lawful reverse engineering is unlikely.

### 1.7.5. Trade Secret Protections in the Balance

A sound TSPP guards what matters—but also aligns with the organization's values, competitive goals, and obligations to employees and society. As you begin Chapter 2, you will start the process of identifying, classifying, and protecting your confidential assets. That process is not just legal. It is strategic.

## 1.8. From Legal Definitions to Practical Protection

Trade secrets occupy a unique position within intellectual property law. Unlike patents or trademarks, they are not created by filing paperwork or satisfying a formal statutory test. They exist only so long as they are actively and effectively kept secret. This feature makes trade secret law both powerful and fragile. It protects some of the most valuable assets in business—formulas, processes, strategies, and data—but only if the owner treats them like secrets worth guarding.

As this chapter has shown, a trade secret must meet three core criteria: it must be information, it must derive independent economic value from not being generally known or readily ascertainable, and it must be subject to reasonable efforts to maintain secrecy. Those requirements define what qualifies as a trade secret, but they also set the foundation for everything that follows. A business that does not know what its secrets are, cannot articulate why they matter, or has not built a culture of confidentiality will struggle to enforce its rights.

We have also seen that trade secret law is not passive. Remedies—whether damages, injunctions, or equitable relief—are not automatic. They require evidence, speed, and credibility. Courts respond to clear documentation, consistent enforcement, and timely legal action. Without those things, even egregious misappropriation may go unpunished. In this regard, trade secret protection is not merely a matter of legal theory but rather a matter of organizational discipline.

This book is built on that idea. The chapters that follow do not assume that trade secrets can be protected with a single policy or contract. Instead, they explore what real protection requires: identifying your trade secrets with precision, assessing their value and risk, establishing layers of internal and external safeguards, and responding effectively to breaches when they occur. The law provides tools—but it is up to businesses, lawyers, and courts to use them wisely.

In short, trade secret protection is not something that happens in courtrooms. It happens in conference rooms, product labs, and shared servers. It is embedded in who has access to what, how information flows within an organization, and how leaders set expectations for confidentiality. What the law recognizes as a trade secret depends entirely on what the business chooses to protect and how well it does so.

The rest of this book will show you how to do exactly that.

## References

Mark A. Lemley, *The Surprising Virtues of Treating Trade Secrets as IP Rights*, 61 Stan. L. Rev. 311 (2010).

Orly Lobel, Talent Wants to Be Free (Yale University Press 2013).

Amy Kapczynski, *The Public History of Secrets*, 55 U.C. Davis L. Rev. 1367 (2022).

William Landes & Richard Posner, The Economic Structure of Intellectual Property Law (Belknap Press 2003).

I.P.L. Png, *Secrecy and Patents: Theory and Evidence from the UTSA*, 2(3) Strategy Science 176–93 (2017).

Camilla Hrdy & Christopher Seaman, *Beyond Trade Secrecy: Confidentiality Agreements That Act Like Noncompetes*, 133 Yale L.J. 669 (2024).

David S. Levine, *Secrecy and Unaccountability: Trade Secrets in Our Public Infrastructure*, 59 Fla. L. Rev. 135 (2007).

Ronald Gilson, *The Legal Infrastructure of High Technology Industrial Districts*, 74 N.Y.U. L. Rev. 575 (1999).

# Chapter 2

# Inventorying and Classifying Trade Secrets

You cannot hit a target you cannot perceive—and you cannot protect a trade secret of which you are unaware.

Trade secret protection begins with one unshakable truth: you must know what you are protecting. There is no such thing as a secret that protects itself. The law only helps those who help themselves—and the first step is identifying which pieces of information qualify as trade secrets in the first place.

This chapter marks the beginning of that process. Before a company can reduce risk, impose restrictions, or take legal action, it must first recognize the assets at stake. That means conducting a thorough inventory of its confidential knowledge—identifying what secrets exist, where they reside, how they function, and why they matter.

Inventorying is not about documentation for its own sake. It is about clarity. A well-executed trade secret inventory allows a business to prioritize what matters most, classify different kinds of secrets, and build a protection strategy tailored to its unique operations. Without it, even the best legal theories or policies will fail.

Every other chapter in this book depends on this one. Although you now understand what trade secrets are and how they fit into the framework of intellectual property (Chapter 1), you cannot evaluate risks (Chapter 3), mitigate threats (Chapters 4 and 5), enforce your rights (Chapter 6), or implement an organization-wide plan (Chapter 7) unless you have first inventoried and classified your trade secrets (this Chapter 2). This step is not optional. It is the foundation for everything that follows.

## 2.1. Identification Is the Foundation for Protection

Trade secrets are protected only when they are identified, valued, and actively guarded. Unlike patents or copyrights, trade secrets are not registered or granted by the government. They have no fixed term and no official recognition. They exist only because someone treats them as secrets—and if someone stops treating them that way, they disappear.

The first step in protecting a trade secret is knowing that it exists. That's the purpose of a trade secret inventory. It gives a business a structured way to identify and classify the confidential information that drives its competitive edge. Without an inventory, protection is impossible. You cannot enforce a right to something you never documented. You cannot prioritize safeguards for assets you have never named.

This chapter walks through how to create that inventory. It explains how to recognize different kinds of trade secrets, how to apply the legal test for protection, and how to assign priority levels based on economic importance. Along the way, it offers practical tools for making the inventory a living part of your business: not a static list, but an ongoing process.

Trade secret protection is a system, not a filing cabinet. That system starts here.

## 2.2. Identifying Trade Secrets for the Inventory

You cannot protect a trade secret until you recognize that you have one. That simple insight underlies the most important task in building a Trade Secret Protection Plan: identifying what qualifies as a trade secret in the first place. Most businesses are surprised by how much information qualifies—and by how much does not.

This section explains how to recognize a trade secret when you see one. It distinguishes between three major categories of secrets—technical, business, and hybrid—and shows how each can qualify for legal protection. These categories do not create legal rights on their own. But they help teams inventory their secrets more clearly, making it easier to apply the legal test from Chapter 1 and assess risk in Chapter 3.

Effective identification is not about reciting doctrine. It is about learning to look at your own operations—products, processes, strategies, and data—and recognizing which parts give you an edge. Many of those edges exist only because others do not know how you do what you do. Once you see your business through that lens, you can begin identifying what needs protection.

### 2.2.1. Technical Trade Secrets

Technical trade secrets are often the easiest to recognize. They include product formulas, manufacturing processes, engineering designs, source code, algorithms, and scientific methods. If the information is used to build, create, test, or operate a product or service and is not generally known, it may be a technical trade secret.

These secrets usually reside with engineers, developers, or scientists—but not always. A sales team's proprietary scoring model or an IT department's internal cybersecurity architecture might also qualify. What matters is that the knowledge is technical in nature and used to accomplish a specific functional task.

To qualify as a trade secret, a technical process must be sufficiently detailed to be replicated. Courts do not protect vague ideas like "make the software run faster" or "improve product quality." The process must be defined with enough specificity that, if stolen, it could be used by a competitor to replicate the benefit.

**SOFTWARE ALGORITHMS CAN BE TRADE SECRETS**

*ClearOne Communications, Inc. v. Bowers*
643 F.3d 735 (10th Cir. 2011)

ClearOne developed proprietary echo cancellation software for use in its audio conferencing systems. When a competitor acquired the software through a third party and integrated it into its own products, ClearOne sued for misappropriation. The court upheld an injunction, finding that ClearOne's underlying algorithms were protectable technical trade secrets. This case reinforces that advanced software logic, even if not patented, can receive trade secret protection if kept confidential and technically detailed.

## 2.2.2. Business Trade Secrets

Business trade secrets are equally important, though sometimes less obvious. They include customer lists, pricing strategies, supplier terms, marketing tactics, sales forecasts, and operational methods. Unlike technical secrets, business secrets are not about how to build a product—they are about how to sell it, manage it, or gain a market advantage.

Business secrets often live in spreadsheets, databases, and employee knowledge. They are especially vulnerable when employees leave to join a competitor or start a new business. A well-maintained customer relationship management (CRM) system, if protected by confidentiality agreements and limited access, can be one of the most valuable trade secrets a company owns.

The key question is whether the information is more than general business experience. Courts distinguish between an employee's general knowledge (which is portable) and the employer's confidential methods (which are protectable). If the information gives the business a competitive edge and is not available to others without effort, it may qualify as a trade secret.

**CUSTOMER LISTS AND PRICING INFORMATION CAN BE TRADE SECRETS**

*Chefs Diet Acquisition Corp. v. Lean Chefs, LLC*
2016 U.S. Dist. LEXIS 133299 (S.D.N.Y. 2016)

Former executives of Chefs Diet launched a competing company, using customer lists, proprietary recipes, and pricing data taken from their previous employer. The court allowed trade secret claims to proceed, finding that such business-side data—when actively protected—could qualify for legal protection. This case shows that customer and pricing information is not just administrative detail; it can be a core asset if treated as a secret.

### 2.2.3. Hybrid Trade Secrets

Some trade secrets blur the line between technical and business. These hybrid secrets combine engineering or scientific content with strategic, financial, or operational components. For example, a software tool that calculates optimal pricing based on real-time data inputs involves both technical algorithms and business decision-making. Neither part alone may be groundbreaking, but together they can produce a high-value system.

Hybrid trade secrets are increasingly common in data-driven businesses. A predictive analytics platform might use confidential client data and a proprietary algorithm. A marketing campaign might rely on a custom-built segmentation model and an internal dataset. These are not purely technical or purely strategic—they are both.

What makes hybrid trade secrets powerful is the way they integrate multiple types of knowledge into a cohesive advantage. Courts have recognized this fusion as protectable when the individual components are confidential and the combined system delivers unique value.

**HYBRID BUSINESS-TECHNICAL INFORMATION CAN BE TRADE SECRETS**

*ClearOne Advantage, LLC v. Kersen*
2024 U.S. Dist. LEXIS 205636 (D. Md. 2024)

ClearOne sued a former employee who allegedly stole client-targeting algorithms used to optimize digital marketing campaigns. The algorithms combined technical logic with behavioral and financial data, making them valuable for both engineering and strategic purposes. The court found that the combination of technical components and marketing use could constitute a trade secret. This case illustrates how hybrid information can be protectable when it integrates confidential data and technical methods into a single, high-impact system.

## 2.3. Applying the Three Essential Elements

Before a business can protect its information as a trade secret, it must first determine whether that information meets the legal definition. Trade secret protection is not automatic; it applies only when the information satisfies all parts of a three-element test:

1. The information must qualify as a protectable form of knowledge (referred to here simply as "information");
2. It must have independent economic value because it is kept secret; and
3. The owner must take reasonable efforts to maintain that secrecy.

Each element plays a distinct and necessary role. If even one is missing, the information cannot be treated as a trade secret under state or federal law. Courts look to all three when deciding whether something is legally protected.

The first and third elements—what counts as "information," and what counts as "reasonable efforts"—are relatively straightforward in structure, though they raise important questions in practice. The second element, however, is more complex.

The second element requires that the information's economic value comes from the fact that it is not widely known or easily discovered. Courts have consistently held that this element is not a single fact to prove but rather a combination of interrelated conditions that work together to establish value through secrecy. Specifically, to meet this element, the information must

(a) have independent economic value (that is, its value comes specifically from being secret),

(b) not be generally known in the relevant industry, and

(c) not be readily ascertainable through proper means.

These three qualities are not separate legal elements. Rather, they form a single, compound element: independent economic value from secrecy. In some cases, courts analyze them together as one inquiry; in others, especially where facts are contested, they break them apart. For clarity, this guide takes the latter approach. Understanding how this second element works is key to identifying what information qualifies for trade secret protection and what does not.

### 2.3.1. Information

The first element of the trade secret test requires that the subject matter qualify as "information." At a glance, this might seem obvious, but trade secret law draws a careful line between information that is protectable and information that is not.

The UTSA defines a trade secret as "information, including a formula, pattern, compilation, program, device, method, technique, or process." This list is not exhaustive, but it illustrates the breadth of what can be protected—so long as the other two elements of the trade secret test are met.

In practice, courts have recognized a wide range of content as "information," including:

- Formulas (e.g., chemical recipes, flavor blends)
- Patterns (e.g., textile templates, engineering layouts)
- Compilations (e.g., curated customer lists, pricing databases)
- Programs (e.g., software source code or apps)
- Methods and Techniques (e.g., specialized manufacturing steps or analytical procedures)
- Processes (e.g., production sequences or business workflows)
- Design Specifications (e.g., CAD files, engineering blueprints)
- Prototypes (e.g., mockups embodying novel design features)
- Strategic Plans (e.g., product roadmaps or market-entry strategies)
- Algorithms and Codes (e.g., data-sorting logic or encryption keys)
- Procedures (e.g., internal quality control protocols or training protocols)

What unites all of these information types is that they represent concrete, defined sets of knowledge or instructions that are capable of being protected—provided they are also secret and valuable.

However, not everything a company keeps private is protectable. The law excludes:

- Physical objects themselves (though the design or method behind them may be protectable)
- General employee skill and experience
- Sensory impressions (e.g., the taste of a product, unless tied to a secret formula)
- Abstract ideas or undeveloped concepts

In other words, trade secret law protects knowledge, not things. A machine is not a trade secret, but the confidential process for building or operating it might be. Similarly, a person's accumulated skill is not a company trade secret—even if they acquired that skill on the job—unless they are also taking defined, protectable knowledge along with them.

**TECHNICAL CONCEPTS CAN BE TRADE SECRETS**

*Altavion, Inc. v. Konica Minolta Systems Laboratory, Inc.*
226 Cal. App. 4th 26 (2014)

Altavion developed a method for embedding secure digital stamps into PDF files and shared this idea with Konica Minolta under a confidentiality agreement. When Konica Minolta applied for patents on similar technology without involving Altavion, litigation followed. The court held that Altavion's ideas were sufficiently specific and technically detailed to qualify as trade secrets. Although they had not yet been turned into a product, they were well-developed enough to be protectable. This case illustrates that even early-stage concepts can be trade secrets if they are clearly described and technically meaningful.

Finally, courts focus on the *substance*, not the *form*. It does not matter whether the information is written on paper, stored in a file, or embedded in a prototype. What matters is whether the underlying knowledge is sufficiently concrete, secret, and economically valuable to warrant protection. Trade secret law protects the intangible insight, not the medium it happens to live in.

## 2.3.2. Independent Economic Value from Secrecy

The second element of the trade secret test requires that the information provide a competitive advantage because it is kept secret. Trade secret law does not protect secrecy for its own sake—it protects secrecy that has commercial significance. In other words, the information must be valuable in a way that depends on its not being generally known or easily discoverable. That value must be tied directly to its confidentiality.

For example, a secret formula that allows a company to produce goods more cheaply, a pricing model that gives it leverage in negotiations, or a customer list that allows more targeted sales—all of these might have economic value that comes from being closely held. If the same information were to become widely known, the advantage would disappear.

This second element is more complex than it first appears. Courts have consistently interpreted it as a compound requirement, one that involves several interlocking ideas:

A. The information must have independent economic value—its utility must come specifically from being secret, not merely from being useful.

B. It must be not generally known in the relevant industry—if it is common knowledge, it confers no competitive advantage.

C. It must be not readily ascertainable by proper means—if competitors could easily figure it out on their own, secrecy is not what makes it valuable.

These three ideas together define the legal meaning of "independent economic value from secrecy." Some courts analyze them together; others treat them as distinct factual questions. Either way, all three must be true for this element to be satisfied. If the information is valuable but generally known, or secret but easy to reverse engineer, it will not qualify for protection. Understanding how these factors work together is essential for identifying and prioritizing protectable trade secrets in a business setting.

### *2.3.2.1. Independent Economic Value*

The second element of the trade secret test begins with the idea that the information must be valuable. In this context, "value" refers to usefulness—information that contributes meaningfully to the operations or success of a business. But not all types of value qualify. Trade secret law is concerned only with value that is economic. The information must improve the business's position in the marketplace, whether by increasing revenue, reducing costs, improving efficiency, enhancing quality, accelerating development, or otherwise creating a competitive advantage.

Courts have made clear that other kinds of value—while possibly important in other contexts—do not satisfy this requirement. For example, sentimental value, personal pride, or religious significance do not count. Nor does reputational value, in the sense of simply wanting to prevent embarrassment or criticism. These may support claims in defamation, contract, or other areas of law—but they are not part of the trade secret framework.

This value must be economic in nature. That is, the information must make a difference to the business's profitability, efficiency, or market standing. Courts accept that this value can take many forms. It might increase revenues, reduce costs, improve decision-making, enhance product quality, or position the company to act more effectively than competitors. Crucially, the information need not be currently monetized—it may qualify even if it has only potential economic value, so long as there is a reasonable basis to believe it could be leveraged for competitive gain in the future.

**SECRECY CAN EVIDENCE ECONOMIC VALUE**

*Religious Technology Center v. Lerma*
908 F. Supp. 1362 (E.D. Va. 1995)

The Church of Scientology claimed trade secret protection over confidential religious training materials known as the "Advanced Technology" documents. The Church charged members substantial fees to access these materials and imposed strict confidentiality rules. This commercial model showed that spiritual or ideological information can generate independent economic value when access is monetized and restricted through secrecy. However, the Church ultimately lost trade secret protection after the materials were placed in a public court file for 28 months and then posted on the Internet. The court held that once the documents entered the public domain, they could no longer qualify as trade secrets, regardless of their prior economic value. The case illustrates that even religious or philosophical materials may receive trade secret protection based on economic value stemming from secrecy, but that protection is irrevocably lost when information becomes publicly available.

Importantly, the economic value must also be independent, meaning it comes specifically from the information's being secret. It is not enough that the information is useful to the company; the value must derive from the fact that others do not know it. If the same benefit would remain even after public disclosure, the information does not meet this standard. This exclusivity is the foundation of trade secret protection: it rewards businesses that develop valuable knowledge and successfully keep it out of competitors' hands.

Some courts describe this as a test of competitive harm: Would a rival gain a meaningful advantage by acquiring the information? If so, that's a strong indication that the information has independent economic value. If not—if the information provides no edge or is already in general use—then trade secret law offers no protection. To illustrate this point, it helps to consider examples of what does and does not count.

Information that may have independent economic value includes:

- Confidential manufacturing techniques that lower production costs
- Internal pricing data and customer profiles that improve sales targeting
- Strategic business plans, market entry timing, or investment forecasts
- Proprietary software source code or machine-learning algorithms
- Unreleased product specifications or research data

Information that does not have independent economic value includes:

- Routine internal data, like employee schedules or vacation calendars
- Holiday party plans or internal communications with no competitive impact
- Common industry practices or generic strategies everyone uses
- Public filings or promotional materials
- Outdated projections or specifications no longer in use

Finally, it is worth distinguishing this requirement from secrecy itself. Economic value and secrecy are related, but not identical. Some information may be secret but trivial—and therefore not protectable. Other information may be useful, but widely known—and thus not protectable either. The point of this element is to focus on value that is created or preserved by the fact of secrecy.

This test ensures that trade secret law protects knowledge that is both meaningful in the marketplace and unavailable to the public. The next section examines the first of the two secrecy-related components: whether the information is not generally known to others in the relevant field.

### 2.3.2.2. Not Generally Known

The second component of the "independent economic value" element is that the information must be not generally known. This reflects the fundamental insight behind trade secret law: if a business advantage comes from keeping information secret, that advantage disappears once the information becomes widely available. Trade secret protection ends where public knowledge begins.

But the law does not demand total or absolute secrecy. Courts recognize a standard of relative secrecy. Information can still be protected even if it is known to a small number of people so long as those people are bound by confidentiality obligations or internal security controls. What matters is whether the information is generally accessible to those who could profit from it—competitors, industry peers, or other actors in the marketplace.

This is not a bright-line rule. Courts assess whether the information is known by enough people, in enough places, and through enough channels to eliminate its competitive value as a secret. If so, it no longer qualifies for protection. Even a company's internal knowledge can lose trade secret status if it has been too widely shared internally without proper safeguards.

There are many ways that information can become generally known, some deliberate, some accidental:

- Filing for a patent will make the disclosed content public, even if the patent is later denied or withdrawn.
- Publishing information in academic journals, industry whitepapers, or marketing materials makes it accessible to competitors.
- Disclosing content in court filings or regulatory submissions can strip it of protection unless specific confidentiality procedures (such as protective orders) are in place.
- Broad dissemination within a company, without access controls or confidentiality markings, can undermine claims that the information was secret.

Conversely, courts have held that information is *not* generally known when:

- It is shared only with employees or partners under nondisclosure agreements.
- It is discussed in closed business negotiations where confidentiality is implied or formalized by customary practices and commercial morality.

- It is known to a small number of companies in the industry but is not publicly available.
- It is based on original internal research, planning, or design, and not duplicated elsewhere.

**CONTROLLED DISTRIBUTION PRESERVES CONFIDENTIALITY**

*Board of Trade of City of Chicago v. Christie Grain & Stock Co.*
198 U.S. 236 (1905)

The Board of Trade created valuable grain pricing data, which it distributed only to paying subscribers under strict conditions. A competitor acquired and republished the data. The Supreme Court held that the Board's data remained confidential because it was not available to the general public. Its value came from its controlled and limited distribution: a key example of how relative secrecy can still support legal protection.

What this element ultimately asks is whether the information gives the business a competitive advantage because others in the industry do not have access to it. If so, then it is not generally known—and it satisfies this part of the test.

But if the information has already "leaked out" into the public domain—whether through external disclosures, shared practices, or failure to restrict internal access—it is no longer a secret in the eyes of the law. That is true even if the company continues to treat it as confidential. Once secrecy is lost, legal protection ends.

This concept is closely related to yet distinct from the next element: whether the information is readily ascertainable. "Not generally known" asks whether the information is currently available to others. "Not readily ascertainable" asks whether others could easily figure it out, even if they haven't yet. Both tests must be satisfied. The next section turns to that question.

### *2.3.2.3. Not Readily Ascertainable by Proper Means*

The final component of the "independent economic value" element focuses not on what others do know but rather on what they could know. Specifically, it asks whether the information could be discovered by others using lawful and legitimate efforts. To qualify as a trade secret, the information must be not readily ascertainable by proper means.

This requirement plays a critical role in separating protectable secrets from open knowledge. Even if information is currently unknown to competitors, it may not be eligible for protection if it can be easily uncovered through commonly accepted methods. The law does not shield businesses from the risk that others might independently figure things out. Instead, it rewards secrecy only when secrecy is necessary to preserve a competitive advantage—when the information would be difficult for others to obtain without improper conduct.

The term "readily ascertainable" refers to whether the information could be learned with reasonable effort. The threshold is not impossibility. The question is whether the information is sufficiently accessible that a skilled person, acting lawfully and without deception, could reproduce or reconstruct it using public tools, market knowledge, or direct analysis.

For example, a company that releases a physical product into the market cannot claim as a trade secret any aspect of that product that could be easily reverse engineered. Courts have consistently held that reverse engineering—carefully examining a product to understand how it works—is a proper means of discovery. If the secret can be determined by disassembling the product, conducting standard chemical testing, or observing its behavior in the field, then that secret is legally exposed, even if no one has taken the time to uncover it yet.

Similarly, courts recognize that companies may arrive at the same information through independent development. If two firms, working separately and without collusion, reach the same technical or strategic insight, each has the right to use that information. Trade secret protection does not grant exclusivity over knowledge that others can lawfully invent on their own.

Likewise, courts reject claims that rest on information found in public sources, even if a company was the first to compile or organize that data. If the core details are published in regulatory filings, government databases, academic journals, or other public repositories, the fact that a competitor could gather and synthesize them without wrongdoing makes the resulting information unprotectable.

The defining theme here is accessibility through honest effort. If the path to discovery is short, clear, and lawful, the law does not bar others from taking it. That is why courts assess not only the originality or usefulness of the information but also how difficult it would be for others to learn it using conventional tools or standard professional diligence.

However, there are many situations where information is not readily ascertainable. A process that is used behind closed doors, embedded in a secure system, or tied to subtle refinements not visible from the final product may remain secret even if the end result is public. In *Hertz v. Luzenac Group*, the court recognized that although each individual step in the talc manufacturing process was known in the industry, Luzenac Group's specific combination and sequence of those steps had not been discovered. The court emphasized that it was not obvious how to arrange the process in the same way, and that difficulty is what made the process not readily ascertainable.

What matters is the effort and expertise required. If reverse engineering would take weeks of trial and error, require special equipment, or depend on unlikely insight, courts may find that the information is not readily obtainable. But if the discovery could be made quickly and easily by someone with standard tools and industry knowledge, protection will not apply.

At the same time, trade secret law draws a bright line between proper and improper means of discovery. Only discovery by proper means—meaning honest, lawful, and ethical conduct—counts against protection. If a competitor learns the information through theft, deception, bribery, hacking, or breach of contract, that acquisition is legally improper, and the trade secret remains intact.

Statutes like the UTSA and the DTSA define improper means to include theft; bribery; misrepresentation; breach of a confidentiality duty; or espionage, whether physical or electronic. Courts have expanded on these examples to include cyber intrusions, phishing schemes, employee disloyalty, and violations of nondisclosure agreements. In these cases, the use of the information is misappropriation, and trade secret law provides remedies even if the information could theoretically be reverse engineered. The issue is not whether discovery was possible but instead whether it was done the right way.

This distinction serves a fundamental policy goal: encouraging fair competition without endorsing misconduct. If a competitor works independently to replicate a product or process using proper techniques, the law protects their right to do so. But if they cross ethical or legal boundaries to gain access to confidential information, that conduct violates trade secret protections—even if the information might have been discoverable by other means.

### REVERSE ENGINEERING IS (GENERALLY) NOT MISAPPROPRIATION

*Chicago Lock Co. v. Fanberg*
676 F.2d 400 (9th Cir. 1982)

Chicago Lock sold high-security locks that shared a common key code system. Locksmiths who purchased the locks began reverse engineering the codes and publishing them in reference guides. The company sued to stop this, arguing that the keying system was a trade secret. The court disagreed. It found that the locks were publicly available and the internal coding could be discovered through lawful examination. Because the information was readily ascertainable by anyone who purchased the product and studied it, it did not qualify as a trade secret. This case demonstrates that trade secret protection ends where lawful discovery begins.

In sum, the third and final part of the "independent economic value" element asks whether the information is difficult to obtain through lawful methods. The law favors protecting information that cannot be easily reconstructed or found using proper diligence. When secrecy makes discovery genuinely difficult, the owner retains protection. When discovery would be obvious, routine, or trivial, the law steps aside.

With this final component established, we have now fully unpacked the second element of the trade secret test. We turn next to the third and final requirement: whether the information has been subject to reasonable efforts to maintain its secrecy.

## 2.3.3. Subject to Reasonable Efforts to Maintain Secrecy

Trade secret law protects secrets—but only when the owner acts like they are secret. The final and perhaps most important element in the legal test is whether the information has been subject to reasonable efforts to maintain its secrecy. This is not a question of perfect security. It is a question of seriousness, discipline, and consistency.

The law does not require that only one person know the secret. Nor does it require vaults, encryption, or locked rooms in every case. What it requires is evidence that the business took affirmative steps to limit disclosure and prevent unauthorized use. That includes policies, contracts, markings, access restrictions, training, and other internal practices that signal to employees and partners that the information is not for public consumption.

Courts ask whether the company behaved in a way that reflects an expectation of confidentiality. If a business shares information casually, fails to use nondisclosure agreements, leaves documents unprotected, or allows access without controls, it may lose trade secret protection even if the information itself remains unknown to the public. The law will not save a company from its own carelessness.

At the same time, the efforts must be proportionate. What counts as reasonable depends on the nature of the business, the sensitivity of the information, and the resources available. A small company with limited infrastructure is not held to the same standard as a multinational corporation. But both are expected to do what is reasonably within their power to preserve secrecy.

One of the most common failures occurs when businesses require signed NDAs but do nothing else. A nondisclosure agreement is a good start, but it is not enough on its own. If the NDA is never explained, enforced, or integrated into company culture, courts may see it as window dressing rather than real protection. The same is true for confidentiality labels that are never backed up by meaningful access controls or consistent reminders.

On the other hand, when companies combine contractual protections with access limitations, employee training, document labeling, and internal discipline, courts are far more likely to uphold the existence of a trade secret. What matters is the overall pattern. The company must treat the information like a secret at every stage of its use and handling.

**NDAS ALONE ARE NOT ENOUGH FOR "REASONABLE EFFORTS"**

*nClosures Inc. v. Block & Co.*
770 F.3d 598 (7th Cir. 2014)

nClosures developed a metal iPad case and entered into a manufacturing relationship with Block & Co. under a confidentiality agreement. Block later brought a similar product to market, and nClosures sued for trade secret misappropriation. The court found that although there was an NDA in place, nClosures had failed to take other reasonable measures to maintain secrecy. It had shared design files without restriction, displayed the product publicly, and taken no additional steps to guard the information. The court ruled that the alleged secret had not been adequately protected and therefore did not qualify for trade secret status. This case illustrates that formal agreements alone are not enough; businesses must actively maintain secrecy in practice.

The legal standard is reasonableness, not perfection. But reasonableness means more than good intentions. It means acting in a way that a court can recognize as consistent with secrecy. When companies show that they care about protecting information, courts are willing to help. When companies are careless, courts will not intervene. Trade secret law protects the diligent, not the indifferent.

## 2.4. Prioritizing Trade Secrets by Economic and Strategic Importance

Once a company identifies what qualifies as a trade secret, the next challenge is deciding which secrets matter most. Not all secrets are equally valuable. Some drive revenue, shape strategy, or protect the business from collapse. Others are useful but replaceable. Treating every trade secret as equally important leads to wasted effort. Trade secret protection is resource-intensive. A company must know where to concentrate its energy.

Prioritization is a matter of both economics and judgment. The legal test tells us whether something qualifies as a trade secret. But the inventory is also a business tool, and businesses need to know which secrets are most worth defending. A small startup might have only a handful of high-priority secrets. A large firm might have dozens spread across departments. Regardless of size, every organization must make distinctions.

Some secrets protect what no competitor can match. Others allow the company to move faster, cheaper, or more effectively than rivals. Still others are important but not critical; they contribute to the business but their loss would not cripple it. A few may be legacy items that once mattered but no longer define the company's position in the market. The goal of prioritization is not to minimize protection for the lower tiers but rather to recognize that not everything can be treated as mission-critical.

The inventory must reflect these differences. Each trade secret should be categorized by priority level based on what would happen if the secret were exposed. That exposure might come through misappropriation, reverse engineering, lawful disclosure, or carelessness. The point is to evaluate how much harm would result and how difficult it would be to replace the advantage.

There are no rigid formulas. But companies can generally classify their secrets into three broad tiers. Some trade secrets are high priority—these are the crown jewels, the secrets that shape everything else. Others are medium priority—they matter, but they can be rebuilt or worked around. The rest are low priority—they still qualify as trade secrets, but their strategic value is modest or declining.

The next three sections explain each of these categories in more detail. The distinctions are not just for theory. They shape how the company allocates protection, assigns responsibility, and prepares for potential litigation. A good inventory does more than identify secrets. It tells the business which secrets it cannot afford to lose.

## 2.4.1. High-Priority Trade Secrets

High-priority trade secrets are the ones a business cannot afford to lose. These are the assets that provide a decisive competitive advantage—knowledge that would cause serious harm if it were disclosed or misappropriated. They often support core products, proprietary technologies, key customers, or strategic relationships. Without them, the business would suffer immediate commercial damage or long-term strategic erosion.

In many cases, these secrets are directly tied to revenue. A proprietary manufacturing process that allows a company to produce at half the cost of its competitors belongs in this category. So does an algorithm that powers a flagship product, a design no one else can replicate, or a dataset that underpins high-value decision-making. When a trade secret loss would mean loss of customers, collapse of margins, or the end of a product line, the priority is obvious.

But not all high-priority secrets are visible on a balance sheet. Some are early-stage technologies that have not yet reached the market. Others are strategic roadmaps or internal playbooks that guide future growth. If a competitor gained access to those documents, they might not destroy the company, but they could erode its ability to lead. Priority is about more than present value. It is also about vulnerability, timing, and the company's broader trajectory.

These are the secrets that demand the most protection. They should be subject to the strongest contractual safeguards, the tightest access restrictions, and the most rigorous monitoring. In some cases, they should be kept entirely out of vendor relationships or third-party platforms, even if doing so creates operational friction. The cost of inconvenience is small compared to the cost of exposure.

Courts are more likely to enforce trade secret claims when the information clearly mattered to the business. A company that can point to a carefully guarded secret that underpins a flagship product will have a far easier time proving misappropriation than one that over-claims routine procedures. Prioritization signals to courts that the company understands its own assets and has acted accordingly.

**HIGH ECONOMIC VALUE BOLSTERS TRADE SECRET STATUS**

*Boeing Co. v. Sierracin Corp.*
738 P.2d 665 (Wash. 1987)

Boeing developed proprietary methods for manufacturing aircraft windshields and treated these techniques as trade secrets. When a supplier began using similar processes, Boeing sued. The court upheld the claim, emphasizing the commercial importance of the techniques and Boeing's efforts to protect them. The decision reinforced that where a secret is both highly valuable and carefully guarded, the law will provide strong protection. Boeing's success in the case reflected not only the uniqueness of the information but also the clarity with which the company had treated it as a critical asset.

A business does not need to have many high-priority secrets, but it must know which ones fall into that category—and treat them accordingly. These are the assets that define the company's edge. Without them, the business is just another competitor.

## 2.4.2. Medium-Priority Trade Secrets

Medium-priority trade secrets matter. They contribute to the business's performance, efficiency, or strategy. But they are not essential to survival. If lost, they would cause friction, not failure. The company might need to retool a process, adjust pricing, or rebuild relationships. But it could do so without catastrophic disruption.

These secrets often reflect operational experience. A pricing formula that helps optimize margins across multiple markets might fall in this category. So might a vendor negotiation strategy, a bundled service approach, or an internal workflow that shortens production time. These are not secrets that competitors could never develop. They are secrets that the company developed first and that still offer a meaningful edge.

In some cases, a trade secret's priority is a function of time. A strategy document might be high priority before a product launch but drop to medium priority after the product is released. A supplier arrangement might be sensitive while a deal is in negotiation but less important once terms are locked in. Prioritization is dynamic. It reflects the secret's current role in the business, not just its theoretical value.

Medium-priority secrets deserve protection, but not at all costs. A company might share these secrets with trusted partners under contract. It might allow broader internal access with appropriate training and reminders. What matters is proportionality. The security measures should reflect the value of the secret and the risk of loss. Over-protecting these assets can waste resources or slow down operations. Under-protecting them can invite preventable loss.

Companies sometimes try to inflate the importance of these secrets during litigation. Courts are not persuaded by exaggeration. If the information was not treated as high-value at the time of the alleged misappropriation, courts are unlikely to elevate it after the fact. A business that classifies its secrets realistically is in a better position to defend its actions and protect its rights.

### MODERATE EFFORTS SUFFICE FOR MODERATE-VALUE SECRETS

*Fred's Stores of Tennessee, Inc. v. M & P Partners, LLC*
2015 U.S. Dist. LEXIS 178745 (N.D. Miss. Dec. 30, 2015)

Fred's alleged that a former business partner misappropriated information about site selection for new store locations. The court found that while the information was not publicly available, it was developed using standard techniques and available data. The business methods had some strategic value, but they were not unique or transformative. The court treated the information as potentially protectable, but it emphasized that the level of protection must reflect the information's actual role in the business. This case illustrates how courts recognize medium-priority secrets when they are realistically framed and reasonably guarded.

Medium-priority secrets fill the middle of the inventory. They are the tools and tactics that help a business compete day to day. Losing them would hurt. But it would not end the game. They require careful protection—not the highest wall, but a strong fence.

## 2.4.3. Low-Priority Trade Secrets

Some trade secrets qualify for protection under the law but carry little weight in the life of the business. These low-priority secrets may reflect routine operations, internal preferences, or legacy practices that no longer shape competitive performance. They still meet the legal definition, and they still deserve reasonable safeguards. But they do not demand the same level of attention, investment, or urgency as more critical assets.

Low-priority secrets might include administrative procedures, marginal product tweaks, or legacy data that has not been purged. A company's old pricing models, outdated technical documentation, or internal training slides may all be confidential and nonpublic. But their exposure would not materially damage the business. These items are worth keeping private, but they are not worth a lawsuit.

In practice, low-priority trade secrets often enter the inventory not because they are vital but because they qualify. The goal of the inventory is to be comprehensive. Once an item is identified as a trade secret, it should be documented. But once documented, it should also be evaluated. Companies should not pretend that every secret is a crown jewel. Doing so undermines credibility and creates noise that distracts from what really matters.

Protection for low-priority secrets should be efficient and proportional. Labeling, basic internal access controls, and standard nondisclosure policies are often enough. If the business later discards the information, removes it from operations, or shares it more broadly, it can be removed from the inventory. The point is not to protect everything forever. The point is to manage secrets wisely.

Occasionally, a low-priority secret becomes more important over time. A small internal tool might become the foundation for a customer-facing product. A minor data set might grow into a strategic asset. Regular inventory updates help businesses spot these changes before it is too late. What starts as low-priority can become critical. But most secrets stay in their lane.

**LOW-VALUE INFORMATION MAY NOT QUALITY AS TRADE SECRETS**

*Paragon Techs., Inc. v. United States*
567 F.3d 1329 (Fed. Cir. 2009)

Paragon claimed that certain information in its contract bidding process was confidential and misused. The court accepted that some of the information may have been nonpublic but found that it was routine and of limited strategic value. The company's failure to demonstrate commercial harm or competitive consequence led the court to treat the secrets as low-priority, with little justification for heightened protection. The case illustrates that trade secret law does not exist to protect everything a business prefers to keep private. The information must matter.

A trade secret inventory is not just a list. It is a map of what the business values. Low-priority secrets have a place on that map, but they should not draw disproportionate attention. A good inventory gives each secret the protection it deserves—and no more than that.

## 2.5. Creating the Trade Secret Inventory

Once a company knows what qualifies as a trade secret and how valuable each one is, it must take the next step: putting those secrets into a usable form. The inventory is that form. It is not just a document—it is the backbone of the entire protection plan. A well-built inventory clarifies what needs to be protected, how it is being used, and why it matters. Without one, even the best legal strategies have no foundation.

The inventory should be structured as a living document. It is typically organized as a spreadsheet or secure database, with each row representing a single trade secret and each column capturing key information about it. That includes a short, descriptive name; a clear explanation of what the secret is; its classification as technical, business, or hybrid; its physical or digital location; its priority level; and any special considerations for how it is used or protected. Some companies include additional fields—such as access controls, department ownership, or dates of last review—but the core elements are the same across industries.

Creating the inventory requires both legal and operational judgment. The legal team ensures that each item meets the legal definition of a trade secret. The business team identifies what knowledge is actually in use and what value it provides. Neither side can do the work alone. A legal team working in isolation may miss strategically important assets. A business team working without legal guidance may include items that do not qualify or overlook risks in how secrets are shared. The process only works when both perspectives are involved.

The inventory is not a dumping ground for all confidential information. It should not include internal chatter, minor process tweaks, or marketing slogans unless they genuinely meet the legal test. At the same time, the threshold for inclusion should not be too high. Many valuable trade secrets are easy to overlook because they are embedded in daily routines. A company's ability to identify those quiet advantages often determines how well it protects itself in the long run.

Precision matters. Each trade secret must be described in terms that are specific enough to be understood by someone outside the company yet clear enough to be useful internally. A vague entry like "customer strategy" or "pricing tool" provides little guidance and little protection. A strong inventory entry tells you what the secret is, where it resides, how it works, and why it matters. It can be read and understood by a judge, a new executive, or a compliance officer without guesswork.

A strong inventory is also defensible. If a dispute arises, the company can point to its inventory to show that the information was identified, reviewed, and classified long before the conflict. This is powerful evidence that the secret was real—and that the company took reasonable efforts to protect it. Courts are more likely to credit trade secret claims that are supported by internal documentation prepared in the ordinary course of business, not just materials created for litigation.

Because the inventory becomes a legal and operational tool, it must be updated regularly. But it must first be created with care. Many companies start with a working version focused on the highest-priority secrets and expand over time. What matters is not that the inventory is perfect on day one, but that it is structured and taken seriously from the beginning. A sloppy or overinclusive inventory can do more harm than good.

The following example illustrates how a well-organized inventory spreadsheet might be structured. Each entry includes a specific name, a functional description, a classification type, a priority level, and other relevant metadata. This is not a checklist of labels. It is a blueprint for protection.

**Table 1. Sample Trade Secret Inventory Spreadsheet—**
***Basic Structure for Classification and Prioritization.***

| Trade Secret Name | Description | Type | Location | Priority |
|---|---|---|---|---|
| Flavoring Algorithm | Software module that optimizes recipe ratios | Technical | Internal Git repo | High |
| Enterprise Client List | Curated list with sales notes and renewal history | Business | CRM system | High |
| Targeting Formula | Digital marketing bid allocation logic | Hybrid | AdTech team files | Medium |
| Internal Admin Portal | Custom backend tool with employee usage data | Technical | Cloud instance | Low |
| Vendor Rate Table | Negotiated terms across regions | Business | Legal Drive | Medium |

A spreadsheet like this can evolve over time. It becomes more useful as the company refines how it describes its secrets and how it understands their role in the business. Ultimately, the inventory is not just a document—it is a way of thinking. It shifts the organization from vague awareness to concrete control. That shift is what turns confidentiality into protection.

## 2.6. Common Pitfalls and Best Practices in Inventorying

Creating a trade secret inventory is a high-leverage task. When done well, it becomes a cornerstone of legal protection and operational clarity. When done poorly, it becomes a liability—confusing, overbroad, or dangerously incomplete. Many companies fall into familiar traps during the inventorying process. These pitfalls are avoidable, but only if they are recognized early.

The most common mistake is overinclusion. Businesses sometimes attempt to label every internal document, communication, or idea as a trade secret. They believe that casting a wide net will maximize protection. In reality, it undermines credibility. Courts are skeptical of sweeping claims. An inventory that includes routine emails, vague strategies, or public-facing content suggests that the company does not understand what a trade secret is. Worse, it dilutes focus. When everything is marked high-priority, nothing really is.

The opposite mistake is underinclusion. Some companies build inventories that are too narrow by listing only formal technologies or customer lists while ignoring embedded knowledge that lives inside teams. A unique onboarding process, a high-performing internal dashboard, or a supplier negotiation sequence may not feel like "IP" but can be a valuable trade secret. Businesses that focus only on patents, products, or technical files often miss their own competitive advantages. A good inventory demands curiosity, not just compliance.

Another frequent error is lack of specificity. Entries like "sales playbook," "product roadmap," or "pricing method" are too vague to support legal enforcement. Courts will not protect abstractions. If a trade secret cannot be described with precision, it cannot be defended. The inventory must describe what the secret is, how it works, and what makes it distinct. Specificity also helps internally. When teams know exactly what the secret is, they are more likely to treat it properly.

Some inventories fail because they are treated as static. A one-time list created during a compliance sprint is not a protection plan. Trade secrets change as businesses evolve. New products launch, old methods are retired, strategies shift. A useful inventory must be reviewed and revised regularly. Companies that revisit their inventory once a year or during major operational changes are far better positioned to respond to risk or litigation than those that treat it as a finished product.

Ownership is another challenge. In many organizations, no one is clearly responsible for the inventory. Legal teams may draft the framework but have no visibility into day-to-day practices. Business teams may understand the secrets but see inventorying as someone else's job. The result is an incomplete or outdated list. Successful companies designate a responsible party or team, ensure collaboration across departments, and integrate inventory maintenance into regular workflows.

Finally, many businesses fail to link the inventory to enforcement. When a trade secret is misappropriated, the company must be able to prove that the information was identified, protected, and valued before the breach. A trade secret that appears only in a litigation brief will not persuade a court. But a secret that was clearly listed, carefully described, and periodically reviewed tells a different story. It shows that the company knew what it was protecting—and treated it accordingly.

### OVER-CLAIMING YET UNDER-DOCUMENTING "SECRET" PROCESSES

*Hertz v. Luzenac Group*
576 F.3d 1103 (10th Cir. 2009)

Luzenac claimed that its talc purification process was a trade secret, but it failed to clearly document what the process involved or how it was protected. The company asserted broad rights over multiple elements of its operations, without distinguishing which components were critical or how they had been maintained as confidential. The court expressed skepticism about these sweeping claims and ultimately narrowed the scope of protection. The case illustrates that overclaiming weakens credibility, and that a trade secret inventory must be both specific and supported by evidence of active protection.

A trade secret inventory is only as strong as the process behind it. Simply stamping "CONFIDENTIAL" on every document will not hold up in court. Precision, balance, regular updates, and clear ownership are not just best practices but rather are the difference between protection that works and protection that fails when it is needed most.

## 2.7. Integrating the Inventory Into Business Operations

A trade secret inventory is not useful if it sits on a shelf. It must become part of how the business actually functions. The strongest protection plans are not legal artifacts but rather are operational realities. That means the inventory must be integrated into everyday decisions, not just maintained as a static document for future litigation.

Integration begins with access. The people responsible for protecting trade secrets must know what those secrets are. That includes legal counsel, security officers, team leads, and business executives who work in areas where the secrets are used. If these individuals cannot easily find, understand, or reference the inventory, it cannot guide behavior. The inventory must be secure, but it must also be usable.

Integration also requires alignment. Internal policies should reflect the distinctions made in the inventory. If a trade secret is marked high priority, it should be subject to stronger protections than a low-priority item. Contracts, training programs, and access protocols should all respond to the classification and prioritization decisions embedded in the inventory. When a secret is labeled as important but treated casually, the inconsistency undermines legal credibility and creates operational risk.

The inventory should influence who gets access to what. This is not just about cybersecurity. It is about personnel decisions. Teams working with sensitive information should be trained in how to handle it. Employees should be briefed on what qualifies as a trade secret and why it matters. Contractors and vendors should be given access only to what they need—and only after appropriate agreements are in place. The inventory can help structure these controls by identifying where the risks lie and which assets require careful handling.

Business planning is another place where the inventory must play a role. If a team is preparing to launch a new product or enter a new market, the inventory should be consulted. Are any of the relevant assets already in the inventory? Do new trade secrets need to be added? Are existing secrets being used in new ways that create different exposure risks? Treating the inventory as a living reference helps ensure that trade secret protection is part of strategy, not just an afterthought.

Litigation readiness also depends on integration. If a company alleges trade secret misappropriation, it must show not only that the secret was documented but also that it was treated as confidential in practice. Courts look for consistency between the inventory and the company's operational behavior. If the inventory is maintained separately from the way the business runs, it is unlikely to carry much weight when it matters most.

The goal is not to turn every employee into a trade secret lawyer. The goal is to create an organization that knows what its secrets are and acts accordingly. That culture starts with visibility. It grows through habits and structure. And it succeeds when the inventory moves out of the legal department and into the heart of the business.

# 2.8. Maintaining and Updating the Inventory

A trade secret inventory is not a one-time project. It must be updated, maintained, and revisited as the business evolves. Information that qualifies as a trade secret today may lose its value tomorrow. A new initiative may generate protectable knowledge that is never captured unless someone adds it to the record. Without updates, even the best inventory becomes stale, and a stale inventory is almost as dangerous as no inventory at all.

Trade secrets change because businesses change. New products are launched. Old services are retired. Employees come and go. Vendors are replaced. A process that was once confidential may become public. A customer list may grow outdated. A confidential tool may be made obsolete by new technology. If the inventory does not reflect these changes, it creates a false sense of security.

Regular updates should be scheduled and structured. Many companies align inventory reviews with annual audits, major product cycles, or key moments in personnel transitions. The right interval depends on the pace and nature of the business. A fast-moving tech company may need quarterly updates. A more stable operation may find that once or twice a year is enough. What matters is that updates happen as a proactive matter of process, not as a reaction to litigation or crisis.

Maintenance is not just about adding new secrets. It is also about removing or reclassifying old ones. If a trade secret is no longer used, or if the company has stopped taking steps to protect it, it may no longer qualify. Leaving it in the inventory anyway weakens the credibility of the whole system. It suggests that the company does not really know which of its assets are confidential. Pruning the inventory is just as important as expanding it.

Updating also means revisiting classifications and priority levels. A secret that was once low-priority may become critical if a new product depends on it. A high-priority secret may be downgraded if the business shifts direction. These changes often go unnoticed unless the company builds time for reflection into its process. Without that discipline, the inventory becomes frozen in the past, even as the business moves forward.

Ownership is key. Someone must be responsible for keeping the inventory current. That person or team must have access to the legal, operational, and technical knowledge needed to evaluate what has changed. They must also have the authority to prompt revisions and the judgment to know when they are necessary. In some organizations, this role falls to in-house counsel. In others, it is handled by compliance, risk management, or information security. The right structure varies. The need for clear responsibility does not.

A well-maintained inventory tells a story of awareness. It shows that the company knows what matters, monitors how its assets are used, and adjusts its protection accordingly. Courts are more likely to respect that kind of system. So are employees, partners, and investors. A trade secret inventory is not just a document. It is a record of care. Keeping it current is how that care becomes credible.

## 2.9. Creating an Organizational Culture Around the Inventory

The trade secret inventory is more than a record. It is a reflection of how seriously a company treats its own knowledge. The best protection plans do not depend solely on legal documents or technical safeguards. They depend on people—on the habits, expectations, and norms that guide how information is handled every day. For the inventory to work, it must be embedded in the company's culture.

A culture of confidentiality does not arise on its own. It must be modeled, communicated, and reinforced. Employees must understand what qualifies as a trade secret, why those secrets matter, and how their own actions contribute to or undermine protection. That understanding begins with visibility. The inventory makes secrecy visible. It shows that the company takes its knowledge seriously and expects others to do the same.

Creating a culture around the inventory means that confidentiality is not just a legal requirement but rather is part of how people do their jobs. Employees are trained to recognize sensitive information. New hires are briefed on the types of trade secrets they may encounter. Departing employees are reminded of their continuing obligations. When people see that the company knows what its secrets are and that it monitors how they are treated, behavior changes.

**A CULTURE OF SECRECY SUPPORTS A FINDING OF TRADE SECRETS**

*Data General Corp. v. Digital Computer Controls, Inc.*
357 A.2d 105 (Del. Ch. 1975)

Data General sued a competitor and former employee for misappropriating internal schematics used in computer hardware design. The court found that Data General had built a strong culture of confidentiality by using access controls, training, and internal policies to ensure its employees understood their obligations. Because the company took secrecy seriously in both policy and practice, the court found its trade secret protections enforceable. This case illustrates how a company's internal discipline and cultural reinforcement can tip the balance in favor of legal protection.

This culture also depends on access and collaboration. The inventory must be known to those who work with the secrets. Engineers, salespeople, product teams, legal, and IT must all play a role in identifying, classifying, and protecting information. When different parts of the organization treat secrets differently, the gaps become risks. But when everyone works from the same map, the business acts with coherence and purpose.

Accountability is another key. Culture is not created by slogans or policies alone. It is created by what people see happening around them. If violations go unaddressed, the inventory becomes irrelevant. If secrecy is enforced only during litigation, the protection effort will be too late. A culture of confidentiality takes root when people understand that the inventory matters—and that failing to follow it has consequences.

### LAX MAINTENANCE DOOMS TRADE SECRET CLAIM

*Fail-Safe, LLC v. A.O. Smith Corp.*
674 F.3d 889 (7th Cir. 2012)

Fail-Safe developed a pool safety technology and shared it with a prospective partner without using any confidentiality agreements, markings, or internal secrecy practices. The court found that Fail-Safe had failed to treat the information as a secret in any meaningful way. It lacked training, internal documentation, and consistent enforcement. As a result, the court held that the information did not qualify as a trade secret. The case demonstrates that without a functioning culture of confidentiality, even valuable business knowledge may be unprotected.

Some of the strongest trade secret programs are those where the inventory is not treated as a compliance tool but rather as a strategic asset. The people who create and manage the secrets understand their importance. The executives who lead the company use the inventory to set priorities. The culture that grows from that alignment is not just protective—it is productive. It encourages focus, reduces duplication, and builds shared understanding across teams.

Trade secrets do not live on paper. They live in people's heads, in the systems they build, and in the relationships they manage. A trade secret protection plan only works when the inventory becomes part of how those people think and act. That is what it means to build a culture around it. Once that culture takes hold, the inventory is no longer a document. It is a mindset.

## 2.10. From Classification to Action

Every effort to protect trade secrets begins with a single step: identifying what you are protecting. That step is not theoretical. It is concrete. It requires clear descriptions, principled classifications, and hard decisions about what matters most. A strong inventory captures those judgments. It forces a business to recognize the shape and value of its own knowledge—sometimes for the first time.

The legal test provides the boundary. Not everything a company wants to protect will qualify. But within those boundaries, the inventory gives structure to what was previously scattered and unspoken. It distinguishes between different kinds of secrets and different levels of strategic weight. It replaces vague intuitions with organized insight.

But the inventory is only the beginning. It is a snapshot of knowledge, not a shield. For that knowledge to remain protected, it must be actively managed. The inventory must become part of the business—not just a record of what the business knows, but a guide for how it operates.

That work continues in the next chapter. Once a company has identified its trade secrets and prioritized them, it must confront the next challenge: how those secrets might be lost. Legal protection depends not only on what you have but also on how vulnerable it is to exposure. Classification without risk assessment is incomplete. The question now is not what the secrets are but rather how likely they are to escape.

# Chapter 3

# Assessing Risks and Mitigating Vulnerabilities

Trade secrets are only valuable as long as they remain secret. That simple premise underlies every chapter in this book, but nowhere is it more critical than here. Even the strongest legal claim cannot protect information that has already leaked. Once secrecy is lost—whether through theft, error, or indifference—the trade secret disappears. This chapter addresses that challenge directly. It explains how companies can anticipate, analyze, and manage the many ways in which their secrets might be exposed.

Effective protection begins with understanding what can go wrong. Trade secret law is reactive by nature: it allows owners to sue after a misappropriation occurs. But smart organizations do not wait for a breach—they identify where they are most vulnerable and act to reduce those risks. This chapter builds that capacity. It begins by defining the difference between risk and uncertainty, two related but distinct challenges in managing secrecy. It then explores common sources of exposure—from insider threats to external partners to technology-driven leaks—and outlines structured methods for assessing which secrets are most at risk. Finally, it shows why risk assessment is not just a technical exercise but a strategic discipline, one that blends analytics with judgment, and law with leadership.

For organizations seeking to protect their competitive edge, this chapter provides the tools and frameworks to identify threats before those threats turn into losses they cannot reverse.

## 3.1. The Centrality of Risk Assessment

Trade secret law offers powerful remedies, but only after the damage has been done. A successful lawsuit might lead to an injunction, damages, or even criminal penalties—but none of those outcomes can restore the value of a secret that has already spread. This makes trade secrets uniquely vulnerable. Unlike other forms of intellectual property, their legal existence depends on the practical reality of ongoing secrecy. Once that secrecy is compromised, the right disappears with it.

That is why risk assessment is not just a legal tool. It is a strategic imperative. To protect what is secret, a business must first understand where its secrets are exposed. Risk is not something that can be wished away. It comes from employees, contractors, vendors, outdated systems, poor training, loose policies, or simple human error. Most trade secret failures are not dramatic acts of theft. They are slow leaks, casual oversights, or breakdowns in process. And they are almost always foreseeable—if someone had taken the time to ask the right questions.

This chapter begins with a foundational distinction: risk is different from uncertainty. Risk involves quantifiable threats—things that can be measured, modeled, and prioritized. Uncertainty involves the unknown and the unknowable—scenarios where no amount of data can predict what will happen. Trade secret protection requires attention to both. A company might know that its sales algorithm is exposed to a certain type of cybersecurity breach (a risk). But it cannot know whether a court will find that algorithm legally protectable if enforcement becomes necessary (an uncertainty). Both must be managed, but they require different strategies.

In the sections that follow, we will show how businesses can approach risk analytically and uncertainty qualitatively. We will explore how secrets are lost, what kinds of vulnerabilities matter most, and why some threats cannot be measured at all. Most of all, we will emphasize that risk assessment is not a checklist—it is a way of thinking. It requires judgment, foresight, and an honest appraisal of how the business actually operates. Trade secret protection begins long before a lawsuit is filed. It begins with a question: What could go wrong, and what would it cost if it did?

## 3.2. Understanding Risk and Uncertainty

Trade secret law assumes that information remains secret unless a firm allows it to slip. Yet the line between "accidental exposure" and "unforeseeable threat" is often blurred. A trade secret can disappear in a moment, through a carelessly forwarded email, a misconfigured server, a vendor's lapse in judgment, or a former employee's quiet conversation at a conference. Sometimes the risk was obvious. Other times, no one could have seen it coming.

To protect trade secrets in this environment, businesses must think differently. They cannot rely solely on compliance checklists, firewalls, or legal forms. Those tools matter, but they only work if the company understands where its information is most vulnerable and how that vulnerability might manifest. That process is not intuitive. It requires a deliberate framework for analyzing exposure, anticipating threats, and making judgment calls in conditions of both confidence and doubt. It also requires an honest reckoning with the limits of foresight.

This section introduces the analytical foundation of trade secret risk strategy. It begins by distinguishing between two closely related but fundamentally different ideas: risk and uncertainty. Risk refers to situations where outcomes and probabilities can be estimated with some degree of confidence. Uncertainty, by contrast, refers to situations where such probabilities cannot be known at all. Both appear routinely in trade secret management. A company might calculate the chance that an employee will click on a phishing link. But it cannot quantify how a judge will interpret a vague nondisclosure agreement or whether a new competitor will act opportunistically if it stumbles across unprotected IP.

The problem is not that uncertainty exists. The problem is that it is often ignored. Legal teams may overestimate their ability to predict judicial outcomes. Engineers may place too much trust in encryption. Executives may assume that trade secrets are safe because no breach has occurred—yet. These assumptions lull organizations into reactive postures, where trade secrets are protected only after a threat has materialized. By then, it is often too late.

To guard against this, trade secret holders must build systems that account for both what they know and what they cannot know. They must integrate quantitative models for estimating risks with qualitative judgment for navigating uncertainty. These are not competing modes of reasoning. They are complements. A business that only measures what it can count will miss what it cannot see. A business that relies only on intuition will struggle to prioritize and allocate resources. The goal is not certainty—it is clarity. Clarity about where secrets live, how they might be exposed, and what kinds of events could disrupt their protection.

In the pages that follow, we will break down risk and uncertainty with precision. We will explain why each matters, how they differ, and what kinds of reasoning each requires. We will then map the specific domains where uncertainty tends to arise—legal, technological, strategic, and behavioral—and show how those domains shape the modern landscape of trade secret vulnerability. Together, these frameworks provide the foundation for understanding how trade secrets are lost, how threats should be prioritized, and how decision-makers can act wisely even when the future is unclear.

## 3.2.1. Defining Risk

Risk is often treated as a vague or generalized threat, but in structured trade secret management, it has a specific meaning. Risk exists when outcomes are uncertain but measurable. It is the product of two elements: the likelihood that an event will occur and the magnitude of harm that would follow. The standard formulation expresses this as:

**Risk = Probability of Event × Magnitude of Harm**

This simple equation provides a powerful starting point. It allows organizations to evaluate threats not by intuition but by structured reasoning. A vulnerability that is extremely likely but would cause only minor disruption may warrant only modest protection. A low-probability event that could destroy the company's competitive position might demand aggressive safeguards. The framework provides a language for making such trade-offs explicit.

Consider a software firm whose flagship product relies on a proprietary algorithm. The probability of a data breach may be informed by prior cybersecurity incidents, industry benchmarks, or technical assessments. The magnitude of harm could include not only financial loss but also reputational damage and diminished investor confidence. By assigning values—quantitative or categorical—to these dimensions, the firm can begin to prioritize risks across its portfolio of secrets.

Structured risk assessment serves multiple purposes. It helps justify resource allocation. It provides a rationale for why some secrets receive more protection than others. And it offers a way to communicate with senior leadership about the trade-offs between cost, convenience, and exposure. Without such a framework, protective measures may be inconsistent, reactive, or politically driven rather than strategic.

But even the best risk models rely on assumptions. The accuracy of a probability estimate depends on the availability and reliability of data. Magnitude is often easier to approximate in retrospect than in advance. Still, even imperfect models are valuable. They shift the conversation from vague concerns to concrete judgments. They reveal what a company believes about its own exposure and whether that belief is grounded in evidence or hope.

In practice, many trade secret threats fall into well-understood categories. Insider theft, phishing attacks, lost devices, shared credentials—each has a known pattern and a body of industry data. This makes them amenable to quantification. And because they are quantifiable, they can be ranked, tracked, and monitored over time.

What risk assessment cannot do is eliminate judgment. Numbers must be interpreted. Categories must be defined. Models must be updated as the business environment changes. Still, when built correctly, a structured approach to risk can help organizations act before a breach occurs—not just respond afterward.

## 3.2.2. Defining Uncertainty

Uncertainty is not a fuzzier form of risk. It is a different category altogether. Where risk involves probabilities that can be estimated, uncertainty arises when such probabilities are unknown or unknowable. It marks the limits of prediction, the boundary where quantitative models lose their grip. For trade secret holders, that boundary is closer than many assume.

Uncertainty pervades the legal environment in which trade secrets exist. A company may have strong internal controls but cannot know how a judge will interpret "reasonable efforts" under the Defend Trade Secrets Act. It may disclose confidential information under an NDA but cannot predict whether a jury will find the agreement enforceable or the disclosure sufficiently limited. The law of trade secrets is fact-intensive, jurisdictionally fragmented, and often shaped by evolving norms. There is no algorithm that can assign a reliable probability to a future court ruling.

The same is true in the competitive landscape. A startup might rely on secrecy to protect a novel product design, believing that its competitors will play by the rules. But what if a well-funded rival disregards the risk of litigation? What if a foreign partner copies the product, knowing that enforcement abroad will be slow or ineffective? These are not simply low-probability events. They are uncertain events—unbounded by usable data, driven by strategic behavior, and subject to externalities that cannot be modeled.

Technological uncertainty adds another layer. New tools and platforms emerge constantly. Today's secure system may be tomorrow's liability. A company might encrypt its customer analytics with what it believes is a state-of-the-art protocol, only to learn that an advance in machine learning makes it possible infer much of the data from metadata alone, or that a new device can scan for electromagnetic signatures from monitors, thus allowing outside actors to reconstruct sensitive visual content. These are not science fiction scenarios. Rather, they demonstrate the reality that protection strategies must evolve faster than traditional legal doctrines can respond.

There is also human uncertainty: the internal variables that resist control. Will a departing employee honor their obligations? Will a junior developer share proprietary knowledge at a meetup? Will a manager, under pressure to hit deadlines, authorize a risky disclosure to a vendor? These questions cannot be answered with statistics. They demand judgment, culture, and foresight.

None of this means that trade secret protection is futile. But it does mean that protection cannot rest solely on risk models. In conditions of uncertainty, decision-makers must rely on qualitative reasoning. They must use analogy, pattern recognition, and scenario thinking. They must weigh worst-case outcomes, not just average-case projections. And they must learn to act even when no clear metric tells them what to expect.

Understanding uncertainty is not a retreat from rationality. It is an extension of it. It acknowledges that many important decisions are made with partial information, in evolving environments, by actors who are not fully predictable. In such settings, strategy does not mean calculating the odds. It means preparing for what cannot be calculated at all.

## 3.2.3. Domains of Uncertainty in Trade Secret Strategy

Uncertainty is not random noise. It follows patterns. Although individual outcomes cannot be predicted, the sources of unpredictability often fall into recurring categories. For trade secret holders, four domains of uncertainty tend to dominate strategic decision-making: entrepreneurial, legal, technological, and human-behavioral. Each requires a different form of judgment and a different kind of response.

### *3.2.3.1. Entrepreneurial Uncertainty*

Business conditions change, often without warning. A company might launch a product under the assumption that its pricing algorithm or supply chain method will remain valuable for years—only to watch a competitor introduce a more efficient model that renders the original advantage obsolete. Markets shift. Customer preferences evolve. New entrants disrupt cost structures or distribution channels. These dynamics reshape the value of a trade secret long before a breach occurs. In fast-moving sectors like software, logistics, and consumer technology, even a well-guarded secret can become irrelevant if the strategic assumptions behind it no longer hold.

Entrepreneurial uncertainty is especially salient for startups and growth-stage firms. These organizations often rely on secrecy because they lack the resources for patent filings or trademark campaigns. But they also face a volatile environment in which the most dangerous threat is not necessarily misappropriation but rather that their business model will be overtaken before their secret can generate value. In such cases, the most important strategic question is not how to guard the secret but whether the secret is likely to matter six months from now.

### *3.2.3.2. Legal Uncertainty*

Even when companies make serious efforts to protect their secrets, the law may not respond as expected. Courts evaluate trade secret claims through fact-specific analysis that varies by jurisdiction and evolves over time. What one judge considers a "reasonable effort" to maintain secrecy, another may dismiss as inadequate. Legal standards are often framed in general terms such as "not readily ascertainable" or "deriving value from not being known" but applied inconsistently in practice.

This unpredictability extends to enforcement. An NDA may appear airtight until a jury finds it vague or overbroad. A protective order may be granted in one court but denied in another, based on a different reading of procedural rules. Some doctrines, such as inevitable disclosure or threatened misappropriation, remain controversial and unevenly applied. Even if a company ultimately prevails, delays, appeals, and evidentiary burdens can drain resources and erode the practical value of success.

Legal uncertainty is not just about doctrine. It is about institutions. Judges have different levels of technical sophistication. Courts move at different speeds. Discovery may reveal more than it protects. Strategic decisions about whether to sue, settle, or stay quiet must account for these variables, even if they cannot be quantified.

### *3.2.3.3. Technological Uncertainty*

No technology remains stable for long. Advances in computation, data analysis, connectivity, and surveillance continuously reshape the landscape of trade secret protection. Techniques that were once considered secure—such as simple password protection, VPN access, or non-indexed web storage—are now widely recognized as inadequate. Encryption standards evolve. Collaboration tools change how information is shared. Artificial intelligence opens new avenues for reverse engineering and pattern detection.

These developments create uncertainty not only about threats but also about safeguards. Will a new platform introduce vulnerabilities the company has not anticipated? Will a patch resolve a weakness or introduce another? Will a storage provider's terms of service inadvertently authorize broader access than intended? These are not idle questions. They are daily concerns for companies whose secrets reside in codebases, databases, design files, and distributed workflows.

Trade secrets depend on control. Technology, by its nature, disperses control. That tension cannot be eliminated, but it must be acknowledged. A robust strategy accounts not just for what is known today, but for what could change tomorrow.

#### *3.2.3.4 Human-Behavioral Uncertainty*

Perhaps the most pervasive and least predictable domain of uncertainty is human behavior. People make mistakes. They act in bad faith. They respond to incentives, pressures, loyalties, and frustrations that are often invisible to the organizations they serve. An engineer may believe they are acting ethically by reusing design ideas at a new job. A manager may bypass protocols under deadline pressure. A vendor may assume that shared files are not confidential unless explicitly labeled as such.

Policies can mitigate these risks, but they cannot eliminate them. Contracts can establish obligations but cannot guarantee performance. Even good training may not overcome distraction, carelessness, or personal ambition. Human behavior does not follow the logic of a spreadsheet. It follows emotion, habit, and context. Trade secret strategy must make room for that reality.

This domain also includes internal dynamics. Does the organization take secrecy seriously? Do managers model good behavior? Are violations treated with appropriate consequence? A company's internal culture is one of the most powerful predictors of whether its secrecy measures will succeed. But culture is not a variable that can be programmed. It must be cultivated, sustained, and—when necessary—corrected.

## 3.3. Vectors of Loss of Secrecy

A trade secret is only protected for as long as it remains secret. That protection can be lost in many ways—some lawful, some unlawful, and many that fall into a gray area. Understanding how secrecy is compromised is not just an academic question. It is the practical starting point for every protection plan. Without a clear view of how secrets might be lost, it is impossible to assess risk, prioritize resources, or design meaningful safeguards.

This section focuses on the concept of loss vectors: the distinct pathways through which a trade secret can lose its protected status. These vectors matter whether the loss comes from misappropriation, mistake, or necessity. They include internal exposures, like employee misconduct; external exposures, like vendor leaks; technological vulnerabilities, like unsecured storage; and even lawful conduct, like reverse engineering or independent discovery. Each vector poses a different kind of threat and calls for a different kind of analysis.

Mapping these vectors is a central component of the Trade Secret Protection Plan. It is also essential to understanding real-world litigation. Many of the most important trade secret cases hinge on how the information was lost. Was the employee bound by a confidentiality agreement? Did the vendor have access to labeled secrets? Was the technology reverse engineered from public materials? These questions are not always easy to answer. But they begin with a clear sense of what the vectors are.

The following subsections provide a detailed framework for identifying and analyzing loss vectors. They serve both as a conceptual guide and as a checklist for practical application. Each vector is examined not only in terms of what it is but also in terms of why it matters and how it tends to arise in business operations. Understanding these pathways is the first step in designing defenses strong enough to keep secrets secret.

## 3.3.1. Insider Threats and Employee Mobility

Insiders are often the most dangerous threat to trade secrets—not always because they are malicious but because they already have access. Employees, executives, interns, and contractors are trusted with sensitive information to do their jobs. That trust creates opportunity. When insiders misuse or mishandle confidential material, the damage can be swift and irreversible.

Some insider threats are deliberate. A departing employee may take files to a competitor, download source code for personal use, or share customer data to impress a new employer. Others are the result of carelessness: forwarding confidential emails to a personal account, uploading documents to an unsecured cloud service, or discussing sensitive projects with friends. In some cases, the risk is not action but inaction: failing to delete files, return physical materials, or abide by continuing obligations after employment ends.

Employee mobility compounds this risk. In industries where job switching is frequent and teams are built from overlapping networks of professionals, trade secrets often travel with people. Even when an employee does not intend to steal anything, their knowledge and habits may reflect confidential methods learned at a prior job. This can lead to inadvertent use or disclosure of protected material that ends up triggering legal disputes long after the employee has moved on.

One of the most prominent insider risk cases arose when a senior executive at Bimbo Bakeries prepared to join a competitor while still employed and still accessing confidential information. The court allowed an injunction, even before any misappropriation occurred, based on the risk that the employee's future work would inevitably draw on protected knowledge.

**COURTS CAN ENJOIN THREATENED MISAPPROPRIATION**

*Bimbo Bakeries USA, Inc. v. Botticella*
613 F.3d 102 (3d Cir. 2010)

Botticella, a senior executive at Bimbo Bakeries, accepted a job with a direct competitor but continued accessing confidential files during his final weeks. Bimbo sought an injunction before he left, arguing that Botticella would inevitably use Bimbo's trade secrets in his new role, and the court agreed. Emphasizing the risk of irreversible harm if Botticella were allowed to begin work, it granted a preliminary injunction. The decision turned on his continued access to sensitive information, his misleading statements during the transition, and the similarity of the new role to his prior position.

In other cases, insider threats become criminal. For example, a former Motorola employee was caught boarding a flight to China with thousands of proprietary documents. The company's internal systems had flagged abnormal download activity, which triggered an investigation that led to prosecution under the Economic Espionage Act.

**SYSTEM LOGS CAN SERVE AS EVIDENCE OF MISAPPROPRIATION**

*United States v. Jin*
733 F.3d 718 (7th Cir. 2013)

Hanjuan Jin, an engineer at Motorola, was stopped at the airport with over a thousand sensitive documents in her luggage. Motorola's system logs had detected a surge in downloads before her unannounced departure. Prosecutors charged her under the Economic Espionage Act. The court upheld her conviction, noting that Motorola had both tracked the activity and taken prompt action. The case highlighted the importance of real-time monitoring and documented access control in identifying insider misappropriation.

Trade secret law does not prohibit people from changing jobs. Nor does it forbid them from using their general skills and experience. But it does require that confidential information gained under conditions of trust remain protected. Courts are often careful to preserve this balance. In some cases, they have rejected claims based on speculative concerns, recognizing that employees are entitled to pursue new opportunities—even with competitors.

**"INEVITABLE DISCLOSURE" REQUIRES MORE THAN JOB SIMILARITY**

*LeJeune v. Coin Acceptors, Inc.*
849 A.2d 451 (Md. Ct. Spec. App. 2004)

Coin Acceptors sued a former engineer who left to join a competitor, alleging that his new role would lead to inevitable disclosure of trade secrets. The court denied the injunction, finding no evidence that the employee had taken confidential materials or was likely to misuse them. It emphasized that mere job similarity and prior access were insufficient without proof of a real threat. The decision reinforced the principle that employee mobility is not, by itself, misappropriation.

Companies must therefore think critically about how information is shared internally. Who needs access to what? Are materials clearly labeled as confidential? Are employees trained on what counts as a trade secret and how it must be handled? Are exit interviews used to reinforce continuing obligations? The answers to these questions determine whether a court will view the company as having taken reasonable steps to maintain secrecy or as having allowed its secrets to walk out the door.

Legal disputes over insider threats often turn on documentation and diligence. Courts want to see policies, training, access controls, and enforcement. Without them, even the strongest claim of theft may fall flat. With them, companies can not only protect their secrets, but also deter misappropriation before it starts.

## 3.3.2. Vendor and Partner Exposure

Trade secrets do not stay locked in a single department or secure facility. They move—through contracts, collaborations, shared services, and outsourced operations. When companies work with vendors, suppliers, consultants, or joint venture partners, they often share confidential information to make the relationship function. That exchange creates opportunity but also exposure.

The risk here is not always deliberate theft. More often, it is a breakdown in alignment. A vendor may not realize that a shared schematic is proprietary. A supplier may store confidential data on insecure servers. A consultant may include proprietary process steps in a presentation to another client, believing that they are only describing industry norms. These errors can be just as damaging as outright misappropriation—and harder to detect.

This problem is compounded when there is no direct relationship between the originator of the trade secret and the party who ultimately receives it. Information may pass through layers of contractors or intermediaries, none of whom fully understand the obligations attached. Even when a nondisclosure agreement is in place, courts will look closely at whether it clearly defined what information was protected, whether the receiving party understood those boundaries, and whether reasonable efforts were made to prevent disclosure.

A case from the financial services industry highlights this dynamic. The plaintiff claimed it shared a proprietary investment concept that ultimately reached the defendant through a chain of intermediaries. But because the information passed through informal channels and lacked clearly defined confidentiality obligations, the court declined to find misappropriation.

**DISCLOSER MUST ESTABLISH A DUTY OF CONFIDENCE**

*Novus Group, LLC v. Prudential Financial, Inc.*
No. 12-CV-5279 (S.D.N.Y. Apr. 22, 2014)

Novus Group alleged that it shared a proprietary financial product idea with Prudential through a series of intermediaries. The court found that the plaintiff had not established a direct or sufficiently clear confidential relationship between itself and the defendant. Because there was no evidence that Prudential knew the idea was shared under restrictions and no NDA covered the final exchange, the court declined to treat the information as misappropriated. The decision illustrates the difficulty of asserting trade secret rights when information is passed informally or indirectly across multiple parties.

The takeaway is not that partnerships are inherently risky but rather that they must be structured with clarity. Companies should define what information is confidential, document who receives it, and monitor how it is used. Confidentiality agreements should be tailored, not boilerplate. Just as importantly, those agreements should be backed by practical controls—limited access, version tracking, retention policies—that reinforce the legal framework with operational discipline.

Trade secret law does not penalize companies for collaborating. But it does expect them to take care. When courts assess whether information was treated as a trade secret, they ask not only whether it was labeled confidential but also whether the owner behaved as though secrecy mattered—even when someone else was holding the data.

### 3.3.3. Cybersecurity and Technical Weak Points

Not all trade secret threats come from people. Some come from systems—or from the failure to secure them. As more proprietary information moves into digital environments, trade secret exposure increasingly occurs through technical vulnerabilities: insecure servers, unencrypted files, shared credentials, forgotten access points, or misconfigured cloud platforms. These exposures often arise without malicious intent. But when they are exploited—by competitors, hackers, or even automated tools—the result is the same: the secret is lost.

Unlike traditional theft, technical exfiltration may leave no trace. A contractor might access a shared drive from an unsecured laptop. A former employee's login may remain active after departure. A third-party service may retain copies of uploaded materials even after a project ends. These are not exotic attack vectors. They are ordinary oversights. And they can destroy the legal foundation of a trade secret by making the information "readily ascertainable" to others with only minimal effort.

One of the most striking examples comes from a case in the Fifth Circuit. A technology firm alleged that its competitor had misappropriated confidential software by reverse engineering a data transfer process. The defendant had obtained the software through lawful means, but the plaintiff claimed that internal technical safeguards should have prevented such analysis. The case illustrates how courts examine both the legal and technical context in assessing whether a trade secret was sufficiently protected.

**"REASONABLE EFFORTS" OFTEN REQUIRES TECHNICAL BARRIERS**

*GlobeRanger Corp. v. Software AG USA, Inc.*
836 F.3d 477 (5th Cir. 2016)

GlobeRanger developed software for tracking inventory using RFID tags. It alleged that Software AG misappropriated confidential aspects of the system after obtaining a copy through a reseller. The court found that although Software AG had lawfully acquired the software, questions remained about whether reverse engineering violated an implied duty of confidentiality. The case turned in part on the technical architecture of the system—whether it included adequate protections against disassembly and analysis. The court allowed the misappropriation claim to proceed, emphasizing that trade secret protection depends not only on access restrictions but also on technical barriers to unauthorized use.

This kind of threat cannot be managed solely through contracts. It requires robust information security practices: tiered access controls, encryption in transit and at rest, device management, network monitoring, offboarding protocols, and frequent audits of system permissions. It also requires awareness. Many businesses underestimate how much sensitive information circulates on internal drives, Slack channels, cloud folders, and mobile devices.

The law recognizes that no system is perfect. But it does expect trade secret owners to behave as if secrecy matters. Courts have consistently looked to technical discipline as a signal of intent: Did the company lock down its most sensitive files? Did it restrict access by role? Did it take action when irregular activity was detected? If the answer is no, even well-drafted NDAs may not be enough to preserve the claim.

In a digital world, technical safeguards are not optional—they are foundational. They do not replace legal protections. They make those protections credible.

## 3.3.4. Reverse Engineering and Lawful Discovery

Not all loss of secrecy results from misconduct. Trade secret law does not protect information from being discovered through lawful means. If a competitor independently develops the same process, analyzes a publicly available product, or reverse engineers a commercial device without breaching any duty of confidentiality, the secret is lost—and no legal remedy applies.

This principle distinguishes trade secret law from other forms of intellectual property. Unlike patents, which grant exclusive rights regardless of independent invention, trade secrets are vulnerable to legitimate discovery. That vulnerability is not a loophole. It is a feature of the system. Trade secret protection rewards confidentiality and internal discipline—not exclusivity. If another party can figure out the same idea without cheating, the law allows them to do so.

Reverse engineering is the most important and most common lawful vector of loss. Courts have long held that a product placed in the marketplace can be analyzed, deconstructed, and understood, so long as the analyst does not violate any legal obligation in the process. This includes chemical analysis, software disassembly, physical inspection, and even behavioral testing.

A well-known case from the Ninth Circuit illustrates this clearly. A company that sold mechanical locks claimed trade secret protection over its key codes. But locksmiths had lawfully acquired the locks and decoded the system by observing the key and lock combinations. The court held that the information was no longer protectable because it had become readily ascertainable by proper means.

**LAWFUL REVERSE ENGINEERING RENDERS INFORMATION "READILY ASCERTAINABLE"**

*Chicago Lock Co. v. Fanberg*
676 F.2d 400 (9th Cir. 1982)

Chicago Lock Co. manufactured mechanical locks that used proprietary key codes. Independent locksmiths compiled reference charts of the codes by analyzing locks obtained in the market. The company sued to stop publication of the charts, claiming trade secret misappropriation. The court rejected the claim, holding that the information had been acquired through lawful reverse engineering. Once the locks were sold, nothing prevented customers or third parties from examining them to deduce their internal design.

Reverse engineering is not the only lawful path to disclosure. Some trade secrets are uncovered through independent development. Others must be disclosed in regulatory filings, in contractual negotiations, or for public safety compliance. While legal safeguards can help limit how much is revealed, they cannot always prevent loss of secrecy. If disclosure is required, the information may lose its protected status unless carefully managed through redactions, protective orders, or parallel IP strategies.

The legal standard is clear: if a trade secret becomes **readily ascertainable by proper means**, it ceases to be a trade secret. This places the burden on the owner to anticipate how the information might be discovered and to take steps to delay or prevent that discovery where possible. Techniques may include product obfuscation, modular design, noncompete provisions (where enforceable), and careful release sequencing. But in many cases, the only reliable solution is to avoid releasing the secret at all.

Trade secret protection is strongest when the information stays out of the public eye. Once a product is shipped, reverse engineering is always a possibility. The law will not save a company from exposure it could have prevented.

## 3.3.5. Necessary Disclosure and Operational Sharing

Some trade secrets cannot function unless they are shared. A proprietary manufacturing method may need to be disclosed to a third-party processor. A customer database may be used by a marketing firm to run targeted campaigns. A core algorithm may be embedded in a product sold to end users. In each case, the information must be exposed in order to generate value. That exposure creates risk, even when it is operationally necessary and legally authorized.

The law does not prohibit companies from sharing trade secrets with employees, vendors, or collaborators. But it does require them to do so in a way that maintains secrecy. Courts routinely ask whether the company took **reasonable steps** to preserve confidentiality when information was distributed. This includes legal safeguards, like nondisclosure agreements and licensing terms. It also includes technical and procedural controls, like access restrictions, data labeling, encryption, and audit trails.

The more widely a secret is shared, the harder it is to protect. Each disclosure creates a new vector for loss—not just through malice or error but through misinterpretation as well. A document marked "confidential" may be forwarded to a new team member who has not signed an NDA. A subcontractor may assume that shared files are general know-how. A team in one department may use a process they believe to be routine, not realizing it was originally protected information.

Courts are not sympathetic to companies that rely solely on formalities. They look for evidence that the business took its secrecy obligations seriously. This includes clarity in documentation, care in training, consistency in enforcement, and restraint in distribution. A secret that is shared indiscriminately—without guardrails, tracking, or internal awareness—may lose its legal protection even if it was once confidential.

A recent case from the District of Massachusetts illustrates how even well-intentioned operational disclosures can undermine trade secret status when safeguards are inadequate.

### OPERATIONAL SHARING WITHOUT SAFEGUARDS UNDERMINES TRADE SECRETS

*AnywhereCommerce, Inc. v. Ingenico Inc.*
578 F. Supp. 3d 219 (D. Mass. 2022)

AnywhereCommerce alleged that a former partner misused trade secrets shared during integration work on payment processing systems. The plaintiff had shared information through routine collaboration but failed to establish that the materials were disclosed under specific confidentiality restrictions. The court found that although the information may have had commercial value, the lack of clear protective measures during operational use undermined its trade secret status. The decision emphasized that mere intent to protect is not enough—reasonable efforts must be evident in practice.

Not every trade secret can be locked away. Some must be deployed. Some must be licensed. Some must be explained to customers or integrated with third-party platforms. The challenge is to do so without forfeiting protection. That requires careful planning, disciplined execution, and a clear understanding that necessary disclosure does not mean unprotected disclosure.

Trade secret law rewards those who treat confidentiality as a continuous obligation, not a one-time formality. When sharing is necessary, secrecy must travel with the information.

## 3.4. Strategic Decision-Making Under Conditions of Uncertainty

Trade secret protection is not just a legal function—it is a strategic one. While lawyers may draft NDAs and engineers may implement access controls, the question of how much to protect, how widely to share, and what risks to accept falls to decision-makers operating under uncertainty. These choices are rarely made with perfect information. Most of the time, they involve tradeoffs, assumptions, and an uncomfortable blend of intuition and logic.

Traditional risk analysis works well when probabilities are known. But trade secret decisions often involve uncertainties that cannot be quantified. Courts may apply unpredictable standards. Competitors may behave opportunistically. Employees may defect unexpectedly. Emerging technologies may render current protections obsolete. In these environments, companies must rely on strategic reasoning—structured tools that support sound judgment even when outcomes are unclear.

This section explores several methods that organizations use to make decisions under uncertainty. These are not legal doctrines. They are business concepts with direct relevance to trade secret management. Each helps explain how companies can move forward even when the path ahead is difficult to map.

### 3.4.1. Regret Minimization

One of the simplest and most powerful tools for strategic reasoning under uncertainty is regret minimization. Rather than asking, "What is most likely to happen?" this approach asks, "If I turn out to be wrong, what will I regret most?"

Applied to trade secrets, this often leads companies to overprotect high-value information, even when the probability of exposure seems low. If the downside of disclosure would be catastrophic—loss of a product lead, damage to customer trust, competitive erosion—the company may choose aggressive controls not because the risk is high but because the regret would be severe if the risk materialized.

This approach explains why some businesses require dual-authentication to access sensitive files, or why they limit visibility even within trusted teams. It is not necessarily because they expect a breach; rather, it is because they could not tolerate the outcome if a breach occurred.

Regret minimization is especially useful when comparing two imperfect options. Should a company share a trade secret with a prospective partner before a deal is finalized? If the deal falls through, will the company regret the exposure more than it would regret a delay in negotiations? These are strategic choices. The goal is not to eliminate uncertainty—but to live with it wisely.

### 3.4.2. Option Value and Flexibility

Secrecy preserves flexibility. Information that remains confidential gives a company the option to patent it later, to license it selectively, or to pivot in response to market developments. Once a trade secret is disclosed, even inadvertently, that flexibility may be lost.

This is why many organizations treat secrecy itself as a strategic asset. They delay public filings. They limit disclosures in contract negotiations. They split projects into modules to avoid revealing the full picture to any one outsider. These techniques are not just about compliance—they are about preserving option value.

Flexibility matters most when future outcomes are uncertain. A company may not yet know whether it will pursue regulatory approval, seek outside investment, or partner with a larger firm. By limiting exposure now, it retains the freedom to choose later. This approach borrows from real-options thinking in finance: the idea that waiting has value when the cost of action is irreversible.

Trade secrets are inherently option-like. They do not guarantee exclusivity, but they do allow a firm to keep its strategic hand hidden until the time is right. Protecting that option—through technical, contractual, and procedural means—is a core element of trade secret strategy.

### 3.4.3. Scenario Thinking and Adaptive Planning

When probabilities are unclear, one alternative to forecasting is scenario thinking. This approach asks decision-makers to imagine a range of plausible futures and to plan for how each would affect the trade secret at issue.

What if a key engineer leaves and joins a competitor? What if a foreign jurisdiction refuses to enforce the company's NDA? What if a regulatory filing becomes public despite redactions? Rather than pretending these outcomes are unlikely, scenario thinking prepares for them. It asks: *What would we do if this happened tomorrow?*

The value of this method is not in prediction but rather in preparedness. Scenario thinking allows a company to identify weak points in its current controls, build contingency plans, and assign responsibility before a crisis occurs. It also supports internal alignment: by discussing potential futures in advance, teams are less likely to panic or blame each other when difficult situations arise.

Adaptive planning builds on this by creating mechanisms for response. For example, if a competitor releases a product that appears to reflect internal know-how, who investigates? Who determines whether to litigate? Who controls messaging to customers or investors? These are not legal questions alone—they are also strategic ones. And they are best answered before the pressure hits.

## 3.4.4. Legal Uncertainty and Judicial Risk

Legal uncertainty adds a unique layer of complexity to trade secret decision-making. A company may take extensive steps to protect its secrets, only to find that a court views those steps as insufficient. Or it may pursue enforcement, only to see the case dismissed on procedural grounds or limited by narrow judicial interpretation.

This is not a reason to give up on trade secret protection. But it is a reason to factor judicial risk into strategic choices. Companies should consider not only what the law says but also how courts have interpreted similar facts in the past—and how long, costly, and public enforcement might become.

Legal uncertainty also affects settlement strategy. A business may have a strong claim but choose to resolve a dispute quietly rather than risk unwanted disclosure during litigation. Or it may decline to file suit if the evidentiary burden is too high or the forum is unfavorable. These decisions are not signs of weakness. They are part of a mature risk strategy, one that recognizes the difference between being right and being effective.

## 3.4.5. Organizational Behavior and Bias

Finally, decision-making under uncertainty is shaped not only by information but by human behavior as well. Organizations tend to overestimate their security, underestimate adversaries, and discount rare but catastrophic events. These cognitive and cultural biases can derail even the most carefully designed protection plans.

Overconfidence is especially dangerous. Teams may believe that their employees would "never do that" or that their contracts are "airtight." They may dismiss early warning signs or fail to review access logs because no incident has occurred. This mindset can blind an organization to real vulnerabilities.

Group dynamics also matter. Risk committees may avoid difficult conversations or defer to dominant voices. Legal and technical teams may operate in silos, failing to coordinate their efforts. These behavioral patterns are rarely visible on an org chart, but they shape every aspect of trade secret strategy.

The best practices for protecting trade secrets includes building processes to counteract problematic behavioral tendencies.

- Structure risk reviews:
  - Hold a standing monthly meeting to identify any new or expired "crown-jewel" trade-secret assets.
  - Routinely review who has access to confidential information.
  - Regularly check vendor/contractor exposure via access logs.
  - Maintain a simple checklist and sign-offs so each asset has owner(s) and revue date(s).
  - Summary review results for executive dashboards (e.g., top 3 risks, priority mitigations chosen, and what will be re-checked next time).
- Document assumptions:
  - Maintain an "assumptions register" that lists each key belief about access, controls, third-party safeguards, and monitoring, the evidence for it, who owns it, and a review date.
  - When an assumption proves wrong, note what changed and update controls (e.g., tighten permissions, amend NDAs).
- Invite dissent:
  - Assign a rotating devil's advocate to argue the failure case and record unresolved concerns.
  - Run what-if drills such as "red team" or "black hat" exercises that test leakage vectors and mitigation strategies.
  - Provide a protected escalation channel for employees to raise access or contract concerns without retaliation (and perhaps anonymously).
  - Catalog dissenting opinions via a minority note—a brief paragraph explaining the objection—so it can be revisited later.
- Treat risk management as an evolving practice:
  - Do blameless post-mortems after incidents or near-misses to fix systems, not assign fault.
  - Set simple metrics and cadences: percentage of assets with "need-to-know" enforced, NDA coverage of vendors, time to disable departing users.
  - Refresh training annually and re-test controls quarterly; update the Trade Secret Protection Plan when tech, staffing, or vendors change.

Best organizational practices treat risk management not as a box-checking exercise but as an evolving practice that requires judgment, humility, and continuous attention. Trade secrets are lost not only through theft but also through inattention. Strategic decision-making under uncertainty is how companies guard against both.

# 3.5. Mapping and Profiling the Threat Environment

Understanding risk requires more than knowing what threats exist. It requires a structured picture of who might want access to a trade secret, how they might attempt to get it, and where the organization's defenses are most likely to fail. This means mapping the threat environment in practical, not abstract, terms. Just as engineers create diagrams of system architecture, trade secret managers must build models of exposure—models that reflect the actual flow of information, the real-world behavior of adversaries, and the structure of the organization itself.

Trade secret law expects owners to take reasonable steps to maintain secrecy. But reasonable steps depend on context. A one-person startup with a single proprietary method faces a different environment than a multinational with dozens of overlapping product lines and an extended supply chain. The threats are different. The resources are different. The expectations are different. This section provides a framework for building a threat model that matches the organization's specific posture.

## 3.5.1. Adversary Profiling

Every trade secret threat has a potential actor behind it. Sometimes the actor is external: a competitor, a vendor, a state-backed entity. Other times, it is internal: a disgruntled employee, a careless contractor, a well-meaning executive under pressure. Profiling adversaries means identifying not only who might benefit from misappropriation but also who has the motive, means, and opportunity to act.

Some businesses face specialized adversaries. A pharmaceutical company operating near patent expiration may expect reverse engineering from generic manufacturers. A tech firm in a competitive hiring market may expect staff poaching. A defense contractor may expect surveillance by foreign agents. Profiling helps companies prioritize which secrets to guard most heavily, and which vectors to monitor most closely.

The goal is not to assign blame in advance. It is to develop a realistic understanding of the incentives and capabilities of others. Would a competitor pay for inside information? Would a regulator require disclosure that leaks into the public domain? Would a partner company retain access to confidential files after a joint project ends? These are questions that shape real risk—not hypotheticals, but the specific ways trade secrets may come under pressure.

Profiling also allows organizations to consider patterns. Have similar companies experienced leaks in specific jurisdictions? Are competitors investing in technologies that make reverse engineering easier? Are certain vendors working with both the company and its rivals? The answers to these questions inform both legal strategies and operational decisions, such as who gets access to what and under what conditions.

### 3.5.2. Attack Surface Analysis

An adversary needs an opening. That opening may be technical, physical, procedural, or cultural. The set of all such openings is often referred to as the attack surface. For trade secret protection, the attack surface includes every place a secret is stored, shared, or transmitted. It includes servers, devices, notebooks, emails, conversations, whiteboards, cloud drives, onboarding materials, and exit interviews. If a trade secret can be seen or inferred, it can be taken.

Mapping the attack surface begins with the inventory. What secrets exist, and where do they live? Who has access? How is that access controlled, logged, or reviewed? What policies govern disclosure? What tools monitor compliance? Many companies are surprised by how widely their most valuable information circulates and how few barriers exist to accessing it.

Attack surface analysis also requires understanding indirect exposure. A marketing team may use a proprietary pricing model without knowing how it works. A design partner may receive specifications that reflect years of confidential development. A help desk technician may have access to internal documentation containing trade secrets unrelated to their duties. Each of these exposures increases the surface area and, therefore, the risk.

Cultural practices can widen the attack surface too. If employees routinely share screenshots in messaging apps, download files to personal devices, or use unsanctioned collaboration tools, technical controls may offer little protection. Trade secret security is only as strong as the system that enforces it—and that system includes behavior.

Attack surface analysis does not guarantee prevention. But it enables visibility. It helps companies focus protection where it is needed most, limit unnecessary exposure, and document the kinds of reasonable efforts courts expect to see when evaluating trade secret claims.

## 3.6. Methods for Assessing Risks

Once the organization has identified its trade secrets, understood the nature of risk and uncertainty, and mapped its threat environment, the next task is to assess which secrets are most at risk and why. This is not a matter of intuition or guesswork. It is a structured exercise that combines factual analysis, operational insight, and reasoned judgment.

Risk assessment does not produce perfect answers. It produces visibility. By articulating each trade secret's likelihood of exposure and how damaging that exposure would be, companies can begin to prioritize protections. Some secrets may require substantial investment in safeguards. Others may pose only minimal risk. The point is not to eliminate risk entirely but rather to align protection efforts with actual exposure.

This section outlines three common tools for trade secret risk assessment: vulnerability audits, risk matrices, and integration with existing enterprise frameworks. Each approach has limitations. But when used together, they provide a practical foundation for making defensible, informed decisions about where and how to protect confidential information.

### 3.6.1. Vulnerability Audits

A vulnerability audit begins with a simple premise: the organization must know how its trade secrets could be lost before it can decide how to protect them. The audit process identifies weak points in the systems, processes, and people who handle sensitive information. It evaluates both the existence of protections and their actual implementation.

The process typically starts with access mapping. Who can see each trade secret? Is access limited by role? Are logs kept and reviewed? Are permissions updated when team members change projects or leave the company? Many firms find that theoretical restrictions are not reflected in daily operations. A server may be password-protected, but the password may be shared among dozens of users. A confidential file may be labeled but stored in a shared folder accessible to contractors.

The audit then examines disclosure pathways. When is the information shared outside the company? Are NDAs signed? Are they specific to the information at issue? Is the information labeled, segregated, or protected by technical measures? If the trade secret appears in a pitch deck, is that deck marked as confidential, and is it sent through secure channels?

Vulnerability audits also include cultural and procedural review. Are employees trained in trade secret handling? Are security practices enforced consistently? Is there a clear process for reporting concerns? Do managers reinforce or undermine confidentiality norms? A trade secret is only as secure as the environment in which it is handled.

The value of a vulnerability audit lies not in the number of flaws it uncovers but in the discipline it instills. It forces the organization to articulate how it protects its most valuable information—and where that protection falls short. It also creates documentation. If litigation arises, the audit provides evidence that the company took secrecy seriously, even if not every control was perfect.

### 3.6.2. Risk Matrices

A risk matrix translates complex judgments into structured comparisons. It helps organizations assess which trade secrets are at greatest risk, based on two dimensions: the likelihood of exposure and the magnitude of harm. These assessments may be qualitative or quantitative, but the goal is the same—to prioritize threats and allocate resources accordingly.

A basic matrix divides both axes into three categories: low, medium, and high. A trade secret with high likelihood and high harm appears in the upper-right corner of the matrix and demands urgent protection. A secret with low likelihood and low harm may warrant only routine safeguards. Secrets that fall in between require closer scrutiny. Some may be hard to access but extremely valuable. Others may be frequently shared but only moderately important.

The matrix does not supply exact answers. It supports deliberation. It helps teams articulate why they see a particular risk as serious or manageable. It surfaces disagreement. It forces specificity. Why is this risk labeled high? What makes that one low? What assumptions underlie those judgments?

Risk matrices also help identify outliers. If a secret is extremely valuable but widely accessible, the company may decide to restrict access. If a secret is routinely shared but of low strategic value, the company may decide to relax controls. The point is not to treat every secret the same but rather to match effort to exposure.

Like any model, the matrix depends on input quality. Assessments must be grounded in actual workflows, not abstract fears. They must reflect current behavior, not aspirational policy. But when done rigorously, the matrix provides a defensible, transparent basis for risk classification—one that holds up under internal review and external scrutiny alike.

## 3.6.3. Framework Integration

Many companies already maintain enterprise risk management systems that can accommodate trade secret protection without building parallel infrastructure. These systems often align with international standards from the International Organization for Standardization (known as "ISO"), such as ISO 31000 (risk management) and ISO/IEC 27001 (developed jointly with the International Electrotechnical Commission for information security management), and with United States national frameworks such as the National Institute of Standards and Technology (NIST) Cybersecurity Framework. Trade secret protection integrates into these structures by assigning clear ownership of crown-jewel assets in the risk register, embedding secrecy-specific controls—such as need-to-know access restrictions and vendor/contractor due diligence—into existing information-security protocols, and subjecting trade-secret safeguards to the same governance, audit, and assurance cycles already applied to enterprise risk and cybersecurity.

ISO 31000 offers a general model for risk management: establish the context, identify risks, analyze their likelihood and impact, implement treatments, and review outcomes. This model fits naturally with trade secret protection. The context is the company's competitive position. The risks are vectors of secrecy loss. The treatments are the safeguards described in later chapters. The review process includes audits, monitoring, and updates to the inventory.

The NIST Cybersecurity Framework provides more detailed guidance in digital environments. It emphasizes five functions: identify, protect, detect, respond, and recover. These can be applied directly to trade secrets stored or transmitted electronically. Identification maps what information qualifies as a trade secret. Protection includes access controls and encryption. Detection involves anomaly tracking and log review. Response and recovery include breach protocols and containment strategies.

Integrating trade secret risk into broader systems helps to ensure consistency. It also builds institutional support. When legal, technical, and operational teams work from the same framework, policies are more likely to be implemented, understood, and enforced. Trade secrets do not sit in a legal silo. They exist in code repositories, factory floors, design studios, and vendor databases. Protecting them requires a shared language—and shared responsibility.

Framework integration also supports external validation. When courts, regulators, or investors ask whether a company takes trade secret protection seriously, pointing to a systematic, standards-aligned process sends a stronger signal than ad hoc policies. The goal is not compliance for its own sake. It is coordination, clarity, and credibility.

## 3.7. The Trade Secret Paradox

Trade secret law contains a conceptual puzzle at its core—a paradox that distinguishes it from every other area of intellectual property. Patents are granted by the government. Copyrights arise automatically when an author creates original work. Trademarks protect signs and symbols used in commerce. But trade secrets are different. They are not defined by registration or authorship. They are defined by secrecy.

And yet, secrecy is not a stable category. Under the Uniform Trade Secrets Act and the Defend Trade Secrets Act, a trade secret is information that derives independent economic value from not being generally known and is subject to reasonable efforts to maintain its secrecy. This definition introduces a feedback loop: the existence of legal protection depends on the owner's efforts to prevent misappropriation, but whether misappropriation occurred depends on whether the information was legally protected in the first place.

This creates the trade secret paradox:

You cannot prove misappropriation unless the information was a trade secret.

But you cannot prove something was a trade secret unless you can show that you tried to prevent misappropriation.

The law protects secrets. But whether something is a secret is judged only after a breach occurs. The right arises from conduct. The violation is defined by whether that conduct was enough.

This circularity is not just theoretical. It defines how courts decide cases. When a business sues for trade secret theft, the first question is not whether the defendant acted improperly. It is whether the information was actually a trade secret at the time of the alleged theft. That depends on facts: Did the company label its documents? Limit access? Use NDAs? Train employees? Monitor compliance? Courts will not assume secrecy. They require proof that the company behaved as though secrecy mattered.

This means that even wrongful acts—taking files, disclosing documents, using a rival's proprietary process—may not be considered misappropriation if the plaintiff failed to treat the information as a secret. The legality of the taker's conduct is contingent on the owner's behavior.

This is the paradox in full: Trade secret law does not define a fixed category of protected information. It defines a dynamic relationship between a business and its knowledge. The same piece of information may or may not be a trade secret depending on how it was handled. Secrecy is not a status. It is a function of effort.

That effort must precede the loss. You cannot retroactively create protection once the information is gone. Trade secret law protects only what was already being protected. It judges the past, not the intention. The paradox is that legal protection exists only if the owner acted in a way that assumed legal protection would be needed—before knowing that any violation would occur.

Trade secrets, in this sense, are performative. They exist because the owner treats them as if they exist. And only by treating them that way will the law agree.

## 3.8. Resolving the Circularity Paradox

The circularity at the heart of trade secret law is not a flaw. It is a feature that reflects the nature of secrecy itself. Unlike other forms of legal protection, which begin with registration or authorship, trade secret protection begins with behavior. The law responds not to the content of the information but to the way it is treated. This makes trade secrets deeply contextual, highly fact-dependent, and inseparable from organizational conduct.

The key to resolving the paradox is to recognize that protection and risk are mutually defining. A company's legal ability to stop misappropriation depends on the steps it took to prevent that misappropriation. Those steps do not merely support the legal claim—they are what create the conditions for the claim to exist.

Earlier in this chapter, we explored how threats arise from both lawful conduct, such as reverse engineering or independent discovery, and unlawful conduct, such as insider theft or contractual breach. But whether a given act falls into one category or the other depends on whether the information was legally protected as a trade secret. And that, in turn, depends on what the owner did to maintain secrecy.

This is where strategy matters. As we saw in Sections 3.4 and 3.6, risk assessment is not just about identifying threats. It is about documenting control. It is about making choices—what to protect, how to protect it, and where to draw the line between necessary sharing and unacceptable exposure. These choices establish the factual foundation for legal enforceability.

The risk matrix is one tool. It helps prioritize which secrets require the strongest controls. The vulnerability audit is another. It exposes gaps between policy and practice. But the real solution to the paradox is behavioral. Courts do not enforce rights in the abstract. They enforce evidence of care. When a company can show that it treated its information as secret—not just in policy, but in daily operations—it gives the law something to work with.

This also explains why so many trade secret claims fail. Plaintiffs often assume that the wrongdoing speaks for itself. But the law does not begin with the wrongdoing. It begins with the question of whether the information was protected in the first place. That protection must be visible, consistent, and credible. It must be embodied in NDAs, access logs, labeling practices, training protocols, and audits. It must appear not just in courtroom declarations but also in ordinary routines.

In trade secret law, certainty comes not from rules but from preparation. The circularity is resolved when organizations treat protection as a continuous act—an operational reality that gives meaning to the legal category. Trade secrets are not defined by their value or novelty. They are defined by how they are handled. The information becomes a trade secret because the company acted as if it were one and because it can prove that it did.

## 3.9. From Awareness to Action

Trade secrets do not protect themselves. They exist only because an organization acts—early, consistently, and deliberately—to keep them secret. This chapter has laid out the conceptual and strategic framework for understanding how trade secrets are lost, how risks are assessed, and why protection begins long before litigation. It has shown that secrecy is not a state of nature. It is a state of practice.

By now, the paradox at the heart of trade secret law should feel less puzzling. There is no contradiction in requiring owners to prove they protected what they claim was secret. It is not a trap. It is the bargain that defines the entire system: the law will enforce secrecy, but only if secrecy has already been maintained.

This means that risk assessment is not merely a technical exercise. It is the foundation of legal credibility. Every decision—what to classify as a trade secret, how to limit access, when to share, and with whom—has downstream consequences. These decisions determine whether the law will recognize a violation as misappropriation or dismiss it as fair competition.

Chapters 1 and 2 provided the groundwork: how trade secrets are defined, and how they are inventoried and categorized. This chapter has shown how risk enters the picture, both as a practical concern and as a condition of enforceability. The next step is to act on that awareness—to build systems that prevent loss, mitigate vulnerabilities, and respond to internal and external threats in ways that courts will recognize and respect.

Chapter 4 begins with internal risks. It examines the greatest and most common source of loss: people within the organization. Employees, contractors, executives, and others with authorized access can become the reason a secret no longer qualifies as a secret. Whether through carelessness, misunderstanding, or deliberate breach, insiders represent the most direct challenge to any protection plan.

But as we will see, those risks can be addressed. Protection is not an illusion. It is a discipline. And it begins by turning awareness into action.

## References

Frank H. Knight, RISK, UNCERTAINTY AND PROFIT (Houghton Mifflin Co. 1921).

Kenneth J. Arrow, *Economic Welfare and the Allocation of Resources for Invention*, *in* THE RATE AND DIRECTION OF INVENTIVE ACTIVITY: ECONOMIC AND SOCIAL FACTORS (Nat'l Bureau of Econ. Research ed., Princeton Univ. Press 1962).

Edmund W. Kitch, *The Nature and Function of the Patent System*, 20 J.L. & ECON. 265 (1977).

# Chapter 4

# Mitigating Internal Vulnerabilities

No trade secret protection plan can succeed without controlling what happens inside the organization. Employees, contractors, executives, and advisors all require access to sensitive information to do their jobs. That access creates vulnerability. And while external threats may draw more attention, it is internal exposure that causes most trade secret loss.

Internal vulnerabilities take many forms. A departing executive might join a competitor and apply proprietary knowledge without ever copying a file. A junior engineer might forward documents to a personal account for convenience, not realizing the legal consequences. A former salesperson might solicit old customers, believing that the company's CRM (or sales database) is just a list, not a protected asset. Even well-intentioned insiders can become inadvertent threats if expectations are unclear or protections are inconsistently enforced.

The law reflects this. Courts evaluating trade secret claims routinely ask whether the company took reasonable measures to prevent exposure. That inquiry begins with what happens inside the business: the clarity of its contracts, the structure of its access controls, the discipline of its training and monitoring, and the credibility of its policies. In other words, trade secret status is not just about what the information is. It is about how the organization treats it—every day, at every level.

This chapter provides a detailed guide to mitigating internal vulnerabilities. It covers:

- The use of contractual tools such as nondisclosure agreements, noncompetes, and invention assignment clauses
- Operational safeguards, including access limitation, document labeling, and employee monitoring
- Behavioral and cultural systems: training, onboarding, and exit protocols
- Legal doctrines that determine when internal misuse becomes legally actionable misappropriation

Throughout, we focus on the performative nature of secrecy. Protections must not only exist—they must be legible to a court as well. They must be consistently applied, well-documented, and tied to the reality of how the organization operates. This is especially true in an era of hybrid work, cloud collaboration, mobile devices, and expanding vendor networks. The internal environment is fluid. So must be the organization's control over it.

We use the term vulnerability to capture both risk (which can often be measured) and uncertainty (which cannot). Internal vulnerabilities may be driven by incentives, behavior, oversight, or organizational design. Some are foreseeable. Others are not. The point is not to eliminate all possibility of breach. It is to ensure that if one occurs, the company can show that it did everything the law expects—and more.

The sections that follow provide both doctrinal analysis and practical guidance. Breakout boxes offer clause samples and policy language, summarize key enforcement cases, and unpack contested doctrines and compliance pitfalls. The result is not just a legal chapter but also a strategic one. It is meant to guide action—not just describe consequences.

## 4.1. Internal Risk as the Primary Threat

The most serious threats to trade secrets almost always come from within. It is not the anonymous hacker or the distant competitor who most often compromises confidentiality. It is the employee who has legitimate access, the contractor who misunderstands expectations, the executive who leaves for a rival, or the vendor whose internal controls fall short. These actors are not strangers to the information. They are part of the business. And because they operate with authority, trust, and routine exposure, they represent the single most important category of trade secret vulnerability.

Courts have long recognized this. The majority of trade secret litigation involves individuals or firms who once had legitimate access to the protected information. These cases often arise after a departure or during a transition in roles. Sometimes the breach is overt, as when a departing executive downloads design files and uses them to launch a competing product. Other times, the harm is more subtle and harder to detect, as when confidential know-how is gradually deployed at a new job in a way that undermines the value of the original secret. In both cases, the legal analysis begins with a single question: Did the company take reasonable steps to protect the information before the breach occurred?

Trade secret protection is backward-looking. A company cannot declare after the fact that certain information was valuable and confidential. It must demonstrate, through contemporaneous conduct, that secrecy was consistently maintained. This conduct includes the use of contractual restrictions, internal policies, access controls, and employee education. It includes monitoring, documentation, and enforcement. Most importantly, it includes evidence that the company took secrecy seriously across the organization—not just at the top or on paper, but in practice.

Internal risk is not a narrow category. It includes full-time employees, part-time workers, independent contractors, consultants, and executives. It includes interns, advisors, board members, and temporary staff. In some cases, it even includes individuals outside the formal organizational structure, such as joint development partners or embedded specialists who are given access to systems or materials for operational reasons. What unites these groups is their proximity to the secret. They do not need to hack a system or circumvent a firewall. They already have access.

Because of this proximity, internal protection requires more than generic policies. It requires calibrated systems that align legal obligations with business realities. The protections must match the level of access and the nature of the risk. A senior developer with visibility into proprietary architecture needs a different set of controls than a customer service representative handling routine account inquiries. The key is not to treat everyone the same but rather to design internal safeguards that are both credible and proportionate.

This chapter begins with contractual mechanisms. These include nondisclosure agreements, invention assignment clauses, non-solicitation terms, and where enforceable, noncompetition provisions. It then turns to operational safeguards, including access limitation, document management, and monitoring practices. It examines onboarding and training, both as legal evidence and as cultural reinforcement. It addresses what happens when an employee leaves and how courts evaluate post-employment risk. And it concludes with enforcement doctrine, drawing from case law to show how courts distinguish credible protection efforts from mere formality.

Throughout, the focus remains on how companies can anticipate internal vulnerabilities before they become legal liabilities. Trade secrets do not depend on any one contract or control. They depend on the system as a whole and on the company's ability to demonstrate that secrecy was built into its structure, not assumed after the fact.

## 4.2. Confidentiality Agreements and Contractual Safeguards

The first and most essential method for mitigating internal vulnerability is through contract. When companies grant individuals access to trade secrets, they must define that access in legal terms. Confidentiality agreements do not guarantee protection, but they do create the framework for enforcing it. They establish duties, clarify expectations, and provide evidence that the company took deliberate steps to preserve secrecy.

Courts evaluating trade secret claims routinely ask whether there was a contract in place, what it said, and whether it reflected the actual flow of information within the business. A well-drafted agreement shows that the company did not rely on trust or routine but rather took the affirmative step of spelling out what information was protected, how it was to be used, and what restrictions would remain after the relationship ended. When these elements are missing or vague, courts are more likely to find that the trade secret was not adequately protected.

This section examines the core legal agreements used to control access to trade secrets: nondisclosure agreements, noncompetition and non-solicitation clauses, and invention assignment provisions. These are not one-size-fits-all contracts. They serve different purposes, raise different legal issues, and face different standards of enforceability depending on the jurisdiction and the relationship between the parties. But all serve the same strategic goal: to give the company a legally recognizable foundation for asserting that its information was secret and that its secrecy was maintained.

The law does not expect companies to use the strongest possible restriction in every case. It expects them to use the right restriction for the circumstances. This means tailoring the scope, duration, and geographic reach of restrictions to the role of the person receiving the information. It also means using language that is precise enough to be enforceable but is not so rigid that it becomes impractical. Many trade secret disputes turn not on whether a contract existed, but on whether the terms of that contract were clearly tied to the information at issue and proportionate to the risks involved.

In the subsections that follow, we examine each type of agreement in detail. We review case law illustrating what courts have found enforceable and what they have rejected. We present sample language, drawn from real-world templates, showing how variations in drafting affect legal outcomes. And we analyze how these agreements fit into the broader strategy of mitigating internal vulnerability—not as a substitute for operational controls but rather as the legal anchor that makes those controls enforceable.

## 4.2.1. Core Doctrines in Trade Secret Contracts

Every internal protection strategy begins with the recognition that legal obligations must be clear, enforceable, and appropriately matched to the role of the individual receiving access. Trade secret law does not require a written contract in every case, but it strongly favors the presence of one. Courts routinely cite the existence or absence of confidentiality agreements as a central factor in determining whether the owner of the secret took reasonable steps to maintain secrecy. For employees, contractors, and other insiders, these agreements define the legal boundaries of acceptable conduct.

The core contractual doctrines that govern these agreements begin with notice. Trade secret protection requires that recipients of confidential information understand that it is confidential and that they are not free to use or disclose it beyond the terms of their engagement. A properly drafted agreement provides this notice explicitly, but it must do more than recite a general obligation of secrecy. It must describe what information is protected, under what conditions it may be accessed or shared, and what duties survive the end of the relationship.

Enforceability depends on more than the presence of a signature. Courts examine whether the contract reflects a reasonable balance between the interests of the employer and the employee. Moreover, courts are often constrained by state statutes that vary significantly regarding enforceability on noncompetes. In some states, such as California, certain clauses, particularly noncompetition provisions, are presumptively unenforceable. California's statute broadly prohibits post-employment restraints on lawful work, reflecting a public policy that favors employee mobility and open competition. As of January 1, 2024, California added Business and Professions Code §16600.5 (S.B. 699), which renders noncompetes unenforceable "regardless of where and when the contract was signed," including agreements executed outside California when enforcement is sought against California employees or residents.

Other states take the opposite view and routinely uphold noncompetition agreements so long as they are reasonable in scope and duration. New Hampshire, for example, generally enforces such agreements when they protect legitimate business interests such as trade secrets, customer goodwill, or specialized training, and it requires advance written notice of noncompetes to prospective employees under N.H. Rev. Stat. Ann. §275:70.

A few states have moved toward statutory compromise. Massachusetts' Noncompetition Agreement Act, Mass. Gen. Laws ch. 149, §24L, allows noncompetition agreements only if the employer provides garden-leave pay, by default at least fifty percent of the employee's highest base salary during the restricted period, or other mutually agreed consideration, and it limits duration to twelve months. Oregon's statute, Or. Rev. Stat. §653.295, likewise caps noncompetes at twelve months, requires advance written notice, and conditions enforceability on a minimum salary threshold tied to the state's median family income. If that threshold is not met, the employer must pay during the restricted period at a defined portion of prior compensation.

These approaches illustrate the spectrum of policy choices, from categorical bans to pay-for-restraint models, through which states balance employer protection against employee freedom to work. What matters across jurisdictions is whether the agreement is tailored to the role, the information, and the actual business risks involved.

Confidentiality agreements also exist within a broader structure of employment law. An at-will employee may owe default duties of loyalty and nondisclosure, but those duties are limited. Without a contract, there is often no surviving obligation once the relationship ends. Similarly, without an invention assignment clause, a company may find that it does not actually own the trade secrets developed by its own employees. In disputes over misappropriation, these gaps become liabilities. Courts are reluctant to impose obligations that the company could have required but failed to.

A common mistake in drafting trade secret contracts is to use language that is either too broad or too vague. Agreements that purport to cover all information of any kind or that impose sweeping restrictions without any reference to role or duration are frequently narrowed or struck down. Precision is essential. The agreement must link the duty of secrecy to the actual information at issue, describe how that information is conveyed or used, and identify how long the obligation is intended to last.

Ultimately, these contracts serve two purposes. They establish rights that can be enforced in court, and they signal to employees and others that the company treats its information as a protected asset. They are not the only element in determining whether something qualifies as a trade secret, but they are often the first place a court will look. In the next sections, we examine the different types of contractual safeguards in detail, beginning with nondisclosure agreements and continuing through more complex restrictions on use, competition, solicitation, and intellectual property.

## 4.2.2. Nondisclosure Agreements

A nondisclosure agreement is the foundational instrument of trade secret protection. It creates the first and most explicit layer of legal obligation between a company and anyone who receives access to confidential information. Courts routinely look to the language of the NDA to determine whether the company took reasonable steps to maintain secrecy, whether the information was adequately identified as confidential, and whether the parties understood the terms of use and the consequences of breach.

Not all NDAs are enforceable. Many are drafted with language so broad or vague that courts decline to give them weight. Some define confidential information in terms so expansive that they include public knowledge, personal experience, or general observations. Others fail to state what uses are permitted, how long the obligation lasts, or what disclosures are allowed in compliance with law. Some rely on form templates that do not align with the actual nature of the business relationship.

At its core, a well-drafted NDA must identify what counts as confidential, how the information will be used, to whom it may be disclosed, and for how long the obligation of secrecy will continue. It must match the terms to the facts. An agreement that is intended to cover trade secrets must reflect that goal in both scope and structure. This means defining the "purpose" of the disclosure, limiting use to that purpose, and prohibiting reverse engineering, independent application, or derivative use. It also means specifying whether oral disclosures are covered, how information must be labeled, and what happens when the relationship ends.

Many companies, especially those serving as disclosing parties, favor unilateral NDAs that protect only their information. Others use mutual NDAs where both sides will share information. The choice should reflect the flow of risk. In either case, the agreement must define its terms in a way that allows for enforcement. Courts will look closely at whether the definition of "confidential information" includes only marked materials or also covers information that should be understood as confidential based on context. They will ask whether the duration of obligation is reasonable, whether return or destruction provisions are triggered automatically, and whether the receiving party can delegate access to affiliates or third parties.

The most defensible NDAs use layered definitions and cascading protections. They define "confidential information" with both objective and contextual terms, include illustrative categories, and require the receiving party to exercise at least a reasonable degree of care—if not the same care used to protect its own information. They also specify that trade secrets must remain protected indefinitely, even if other information becomes subject to a time limit. Many include standard language confirming the disclosing party's ownership rights and disavowing any grant of license or use beyond the stated purpose.

An NDA is not a legal substitute for operational trade secret protection. But it is often the clearest signal to a court that the company understood what was at stake. When paired with operational controls and consistent enforcement, it becomes one of the strongest forms of documentary evidence that secrecy was both real and reasonable.

The clauses below illustrate how contract language changes depending on whether the company is in the stronger bargaining position. The first version is written for a disclosing party seeking maximum protection. The second is written for a receiving party seeking flexibility and clarity. Each version reflects real language used in practice.

### CONFIDENTIAL INFORMATION CLAUSE

#### *Pro-Disclosing Party*

"Confidential Information" means all nonpublic information disclosed by the Disclosing Party, directly or indirectly, in written, oral, electronic, visual, or any other form, that the Receiving Party knows or reasonably should know is confidential based on the nature of the information or the circumstances surrounding its disclosure. Confidential Information includes, without limitation, technical data, trade secrets, know-how, product designs, marketing plans, business models, financial data, internal policies, customer and supplier information, employee data, pricing strategies, and any analysis, compilations, or summaries derived from such information.

The Receiving Party agrees to use the Confidential Information solely for the purpose of evaluating or pursuing a business relationship with the Disclosing Party, to restrict disclosure to those employees and agents who have a need to know and are bound by obligations of confidentiality no less protective than those set forth herein, and to protect the Confidential Information with the same degree of care used to protect its own confidential information, but in no event less than a reasonable degree of care. The Receiving Party shall not reverse engineer, decompile, or otherwise attempt to derive the underlying materials from any Confidential Information and shall return or destroy all Confidential Information upon request or upon termination of the relationship.

This Agreement shall continue in effect with respect to any Confidential Information for a period of two years from the date of disclosure, except that the Receiving Party's obligations with respect to any trade secret shall survive so long as the information remains a trade secret under applicable law.

In general, the clause's drafter should draft it favorably to their own side. When a party frequently receives information—such as an inventor-support hotline or a venture-capital firm—that party may draft the NDA in a narrower manner.

**CONFIDENTIAL INFORMATION CLAUSE**

*Pro-Receiving Party*

"Confidential Information" means only such information that is marked in writing as confidential at the time of disclosure, or, if disclosed orally, is designated as confidential in writing within ten (10) business days thereafter. Confidential Information shall not include any information that

(a) was known to the Receiving Party without restriction before disclosure,

(b) becomes publicly available through no fault of the Receiving Party,

(c) is lawfully obtained from a third party without a duty of confidentiality, or

(d) is independently developed by the Receiving Party without reference to the Disclosing Party's information.

The Receiving Party agrees to use the Confidential Information solely for the purpose expressly identified in this Agreement and not for any other purpose. The Receiving Party shall protect the Confidential Information using reasonable care, but no greater than the care it uses to protect its own information of similar sensitivity. The Receiving Party shall not be liable for accidental disclosure so long as it acted in good faith and promptly notifies the Disclosing Party of any unauthorized use.

Unless otherwise stated in writing, the confidentiality obligations under this Agreement shall expire one year after the date of disclosure.

These clauses differ in both structure and effect. The pro-disclosing party version uses broad, layered definitions and extends obligations for the duration of trade secret protection. It avoids requiring written markings and prohibits reverse engineering. It seeks maximum control, including a return or destruction requirement and explicit limits on internal disclosure. The pro-receiving party version narrows the scope significantly. It limits confidentiality to marked or memorialized information, excludes independently known or developed content, sets a fixed duration, and disclaims liability for good-faith mistakes. These distinctions are not just semantic. They determine what rights survive in a dispute, what obligations a court will enforce, and how likely it is that the company will be able to assert a trade secret claim if a breakdown occurs.

When drafting NDAs, lawyers must understand not only what language is standard but also what language shifts risk. Whether representing the disclosing or receiving party, the objective is the same: to define the relationship clearly, allocate responsibility fairly, and anticipate how the agreement will function if something goes wrong.

## 4.2.3. Non-Solicitation and Noncompetition Agreements

Restrictions on solicitation and competition are among the most contentious and heavily litigated clauses in employment agreements. For companies, they are essential tools to prevent insiders from departing and immediately undermining the company's competitive position. For employees, they can feel like career-limiting restraints that persist long after the relationship ends. Trade secret law does not require these clauses, but where they are enforceable, they can serve as a powerful supplement to traditional confidentiality agreements. They restrict the use of information not by limiting access but instead by limiting action.

Courts approach these clauses with caution. Unlike NDAs, which are usually enforced as written unless unreasonably vague, non-solicitation and noncompetition clauses are scrutinized for scope, duration, geographic reach, and the nature of the employer's legitimate business interest. They are typically enforced only to the extent that they are necessary to protect customer relationships, employee stability, or the misuse of confidential information. If the restriction goes further than necessary to serve those goals, it may be struck down in whole or in part. In some jurisdictions, such as California, certain types of restrictions are unenforceable by statute regardless of the employer's interests.

A non-solicitation clause prohibits a former employee from soliciting clients, customers, or employees for a competing business. A noncompetition clause goes further, barring the individual from working for or establishing a competing business altogether. Some agreements include narrow job-specific restrictions; others attempt to bar entire categories of work across wide geographic regions. The broader the clause, the more likely it is to be challenged.

The enforceability of these restrictions depends not only on the wording of the clause but also on the justification offered for it. Courts ask what interest the employer is trying to protect, why that interest cannot be protected through less restrictive means, and whether the employee's new role actually implicates those interests. They also consider whether the restriction is necessary to protect trade secrets specifically or whether it is being used to limit ordinary market competition.

The following clause reflects a pro-employer approach. It includes a two-year duration, prohibits both direct and indirect solicitation, and applies to both customers and employees. It is carefully worded to focus on relationships developed during the term of employment, which increases its likelihood of enforcement.

**CUSTOMER AND EMPLOYEE NON-SOLICITATION CLAUSE**

*Pro-Employer Language*

The Employee agrees that for a period of two (2) years following the termination of employment for any reason, the Employee shall not, directly or indirectly, solicit, induce, or attempt to induce any employee, contractor, or consultant of the Company to terminate their relationship with the Company. The Employee further agrees that, for the same period, the Employee shall not solicit or attempt to solicit, for the purpose of offering competing products or services, any customer or prospective customer of the Company with whom the Employee had material contact during the twelve (12) months preceding the termination of employment.

This restriction shall apply regardless of whether the solicitation is initiated by the Employee, the former colleague, or the customer, and regardless of whether such conduct is undertaken on behalf of the Employee individually or through another business or entity.

This clause illustrates how a well-drafted non-solicitation provision can be targeted without being timid. It ties the restriction to specific relationships, includes a clear time frame, and avoids language that could be seen as punitive or vague. Courts are more likely to enforce clauses that are narrowly tailored in this way.

By contrast, the next clause reflects a pro-employee drafting perspective. It limits the scope of restriction, carves out general advertising and passive receipt of business, and excludes former customers who initiate contact without solicitation. It also caps the restriction at one year and applies only where trade secrets are implicated.

**CUSTOMER AND EMPLOYEE NON-SOLICITATION CLAUSE**

*Pro-Employee Language*

The Employee agrees that for a period of one (1) year following the termination of employment, the Employee will not actively solicit business from any client of the Company with whom the Employee had direct contact and confidential commercial dealings during the last six (6) months of employment, but only to the extent that such solicitation would involve the use or disclosure of the Company's trade secrets or other confidential information.

> Nothing in this clause shall prevent the Employee from engaging in general advertising not targeted at specific clients or from accepting unsolicited business initiated by a former customer without any active encouragement or inducement. This restriction shall not apply to customers with whom the Employee had a pre-existing relationship independent of their employment.

This language reflects a more limited view of post-employment obligations. It narrows the scope of restriction to situations where actual misuse of confidential information is likely, and it explicitly preserves the employee's ability to compete on fair terms. Courts often favor this kind of framing when evaluating whether a restriction is reasonably calculated to protect a legitimate business interest or whether it is designed simply to restrain competition.

The strategic choice between these approaches depends on many factors: the seniority of the employee, the nature of the information at issue, the competitive dynamics of the industry, and the jurisdiction in which enforcement would occur. Companies seeking to protect trade secrets through contract must consider not only what protections are desirable but also what a court will uphold. Likewise, employees and their counsel must evaluate what they are agreeing to give up and whether the clause appropriately balances the employer's interests with the employee's freedom to work.

Well-crafted restrictions on solicitation and competition can reduce the risk that trade secrets will walk out the door and be immediately deployed by a rival. But overreaching language can backfire by rendering the clause unenforceable and undermining the company's credibility in court. The goal is not to prevent all post-employment activity. It is to prevent misuse of protected information by those who once had privileged access to it.

## 4.2.4. Assignment of Inventions and IP Rights

Companies often assume that they automatically own the intellectual property created by their employees. In many cases, that assumption is wrong. Under default rules, the creator of an invention, work of authorship, or proprietary method retains ownership unless a contract clearly assigns it to the employer. This is true even when the invention is developed on company time or using company resources. As a result, the absence of an effective invention assignment agreement can create substantial risk, particularly when trade secrets are developed internally.

Invention assignment clauses serve two functions. First, they transfer ownership of innovations, developments, and other intellectual property from the individual to the company. Second, they reinforce the company's control over related trade secrets by establishing that information developed during the course of employment is not merely confidential—rather, it is owned by the business. This distinction matters.

Ownership strengthens the argument that the company took reasonable steps to protect the information and has standing to assert legal rights over it.

Enforceability depends on scope. Clauses that purport to assign all ideas or inventions conceived by the employee, regardless of whether they relate to the company's business, are often struck down as overbroad. Many states restrict an employer's ability to claim inventions developed entirely on an employee's own time and without use of company resources. California, for example, requires employers to exclude such inventions from the scope of assignment and to provide notice of that exclusion. Other states allow broader assignment but still require a clear connection between the work and the employer's line of business.

From the company's perspective, the goal is to ensure that valuable innovation, including trade secrets, becomes part of the firm's intellectual property portfolio. From the employee's perspective, the concern is often overreach—for example, whether the clause captures work done outside the scope of employment or imposes obligations that persist long after the relationship ends. These tensions can be addressed through careful drafting that links the assignment to specific roles, projects, and business functions, and that limits its reach to what is reasonably necessary to protect the company's interests.

The clauses below reflect these competing approaches. The first version is written to maximize employer ownership. The second includes carveouts and clarifying limitations designed to preserve the employee's independent creative work.

### INVENTION ASSIGNMENT CLAUSE

#### *Pro-Employer Language*

The Employee agrees that all inventions, discoveries, improvements, processes, designs, developments, ideas, trade secrets, and other works of authorship (collectively, "Inventions") conceived, developed, or reduced to practice by the Employee, alone or with others, during the term of employment, and that relate in any manner to the Company's business, operations, research, or anticipated work, shall be the sole and exclusive property of the Company. The Employee hereby assigns to the Company all right, title, and interest in and to such Inventions, whether or not patentable or registrable, and agrees to execute all documents necessary to confirm such ownership.

This obligation applies regardless of whether the Invention was developed during working hours or using Company equipment, and shall survive the termination of employment.

This clause favors the employer by using expansive but business-tethered language. It captures all developments related to the company's field, regardless of when or where they were made, and secures both patent and trade secret rights without limitation. Courts are more likely to enforce such a clause when the employee's role is technical or innovation-oriented, and when the connection to the company's work is direct and provable.

**INVENTION ASSIGNMENT CLAUSE**

*Pro-Employee Language*

The Employee agrees to assign to the Company any invention, discovery, or work of authorship that is conceived or developed by the Employee during the course of employment and that either

(a) results from any work performed for the Company, or

(b) uses the Company's time, equipment, supplies, or proprietary information. This assignment does not apply to any invention that

(i) was developed entirely on the Employee's own time,

(ii) does not relate to the Company's business or anticipated research, and

(iii) was created without use of Company resources. Nothing in this clause shall be construed to require the Employee to assign rights in personal projects or unrelated creative work.

The Company agrees to provide advance written notice of the scope of any assignment obligation imposed on work created outside the scope of regular duties.

This version narrows the employer's claim while preserving core protection. It mirrors statutory carveouts in jurisdictions like California and creates a presumption that unrelated or personal work remains with the employee. It also provides transparency and avoids ambiguity about the scope of the assignment.

Invention assignment clauses are essential to the integrity of a trade secret protection plan. Without clear ownership, it becomes difficult to argue that a given process or method belongs to the company, or that a departing employee had no right to use it. But overreach invites litigation and can weaken the company's position. Precision, balance, and relevance are what make these clauses work, not just strength of language.

# 4.3. Judicial Enforcement of Restrictive Covenants

The strength of a restrictive covenant lies not in how firmly it is written but rather in whether a court is willing to enforce it. Nondisclosure agreements, noncompetition clauses, non-solicitation provisions, and invention assignment agreements each create obligations that exist only to the extent that courts give them legal effect. What matters is not just what the contract says but also how it functions when tested. Trade secret protection depends on this enforceability. If a company cannot show that it used enforceable covenants to limit misuse, it may be unable to prove that it took reasonable steps to maintain secrecy at all.

Courts do not enforce these clauses reflexively. They scrutinize them. The premise of enforceability is that the clause is reasonable, proportionate, and tied to a legitimate business interest. Employers cannot use contract to suppress ordinary competition, restrict employee mobility beyond necessity, or claim ownership over information and relationships that are not directly related to trade secrets. But when the clause is well-drafted, well-matched to the role, and consistently enforced, courts may treat it as central evidence that the company viewed its information as secret—and treated it accordingly.

The cases that follow show how these doctrines are applied in practice. Each illustrates how a court evaluated the text of the agreement, the behavior of the parties, and the connection between the clause and the information at issue. These cases are not simply about contract. They are about credibility: whether the company had a real plan for protecting its secrets and whether the agreement supported that plan or merely gestured at it.

## 4.3.1. Enforcement of Nondisclosure Agreements

Nondisclosure agreements are among the most frequently litigated forms of restrictive covenant. While they are generally favored by courts, they are not automatically enforceable. Their effectiveness depends on the specificity of the language, the context in which the agreement was executed, and the behavior of the parties during the relationship. Courts examine whether the NDA clearly defined what information was confidential, whether that information was actually protected in practice, and whether the use or disclosure that followed constituted a breach.

In one early and influential case, the Seventh Circuit rejected a claim of misappropriation where the plaintiff relied on vague confidentiality language and failed to mark documents or limit access.

**DISCLOSERS MUST PRACTICE THE PROTECTIONS THEIR NDAS REQUIRE**

*nClosures Inc. v. Block & Co.*
770 F.3d 598 (7th Cir. 2014)

nClosures designed custom metal cases for tablets and shared product drawings with a prospective manufacturing partner. The drawings were not marked as confidential, and no NDA was signed. When the partner later released a competing product, nClosures sued for trade secret misappropriation. The court found that nClosures had not taken reasonable steps to maintain secrecy. The absence of confidentiality markings, coupled with the lack of access restrictions or formal contractual protections, defeated the claim. The court emphasized that trade secret protection requires more than hope—it requires structure.

By contrast, in a more recent decision from California, the court upheld a nondisclosure agreement that included specific definitions and was accompanied by consistent security practices, even though the defendant argued that the information was not truly secret.

**FOLLOWING NDA PROTOCOLS SUPPORTS TRADE SECRET CLAIMS**

*BladeRoom Group Ltd. v. Emerson Electric Co.*
331 F. Supp. 3d 977 (N.D. Cal. 2018)

BladeRoom developed modular data-center technology and disclosed key design and process information under a detailed NDA during acquisition discussions. After negotiations failed, Emerson won a contract using a strikingly similar design. BladeRoom sued for trade secret misappropriation. The court allowed the claim to proceed, emphasizing the NDA's specificity, the care taken to limit access, and the company's internal practices for labeling and segregating confidential information. The case shows how a well-executed NDA that is tied to real-world behavior can support a broader enforcement strategy.

Courts are especially cautious about NDAs that rely solely on boilerplate language or that purport to treat all information as confidential. In a Delaware case involving a software startup, the court declined to enforce an NDA where the scope was so broad that it became functionally meaningless.

**OVERBROAD NDAS UNDERMINE TRADE SECRET CLAIMS**

*Great Hill Equity Partners IV, LP v. SIG Growth Equity Fund I, LLLP*
2020 Del. Ch. LEXIS 76 (Del. Ch. Feb. 27, 2020)

In a dispute following the acquisition of a tech company, the buyer claimed that the seller's use of business information violated the NDA. The agreement defined "confidential information" to include virtually all company data, regardless of whether it was public, private, or already known to the receiving party. The court found the definition unreasonably broad and declined to enforce it as written. The decision underscores the importance of tailoring NDAs to actual confidentiality concerns and avoiding language that appears to overreach.

These cases illustrate a clear pattern. Courts expect NDAs to be specific, grounded in operational reality, and proportionate to the information they aim to protect. They reward precision and punish overreach. They also look beyond the text of the agreement to see whether the company behaved like it had something worth protecting. An NDA is not a magic wand. It is part of a system of effort. When it fits that system, it becomes a powerful tool. When it does not, it becomes evidence that the company did not take its own secrets seriously.

## 4.3.2. Enforcement of Non-Solicitation Clauses

Non-solicitation clauses are designed to protect a company's relationships—both with its customers and its employees. Courts evaluate them with more scrutiny than NDAs but less skepticism than noncompetes. Their enforceability depends on how narrowly they are drawn, whether they are tied to protectable interests such as trade secrets or goodwill, and how they operate in practice. While courts are generally more willing to enforce a clause that limits direct outreach than one that prohibits all forms of competition, they still require that the restriction be reasonable and grounded in the actual role of the person subject to it.

Customer non-solicitation clauses prevent former employees from contacting or attempting to do business with the company's clients. These clauses are more likely to be upheld when they are limited to clients with whom the employee had material contact or to relationships developed during a defined period prior to departure. Clauses that attempt to prevent contact with all current or prospective customers, regardless of connection, are often deemed overbroad.

In a case from the Virginia state courts, an employer successfully enforced a customer non-solicitation clause because it was narrowly tailored to cover only those relationships the employee had actively managed.

### CUSTOMER NON-SOLICITATION ENFORCED WHEN NARROWLY TAILORED

*Lasership, Inc. v. Watson*
79 Va. Cir. 205 (2009)

Lasership, a delivery logistics company, sued a former employee who started a competing service and contacted former clients. The employment agreement included a non-solicitation clause prohibiting contact with customers whom the employee had serviced within the past year. The court found the clause enforceable, emphasizing that it was limited in both scope and duration and clearly connected to the protection of trade secrets and customer goodwill. Because the employee had built direct relationships with the affected customers, enforcement was warranted.

In other cases, courts have rejected customer non-solicits that sweep too broadly or are unsupported by evidence that the employee ever accessed sensitive client information. In a Pennsylvania case, the court declined to enforce a clause that applied to all customers, including those the employee had never worked with.

### OVERBROAD NON-SOLICITS ARE UNENFORCEABLE

*WellSpan Health v. Bayliss*
2005 PA Super 76 (2005)

WellSpan Health sought to enforce a non-solicitation clause against a former executive who moved to a competing healthcare provider. The clause prohibited contact with any current or prospective customer of WellSpan, regardless of whether the executive had any relationship with them. The court refused to enforce the restriction, holding that it was not reasonably tailored to protect trade secrets or goodwill. The decision emphasized that non-solicitation clauses must be connected to the employee's actual scope of responsibility and not be used as a general barrier to competition.

Employee non-solicitation clauses are similarly limited. Courts are willing to uphold provisions that prevent a former employee from raiding a team or undermining internal stability, but they are wary of clauses that attempt to prevent all communication or that function as de facto noncompetes. The central inquiry is whether the employee's actions were targeted and whether the clause is proportionate to the company's interest in preventing disruption.

In a case involving a staffing firm, the court upheld a non-solicit because the departing employee had attempted to move several key staff members to a new competitor within days of leaving.

**EMPLOYEE NON-SOLICITS ENFORCED WHEN TARGETED AND PROPORTIONATE**

*TEKsystems, Inc. v. Bolton*
No. 2:19-CV-02355, 2019 WL 237388 (D. Kan. Jan. 16, 2019)

A recruiter for TEKsystems left the company and began soliciting former coworkers to join a direct competitor, despite a one-year employee non-solicitation clause in her contract. The court found that the clause was enforceable and narrowly tailored. The employee had direct relationships with those she solicited, and the court held that the company had a legitimate interest in preventing immediate team disruption. The case demonstrates how enforcement is closely tied to the factual context and the nature of the departing employee's role.

Taken together, these cases reflect a common theme. Courts expect non-solicitation clauses to be used precisely and sparingly. They must match the employee's actual responsibilities, target specific risks such as trade secret misuse or goodwill disruption, and avoid functioning as indirect noncompetes. When drafted and applied in this way, they can be highly effective. But when used broadly, without reference to actual exposure or competitive harm, they are likely to be narrowed or rejected. Enforcement is not a question of whether solicitation occurred. It is a question of whether the restriction was fair.

## 4.3.3. Enforcement of Noncompetition Clauses

Noncompetition clauses are the most controversial and least consistently enforced type of restrictive covenant. While employers view them as necessary to prevent insiders from immediately undermining competitive advantage, courts view them with skepticism. They are disfavored because they restrict an individual's ability to work, earn a living, and use general skills and experience. Courts will enforce them only when the restriction is narrowly tailored, the interest protected is legitimate, and the burden on the employee is not excessive.

The legal standard varies by jurisdiction. In some states, such as California, noncompetes are generally void as a matter of statute, with only narrow exceptions for the sale of a business or protection of trade secrets through other means. In others, such as New York or Texas, courts apply a balancing test that considers duration, geographic scope, industry specificity, and necessity. The clause must be reasonable in light of the employee's role and the nature of the threat to the employer's interest. The employer must show that the restriction is not simply about preventing competition—it must be aimed at preventing unfair competition arising from misuse of confidential information, goodwill, or customer relationships.

Duration is a central factor. Courts are more likely to enforce a clause that lasts six months or one year than one that extends for two years or longer. Scope matters as well. A clause that prohibits work in a specific industry or geographic area may be upheld if the employee held a senior role with extensive access to sensitive strategy. But a clause that attempts to bar all competitive activity regardless of location or function will likely be struck down or modified.

In one leading case, the Seventh Circuit enjoined a departing executive under a theory of threatened misappropriation, even though he had not signed a noncompete agreement. The court found that the executive's intimate knowledge of confidential business strategy would likely influence his work at a direct competitor, making misuse almost inevitable. This reasoning gave rise to the inevitable disclosure doctrine, which allows courts to infer that trade secret misappropriation is likely to occur and enjoin future employment as a remedy. Although not formally a noncompete, the injunction functioned as a de facto noncompete by limiting the employee's ability to work in the same industry based solely on the risk of disclosure.

### "INEVITABLE DISCLOSURE" CAN JUSTIFY *DE FACTO* NONCOMPETE RELIEF

*PepsiCo, Inc. v. Redmond*
54 F.3d 1262 (7th Cir. 1995)

Redmond, a senior executive at PepsiCo, accepted a job with Quaker, a direct competitor. PepsiCo sued to prevent him from taking the role, arguing that he would inevitably disclose or use PepsiCo's confidential marketing and pricing strategies. The court agreed, granting a preliminary injunction even in the absence of actual disclosure. The decision was grounded in Redmond's intimate knowledge of PepsiCo's competitive planning and the similarity of his new responsibilities. The case became a foundational authority for the inevitable disclosure doctrine and remains one of the most widely cited examples of proactive enforcement.

Not all courts accept the inevitable disclosure theory. Some require concrete evidence of actual misuse. Others view the doctrine as a backdoor noncompete and reject it on public policy grounds. Even in jurisdictions that allow the doctrine, it is applied cautiously, typically only where the employee's role at the new company would make it impossible to avoid using the former employer's secrets.

When a noncompete is too broad, courts may modify it under the so-called blue pencil doctrine. In some jurisdictions, courts will rewrite a clause to make it enforceable. In others, they will enforce only the part that is reasonable and strike the rest. But some courts refuse to salvage overbroad clauses at all, especially where the employer appears to have overreached. In a Florida case, the court declined to enforce a sweeping noncompete that barred the employee from working anywhere in the state even though the employer operated in only a few counties.

**OVERBROAD NONCOMPETES ARE UNENFORCEABLE**

*Gupton v. Village Inn Pancake House*
89 So. 2d 847 (Fla. 1956)

Gupton left Village Inn to open his own restaurant. The company sought to enforce a noncompete that prohibited him from working in the restaurant business anywhere in Florida for two years. The court found the restriction excessive, noting that Village Inn had only limited operations in the state and that the clause appeared designed to eliminate lawful competition. The court refused to modify or enforce the clause, emphasizing the importance of drafting covenants that reflect real business needs.

The lesson from these cases is that noncompetes are enforceable only when they are used carefully. Courts will not allow employers to block former employees from earning a living or working in their chosen field unless the clause is clearly connected to the protection of information or relationships that the law recognizes as worthy of special protection. Employers must be prepared to explain why the restriction is necessary, how it is limited, and why no less restrictive option would suffice.

Well-drafted noncompetes can protect the investment a company has made in training, strategy, and client development. But they must be treated as exceptions, not defaults. When they are overused or poorly justified, they risk not only invalidation but also reputational harm. They must be built on real risk—and structured to survive real scrutiny.

In 2024, the Federal Trade Commission issued a final rule banning most noncompete clauses nationwide, citing their negative effects on labor mobility, wages, and innovation. The rule applies prospectively and retroactively in many cases, though it includes limited exceptions for senior executives and in connection with the sale of a business. However, the rule has already been challenged in multiple lawsuits asserting that the FTC lacks statutory authority to regulate in this space. The outcome of this litigation remains uncertain, but the rule reflects a broader regulatory and political shift toward restricting or eliminating noncompete agreements as a matter of public policy.

## 4.3.4. Enforcement of Invention Assignment and IP Clauses

Ownership of intellectual property created during the course of employment is not automatic. Unless the employer has secured a written assignment, the default rule is that the creator—usually the employee—retains ownership, even when the work was developed in the scope of employment or using company resources. Invention assignment clauses are meant to prevent this ambiguity. They assign to the employer any inventions or works of authorship that arise from the employee's work and relate to the company's business. When properly drafted and consistently enforced, these clauses provide a legal foundation for claiming ownership of trade secrets, confidential methods, and other forms of proprietary innovation.

Courts generally enforce invention assignment clauses when the terms are clear, the scope is reasonable, and the connection to the company's business is specific. However, they are cautious about clauses that attempt to sweep in inventions created on the employee's own time, especially when those inventions are unrelated to the employer's field of work. Many states impose statutory limitations. California, for example, prohibits assignment of inventions developed entirely on personal time and without use of employer resources unless the invention relates directly to the company's business or expected research and development. Other states follow similar rules, requiring that the clause reflect the actual relationship between the invention and the employer's interests.

In a key California case, the court refused to enforce an invention assignment clause that sought to claim ownership over an employee's side project developed outside of company time and without company materials.

**INVENTION ASSIGNMENT AGREEMENTS MUST COMPLY WITH STATE LAW**

*Applied Materials, Inc. v. Advanced Micro-Fabrication Equipment, Inc.*
No. 5:07-cv-05248, 2009 WL 10694784 (N.D. Cal. Feb. 17, 2009)

Applied Materials sued a former employee and his new company, claiming that trade secrets and inventions created after his departure should be assigned under his prior employment agreement. The agreement included a broad invention assignment clause, but the court found that California Labor Code section 2870 prohibited assignment of inventions developed entirely on the employee's own time, using no company resources, and unrelated to the employer's business. Because the invention did not fall within the statutory exceptions, the clause was unenforceable as applied.

Cases like this underscore the importance of tailoring invention assignment language to comply with state law. Overly aggressive language may not only fail to protect the company—it may also trigger legal challenges or render the entire clause void. The most effective clauses are those that assign rights clearly, provide notice of statutory carveouts, and create procedures for employees to disclose independent projects for review. Courts are more likely to uphold a clause that respects employee rights while safeguarding the company's legitimate interests.

Companies should also ensure that their assignment clauses are reinforced by consistent onboarding, training, and exit procedures. Signing the clause is only the beginning. Employees should be reminded of their continuing obligations, and procedures should be in place to confirm return of work product and confidential material at the end of the relationship. Without this follow-through, even a well-drafted clause may lose its value in enforcement.

Assignment clauses play a crucial role in trade secret litigation. When a departing employee claims to have developed a method independently, the company must be able to point to a signed agreement that covers the work and establishes ownership. Without it, the legal basis for claiming misappropriation may be significantly weakened. But to be effective, the clause must not only exist—it also must be enforceable. And to be enforceable, it must be both legally compliant and practically connected to the way the company and the employee actually operated.

## 4.3.5. Public Policy Limits on Restrictive Covenants

Even the most carefully drafted restrictive covenant may be unenforceable if it conflicts with public policy. Courts do not evaluate these clauses in a vacuum. They examine the broader context in which they are used—who is subject to the restriction, what the restriction prevents, and whether enforcement would undermine principles such as employee mobility, economic fairness, or statutory protections for innovation. In some states, public policy limits are codified. In others, they emerge from common law decisions that balance the interests of employers against the rights of individuals and the public.

California is the most well-known example of a jurisdiction that prohibits most noncompete agreements. Under section 16600 of the California Business and Professions

Code, any contract that restrains a person from engaging in a lawful profession, trade, or business is generally void. The few exceptions include the sale of a business and protection of trade secrets through narrowly drawn covenants that do not operate as blanket bans. Massachusetts, Illinois, Colorado, and Washington have also enacted statutes limiting the use of noncompetes for low-wage workers, requiring advance notice, or imposing other procedural safeguards. These laws are intended to prevent overuse of restrictions that could suppress labor mobility or chill innovation.

Even in states without specific legislation, courts may refuse to enforce a covenant that appears punitive, anticompetitive, or unnecessary. In one New York case, the court rejected a noncompete imposed on a former employee with no managerial responsibilities, finding that the restriction served no legitimate interest and posed a barrier to ordinary career progression.

**RESTRICTIVE COVENANTS CANNOT VIOLATE PUBLIC POLICY**

*Brown & Brown, Inc. v. Johnson*
25 N.Y.3d 364 (2015)

Brown & Brown, an insurance brokerage firm, sought to enforce a noncompete against a junior employee who left to join a competitor. The clause barred the employee from working in any capacity for a competing firm within a large geographic region for two years. The court found the restriction unenforceable, holding that it was broader than necessary to protect client relationships or trade secrets and imposed an unreasonable burden on the employee's ability to work. The ruling emphasized that covenants not to compete must be justified by a specific, protectable interest—not simply the desire to avoid competition.

Public policy limits also affect how trade secret claims are evaluated. If a restrictive covenant is so broad that it appears to be a substitute for trade secret protection rather than a supplement to it, courts may reject both the contract and the trade secret claim. A company that attempts to prevent competition by labeling all information as confidential or using blanket restrictions on employee activity may lose credibility when it asserts that the information at issue qualifies as a trade secret. Courts are more likely to find secrecy where the company has used calibrated protections, and they are more likely to reject it where the company has used expansive contracts to mask weak internal discipline.

The policy trend in recent years has moved steadily in favor of employee rights. Legislatures and courts alike have sought to limit the use of restrictive covenants that function as tools of control rather than as legitimate protection. Employers must adapt their strategies accordingly. This does not mean that restrictive covenants are obsolete. It means that their role must be narrowly defined, carefully justified, and firmly anchored in the actual risks the company faces.

A covenant that overreaches may not only fail—it may erode the company's ability to enforce more modest protections. A covenant that is well-matched to the task, by contrast, will stand a stronger chance of enforcement and will support the broader claim that the company took its obligation to protect trade secrets seriously. In this way, public policy is not a barrier to trade secret enforcement. It is a reminder that enforcement must rest on real interests, not imagined ones.

## 4.4. Access Controls and Operational Safeguards

Restrictive covenants provide one layer of protection. Operational discipline provides another. Courts will not enforce a contract in the abstract; they look for evidence that the company built secrecy into its everyday systems. The most compelling proof that a business took reasonable steps to protect its trade secrets is not what it said in an agreement but what it did in practice. That inquiry begins with access control.

A trade secret can only be protected if it is treated as secret. If confidential information is accessible to all employees regardless of role, if it is stored in shared folders without restriction, or if it is left unsecured in physical spaces, courts may conclude that the company did not take secrecy seriously. Protection begins with limitation: who can see the information, under what circumstances, and through which systems.

Role-based access is the foundation of control. Each employee or contractor should have access only to the materials necessary for their specific duties. This is not merely a technical best practice—it is a legal signal. If the company can show that only a limited number of individuals had access to a particular dataset, formula, or design, and that those individuals were bound by appropriate contractual and policy safeguards, courts are more likely to find that the information was in fact kept secret.

Access control also includes digital and physical security. Trade secrets often reside in code repositories, product development systems, shared drives, email attachments, and internal messaging tools. They also live on whiteboards, in lab notebooks, in engineering mock-ups, and in physical product samples. Each of these settings creates opportunities for exposure. Courts have looked closely at whether access to sensitive materials was password-protected, whether file permissions were restricted, whether laptops were encrypted, and whether physical rooms were badge-locked or surveillance-monitored. No one safeguard is dispositive, but the accumulation of many small controls creates a compelling record of reasonable effort.

Labeling and version control reinforce these protections. Materials that contain or reflect trade secrets should be clearly marked as confidential or proprietary. Where labels are missing, courts may treat the information as if it were public. Version control also matters. If a trade secret evolves over time, courts may ask whether earlier iterations were separately protected or if the secret as a whole was diluted by open circulation of partial versions. Document management is not just an internal convenience. It is part of the legal infrastructure that supports the claim.

Monitoring and auditing provide the feedback loop. It is not enough to restrict access. The company must also know when restrictions are breached, who has downloaded sensitive files, when unusual access patterns occur, and whether any devices containing confidential information have been lost or compromised. Modern log management systems can generate alerts when access levels are elevated, documents are exported, or downloads exceed baseline norms. These systems do not need to catch every breach. But they must exist, and they must be capable of demonstrating, after the fact, that access to the trade secret was not uncontrolled.

Access controls cannot stand still. As employees move into new roles, as projects change, or as systems evolve, permissions must be updated. Former employees must be removed from repositories immediately upon separation. Temporary permissions must expire when tasks are complete. Vendors and contractors must have defined scopes of access with limitations on onward sharing (further disclosure beyond the original recipient) or retention. Where companies fail to adjust access as circumstances change, courts may conclude that the protections were performative, not real.

When a court asks whether a company took reasonable steps to protect its trade secrets, it is asking whether the organization acted like secrecy mattered. The answer is found not in the contract archive but in the permissions matrix, activity logs, email servers, and badge swipe records. The best legal protection is the one the company already built—before anyone asked to see it.

## 4.4.1. Role-Based Access Limitation

The simplest and most powerful way to reduce internal vulnerability is to ensure that employees can only access the information they need. This principle, often referred to as "least privilege" or "need to know," is central to both operational security and legal protection. Courts routinely ask whether a trade secret was shared only with those who required it and whether the company limited access according to the responsibilities of each role. A business that exposes its confidential information to all personnel, regardless of function, faces an uphill battle in proving that the information was truly kept secret.

Role-based access control means defining, in advance, which individuals or job categories are permitted to see which types of information. In a development-driven company, this might mean that engineers have access to the product architecture but not to customer pricing. Sales personnel may see pricing tiers but not source code. Administrative staff may have access to scheduling tools but not to vendor contracts or prototype designs. Each role carries a different risk, and access must be tailored accordingly.

This tailoring can take many forms. Some companies define access permissions in formal documentation, tying them to job descriptions or system profiles. Others implement access hierarchies through technical systems: password-protected drives, VPN limitations, project-based file shares, or departmental folder structures. The method matters less than the outcome. Courts want to see that the company knew where its secrets lived and made deliberate choices about who could see them.

Role-based limitation also requires organizational discipline. If access controls are defined but not enforced—if credentials are shared, if folders are broadly accessible, or if employees routinely store sensitive files in personal drives—then the existence of a policy will do little to support the claim. Courts do not evaluate intentions. They evaluate structure. The gap between stated policy and actual practice is often the gap in legal protection.

This structure must adapt as roles change. When employees move between departments, are promoted, or shift projects, access should be reevaluated. If a marketing lead transitions to a strategic role, access to analytics or R&D documentation may need to be expanded or newly limited. Similarly, if an employee leaves a project, their access to that material should be revoked. Temporary credentials should expire automatically. Project-based folders should be archived or decommissioned once development ends. The point is that static access frameworks become obsolete, and only dynamic systems can reflect the evolving structure of a real business.

Companies that implement strong role-based access controls have a clear advantage in litigation. They can show who saw the secret, when, and under what conditions. They can demonstrate that disclosure was limited by design, not just by accident. And they can point to a system of permissions that tracks responsibility rather than one that allows information to circulate without restraint. When courts see this structure, they are more likely to credit the company's claim that the information was secret because it was treated as such.

### 4.4.2. Document Control, Labeling, and Classification

A trade secret must be treated as a secret not in theory alone but rather in the way it is stored, circulated, and labeled. Courts do not expect companies to mark every email or Slack message. But they do expect a pattern of discipline—one that signals to employees, contractors, and outsiders that certain categories of information are subject to confidentiality restrictions. Labeling and document management are not formalities. They are part of the factual record that supports a trade secret claim.

The most basic form of document control is marking. When a company consistently labels documents containing confidential information, it strengthens its ability to later claim that the information was understood as secret. Labels might include headers such as "Confidential," "Trade Secret," or "Proprietary," or they may use internal coding systems tied to document sensitivity. What matters is that the labels are visible, used systematically, and understood internally. Courts have given weight to labeling even where the underlying information was later challenged as too obvious or too widely known. The presence of a confidentiality label is not decisive, but it demonstrates that the company made a conscious effort to identify what required protection.

Classification goes further. Many companies use tiered systems to identify levels of confidentiality. A basic framework might distinguish between "Internal Use," "Confidential," and "Restricted." More detailed systems may include role-based clearance, flags for export control, or automatic redaction triggers. These systems serve two purposes. Internally, they inform employees about how information may be shared. Legally, they create a record of how the company handled sensitive material. A file labeled "Restricted—Engineering Only" that resides on a segmented server and whose access is limited to a specific team is far more defensible than an unlabeled document circulating in a shared drive.

Version control supports these efforts. Many trade secrets are not static. They evolve through drafts, iterations, and collaborative input. If earlier versions of a secret are circulated without restriction, or if drafts remain accessible in shared folders long after the final product has been released, the claim of secrecy may be undermined. Companies must be able to show which version of the information was protected, who had access to it, and how the transition between drafts was managed. This is especially important in software, where older versions of code may be reused or stored in repositories with broader access than the final release.

Email and messaging platforms present special challenges. Trade secrets are often discussed, refined, and circulated in fragments—paragraphs, comments, screenshots—within systems that are not built for classification. While companies are not expected to control every informal message, they are expected to control access to attachments, limit circulation of files, and monitor whether key information is being handled appropriately. Policies that require labeling of attached documents, restrict forwarding outside of authorized teams, or archive confidential threads for review can all support the company's case.

Document control also extends to retention and deletion. If sensitive information remains accessible long after a project ends, or if confidential drafts are retained indefinitely in unprotected systems, courts may conclude that the company failed to maintain secrecy. The standard is not perfection. It is reasonableness. But a failure to purge, archive, or restrict obsolete materials can become evidence of indifference, and indifference is rarely consistent with secrecy.

When a trade secret is lost, the company must be able to show how it was handled before the loss occurred. If it was labeled, tracked, versioned, and stored according to defined rules, courts are far more likely to find that secrecy was preserved. If it was treated no differently from any other file, the legal claim may fail before it begins.

### 4.4.3. Monitoring, Auditing, and Insider Activity Detection

Secrecy is not a one-time decision. It is a continuing obligation. A company cannot protect its trade secrets merely by drafting good policies or restricting access. It must also be capable of knowing when those protections are being tested, bypassed, or ignored. Monitoring and auditing are what make the system real. They convert formal controls into practical safeguards. And they generate the kind of evidence courts rely on when evaluating whether a company took secrecy seriously.

Monitoring begins with visibility. A business cannot protect what it cannot see. At a minimum, systems should be configured to log access to sensitive materials, including who accessed what information, when, and from where. These logs provide the historical record needed to identify patterns, detect anomalies, and, in some cases, prove misappropriation. When a departing employee is suspected of taking trade secrets, access logs can reveal whether confidential files were downloaded in the days before departure, whether external storage devices were connected, or whether login activity occurred outside normal working hours.

The presence of these logs can shape litigation. Courts do not require every company to have a sophisticated intrusion detection system. But they do expect that sensitive systems are monitored and that unauthorized or suspicious activity triggers investigation. In some cases, the failure to monitor has been cited as evidence that the company did not genuinely treat the information as a secret. In others, the ability to pinpoint when and how access occurred has made the difference between speculation and proof.

Auditing reinforces these efforts. Regular reviews of access permissions, user activity, and policy compliance help ensure that the system remains effective. Audits can identify dormant accounts that still have access, shared passwords, misconfigured permissions, or other silent vulnerabilities. Courts have given weight to companies that perform regular internal audits and act on the findings. When a business can show that it reviewed its own systems, updated its controls, and corrected deficiencies, it sends a clear message that confidentiality was not left to chance.

Insider activity detection extends beyond technical logs. Behavioral signals also matter. Companies should have processes in place to detect when employees begin to act in ways that suggest intent to leave or to take information with them. These signals may include copying large numbers of files, sending attachments to personal accounts, printing confidential documents, or accessing areas of the system outside the scope of a normal role. Detection tools can flag this activity, but they are only useful if there is a response protocol. A flagged activity must lead to inquiry. A pattern must lead to review.

Monitoring and auditing are also relevant to policy enforcement. A company that monitors activity but does nothing when violations occur will be seen as tolerating breaches. Courts may ask whether policies were enforced uniformly, whether training was followed by verification, and whether known violations were addressed. Inconsistent enforcement can undermine the entire system. By contrast, consistent follow-through reinforces the claim that trade secrets were not only defined—they were defended.

Finally, detection systems help companies respond in real time. When a breach is identified early, the company may be able to seek an injunction, preserve evidence, or limit the spread of the information. If detection is delayed, the opportunity to act may be lost. Trade secret protection is time-sensitive. The sooner the risk is identified, the stronger the legal and practical options will be.

Monitoring, auditing, and detection are not simply security functions. They are part of the legal argument. They demonstrate that the company paid attention, took action, and created systems to ensure that its policies were more than words. Although courts do not expect perfection, they do expect consistent effort, and such effort leaves a trail.

In sum, to promote secrecy and protect its trade secrets, companies should:

- Log access to sensitive files and systems, including date, time, user, and location of access.
- Establish baseline activity patterns for employees in sensitive roles to detect anomalies.
- Monitor for red flags such as large downloads, late-night access, or off-network activity.
- Track use of external storage devices, personal email, and unauthorized sharing platforms.
- Conduct periodic audits of user permissions to ensure access aligns with role requirements.
- Document monitoring policies and ensure they are communicated to employees in writing.
- Create escalation protocols for responding to detected irregularities.
- Retain access and audit logs for a defined period to support potential future investigations.
- Integrate monitoring with exit procedures to review access activity prior to departure.
- Review and update monitoring tools and audit procedures on a recurring schedule.

# 4.5. Onboarding and Training

Even the best systems fail if the people using them do not understand their purpose. Contracts, access controls, and monitoring tools provide the technical and legal framework for trade secret protection, but it is the workforce that determines whether those safeguards are implemented, respected, and sustained. Courts evaluating trade secret claims often look beyond the infrastructure to ask what the company did to educate its employees. Did the organization tell people what counted as confidential? Did it explain how to handle sensitive information? Did it remind them, over time, that the obligation of secrecy continued?

Onboarding is where these answers begin. A new employee must not only sign the relevant agreements but also understand what they mean. This includes the nondisclosure agreement, the invention assignment clause, and any applicable non-solicitation or noncompete provisions. But it also includes the policies that govern day-to-day behavior: how to store documents, where to save work, what systems require credentials, and how to escalate questions or report concerns. Courts give weight to evidence that a company explained its policies at the outset of the relationship and reinforced them through orientation, training, and documented acknowledgement.

Merely providing documents is not enough. Employees often sign stacks of forms at the start of a new role, and courts recognize that signatures alone do not guarantee comprehension. Companies should take steps to ensure that the message of confidentiality is clear. This may include onboarding sessions that explain trade secret protections in plain language, walkthroughs of how access systems work, or confirmation emails summarizing key points. Some organizations require new employees to pass short training modules or quizzes. Others use orientation videos or onboarding portals. What matters is not the format but rather the fact that the company made an effort to inform.

Training should not stop after orientation. Most employees handle confidential information in an evolving environment. New tools, new projects, and new team structures create ongoing risk. Regular training ensures that employees are reminded of their obligations and are kept up to date on procedures. In some cases, courts have cited the absence of any follow-up training as evidence that the company's confidentiality culture was performative. Where training occurs regularly, is recorded, and includes examples tied to the actual business, it reinforces the credibility of the company's claim that it protected its secrets.

Ongoing training is particularly important in organizations where trade secrets are embedded in ordinary workflows. In technical environments, employees may not recognize that internal benchmarks, process improvements, or operational decisions constitute proprietary information. In sales organizations, pricing models or customer segmentation data may not be seen as confidential unless that expectation is clearly stated. Training helps bridge this gap. It makes the boundaries legible to those who are responsible for maintaining them.

Some of the most damaging trade secret losses come not from malice but rather from misunderstanding. A well-meaning employee may reuse a presentation template, include a client list in a resume, or carry forward a coding shortcut without realizing that it contains protected information. Courts recognize that mistakes happen. But when those mistakes occur in a company with no training, no reminders, and no effort to educate, the court may conclude that secrecy was not a real priority.

Training also has cultural significance. It shows that confidentiality is not merely a legal concern but also a shared responsibility. When managers reinforce policies, when teams are briefed before major product launches, or when exit interviews revisit confidentiality obligations, the message becomes institutional. Courts often view this culture as one of the strongest indicators of reasonable effort. A company that trains its people, documents its policies, and reinforces its values is more likely to persuade the court that its secrets were treated as secrets.

To help ensure that employees are educated about and understand company policies, companies should implement an onboarding and training process that includes the following elements:

- Ensure that new employees review and sign all relevant agreements, including NDA, invention assignment, and any applicable noncompete or non-solicitation clauses.
- Explain what qualifies as a trade secret in the context of the company's operations.
- Provide practical examples of confidential information employees will encounter in their role.
- Walk through internal policies on document storage, labeling, and access restrictions.
- Demonstrate how to access secure systems and how credentials are managed.
- Review procedures for reporting security concerns or suspected misuse.
- Explain the employee's ongoing duty of confidentiality after employment ends.
- Require written acknowledgment of orientation completion and understanding.
- Document training delivery, including materials used and attendance records.
- Schedule follow-up or refresher training as part of the employee's integration plan.

# 4.6. Exit Protocols and Post-Employment Risk

The most dangerous moment in the life of a trade secret is often when an employee leaves. Departures concentrate vulnerability. They trigger downloads, file transfers, hasty communications, and quiet copying. They also disrupt workflows, reassign responsibilities, and create uncertainty about what information will be taken, remembered, or reused. Exit protocols are therefore not just administrative processes. They are a final opportunity to assert control.

Courts routinely examine what a company did when a key employee left. Did it disable access immediately? Did it conduct a review of system activity? Did it conduct an exit interview and remind the departing employee of ongoing obligations? Did it retrieve devices, secure documentation, and require acknowledgment of the duty to maintain confidentiality? Each of these questions points to the same larger inquiry: Did the company act as if its secrets still mattered even after the person who knew them was walking out the door?

An effective exit protocol begins before the final day. Companies should have a checklist of procedures tied to trade secret protection. These procedures may include deactivating user credentials, revoking access to repositories, collecting company-owned devices, reviewing recent downloads or transfers, and auditing cloud storage or personal email use. The scope of review should match the sensitivity of the information. A departing executive with access to product strategy requires different scrutiny than a junior team member with limited visibility. Courts do not require overreaction. They expect proportion.

Exit interviews provide an opportunity to clarify continuing obligations. Even where an employee signed a nondisclosure agreement at the outset, the company strengthens its position by restating those duties at the end. This may involve asking the employee to confirm that no confidential information has been retained, copied, or shared. It may include reviewing what qualifies as a trade secret, reminding the employee that contractual obligations survive termination, and confirming that the employee has returned all materials. When these interviews are documented, they provide persuasive evidence that the company took the protection of its secrets seriously.

Some companies use separation agreements to restate key provisions, secure additional assurances, or establish specific representations about information return. These agreements may include confidentiality reaffirmations, reminders about invention assignment, or additional clauses about competitive conduct. Where enforceable, they may also include release language or dispute resolution provisions. Courts often give weight to post-employment agreements, particularly when they are signed with adequate consideration and clearly identify surviving obligations.

Departures should also be followed by internal adjustments. Access logs may need to be preserved. Systems may need to be reconfigured. Teams may need to be reminded not to forward documents or communicate with the former employee. In some cases, competitors may need to be notified that the company considers certain information to be protected. These follow-up actions are not just for show. They prevent misunderstanding, protect against inadvertent leaks, and ensure that the company's trade secret protections remain intact.

When a former employee joins a competitor, the situation becomes more delicate. The company may choose to send a letter to the new employer outlining the departing employee's obligations and requesting assurance that trade secrets will not be accessed or used. These letters are not threats. They are records. Courts have cited them as evidence that the company acted to preserve secrecy and put others on notice. If litigation arises, the company will be able to show that it did not wait passively for harm to occur.

Ultimately, post-employment risk is not just about what the former employee chooses to do. It is about what the company chooses to control. Courts are far more likely to enforce restrictive covenants, grant injunctive relief, or award damages when they see that the company treated the departure as a moment of risk and responded accordingly. Exit protocols turn vulnerability into preparedness. They are the final chapter in the story the company tells the court—and sometimes the most important one.

To minimize post-employment risk, companies should:

- Disable all system access on or before the employee's departure date, including email, VPN, and internal platforms.
- Recover all company-owned devices, including laptops, phones, drives, and access cards.
- Audit recent user activity for irregular downloads, transfers, or access to sensitive systems.
- Conduct an exit interview that includes a review of continuing confidentiality obligations.
- Require written certification that all company information has been returned or deleted.
- Reiterate post-employment restrictions stated in any applicable NDA, noncompete, or non-solicit agreement.
- Document any known projects or files the employee had access to at the time of departure.
- Notify relevant managers and team members of the employee's departure and reinforce noncommunication protocols if needed.
- Consider sending a notice to the new employer if there is a material risk of misappropriation.
- Archive access logs, certifications, and separation documentation for future reference or litigation.

# 4.7. When Internal Safeguards Fail

No system is perfect. Even companies with strong policies, carefully drafted contracts, and well-calibrated controls will sometimes experience losses. A laptop goes missing. A departing employee takes files. A mistake is made, and sensitive information is exposed. When that happens, the question is not whether the company failed. It is how the company responded.

Trade secret law does not require absolute prevention. It requires reasonable efforts. That standard allows for the reality that human error, technical breakdowns, and even intentional misconduct can occur despite a company's best intentions. But when safeguards fail, the company must act quickly and deliberately to preserve its legal rights. Delay, inaction, or confusion may suggest that secrecy was not a real priority and that the company is reacting for the first time rather than executing a plan.

The most important step after a failure is containment. If a breach is suspected, access must be revoked immediately. Relevant logs should be preserved. Systems should be audited to determine what was taken, when, and by whom. If devices are missing, they should be remotely wiped or deactivated if possible. If documents were emailed externally, recipients may need to be contacted. The company should act as if the information still matters—because that is what the court will ask.

Investigation follows containment. The company must determine whether the incident involved a trade secret, whether any contractual obligations were breached, and whether the recipient knew or should have known that the information was confidential. This requires not only technical analysis, but legal evaluation. Counsel must review relevant agreements, policies, training records, and employee acknowledgments. These materials will shape the company's ability to assert claims or defend its actions in court.

Communication must be handled carefully. Internally, managers and affected teams may need to be informed. Access to shared drives may need to be restricted. New policies or reminders may be issued. Externally, the company may choose to send a cease-and-desist letter, notify a competitor, or file a motion for injunctive relief. In some cases, the company may be required to make public disclosures, for example, under regulatory obligations or in the context of an acquisition. But all such communications should be vetted for consistency and strategic alignment.

Documentation is essential. Courts often evaluate not just whether a company responded but also whether it can prove what actions it took. The internal investigation should be documented in a privileged report. Communications should be recorded. Decisions about response, notification, and remediation should be tied to the company's broader trade secret protection plan. If the case proceeds to litigation, this record will help establish that the company did not act out of panic but instead followed a disciplined approach.

Sometimes, internal failure reveals weaknesses in the system itself. A breach may uncover outdated access protocols, overly broad permissions, or poor logging. These issues should be addressed immediately—not just for operational reasons but also because the legal doctrine expects learning. Courts understand that failure is possible. They are less forgiving when failure repeats.

In rare cases, the breakdown is total. A product is leaked. A formula is disclosed. The secret is lost. Even then, legal action may still be available. Courts may grant damages, issue injunctions to limit further use, or require competitors to return or destroy materials. But the company's position will depend heavily on what it can show. If the court concludes that the information was never really protected, the law will not treat its loss as a violation.

This is why failure must be anticipated. A company that prepares for failure is not admitting defeat. It is preserving its ability to recover. Every trade secret protection plan should include a response protocol, escalation paths, legal review procedures, and systems for containment. When those are in place, the company will be ready—not just to limit the damage but also to prove that it never stopped taking secrecy seriously.

## 4.8. Turning Policy Into Practice

Trade secret protection begins inside the organization. It is shaped not only by what the company knows to be sensitive but also by what it does to protect that knowledge—day after day, across systems, contracts, and human behavior. This chapter has traced the full arc of internal discipline, from the drafting of restrictive covenants to the enforcement of operational safeguards. It has shown how trade secret law rewards structure, punishes indifference, and holds companies accountable for whether secrecy was real or merely presumed.

The legal system does not demand perfection. But it does demand seriousness. A company that knows what its trade secrets are, limits access accordingly, trains its people to treat information carefully, and responds promptly to breaches has already done most of the work the law expects. A company that writes ambitious policies but cannot show how they were implemented or that imposes sweeping restrictions without proportion may find that the law does not follow where the paperwork points.

What distinguishes strong internal protection is not formality but credibility. Courts ask whether the protections in place reflected the value of the information, the vulnerability of the system, and the roles of the individuals involved. They examine the words of the contracts and the conduct of the business. They look at what happened not when everything was functioning but rather when something went wrong. A company's ability to respond to that scrutiny is what turns policies into protection.

At its core, trade secret law does not create secrecy. It recognizes it. That recognition depends on whether the company treated its information like a secret in its day-to-day life. That means enforcing restrictions. It means revoking access. It means monitoring, auditing, and responding to threats. It means educating employees and confronting risk. It means aligning internal discipline with external claims. And it means accepting that trade secrets are not self-executing rights—they are fragile assets that exist only when the organization acts to preserve them.

The work of protection does not end at the walls of the company. Many of the most serious trade secret threats arise not from insiders but from third parties: vendors, partners, customers, collaborators. The next chapter addresses these external risks. It examines how companies can preserve secrecy while working with others, how to structure relationships that require information sharing, and how to build contractual and operational safeguards that extend beyond the boundaries of internal control. The principles remain the same. But the terrain becomes more complex.

# Chapter 5

# Mitigating External Vulnerabilities

A trade secret does not lose protection merely because it is shared with others. Yet the moment confidential information crosses organizational boundaries, it becomes subject to a new set of vulnerabilities—some predictable, others uncertain. Unlike internal disclosures, which can be governed by hierarchy, policy, and culture, external disclosures depend almost entirely on the structure of the relationship. Courts do not infer protection simply because information was valuable or shared with caution. Instead, they examine whether the disclosing party took affirmative, reasonable steps to control how the information was used, accessed, and retained by third parties.

External vulnerabilities arise in countless forms: vendors with system-level access, partners in joint development efforts, customers evaluating early-stage prototypes, cloud platforms hosting proprietary code, and distribution channels with little visibility into downstream users. Each interaction brings with it not only the risk of misappropriation but also the uncertainty of misalignment. A company may believe it has limited use to a defined purpose, while the recipient sees the information as freely usable once the formal project ends. These conflicts rarely turn on bad faith. More often, they result from ambiguous contracts, missing boundaries, or failure to anticipate how confidential information will behave once embedded in shared systems or deliverables.

The law's standard remains the same: a trade secret must be subject to reasonable efforts to maintain its secrecy. But in external contexts, what qualifies as "reasonable" is no longer a matter of internal discipline but of design. Contracts must define use and ownership with precision. Technical systems must limit access and record activity. Termination clauses must ensure that trade secrets do not survive the deal but rather disappear from the recipient's possession and systems. Above all, the relationship must be structured to create traceability: a clear path to determine who accessed what, when, and for what purpose. Without that traceability, enforcement becomes speculative, and legal protection collapses into a presumption of waiver.

This chapter examines how trade secret holders can mitigate these external vulnerabilities through thoughtful contract design, segmented access, targeted use restrictions, and enforceable exit provisions. Each section focuses on a different relationship type—vendors, collaborators, customers, or distributors—and explains how courts have evaluated efforts to protect trade secrets in these settings. Case law is integrated throughout, not to catalogue outcomes but to reveal where protection strategies succeed or fail in practice. Breakout boxes offer model contractual provisions along with drafting notes, illustrating how different clause variants shift the legal terrain. The goal is not to eliminate external vulnerability altogether. It is to contain it so that trade secrets remain defensible even when they must be shared.

## 5.1. External Vulnerability as a Structural Problem

Trade secrets do not exist in isolation. They are often embedded in partnerships, shared in vendor relationships, and exposed during customer engagement. What makes these external interactions dangerous is not that they involve outsiders but rather that they introduce a loss of structural control. When information is shared with employees, internal protocols and cultural expectations fill in the gaps. But when information is shared with another organization, the only source of discipline is what the parties have agreed to. That agreement, whether contractual, procedural, or architectural, must carry the full burden of secrecy.

The vulnerability here is both legal and operational. Legally, external disclosures without clear constraints may destroy trade secret status entirely. Courts consistently hold that sharing valuable information without protective conditions is fatal, even if the disclosing party believed it was acting cautiously. Operationally, third-party recipients are not subject to internal access controls or training. They may have their own vendors, subcontractors, and platforms, each of which introduces additional exposure unless explicitly barred or constrained. The trade secret becomes a traveler, not a resident.

These vulnerabilities are compounded by uncertainty. Many external relationships are open-ended or exploratory: collaborative R&D, licensing talks, customer pilots. The parties may not know what will be developed, what will be retained, or who will ultimately own the resulting insight. Ambiguity about scope, ownership, and post-termination rights is not just a business risk—it is a legal vulnerability. Courts evaluating trade secret claims will ask whether the disclosing party took steps to prevent the very ambiguity that now clouds the dispute.

**CONTRACTUAL SAFEGUARDS ARE ESSENTIAL FOR TRADE SECRET PROTECTION**

*Auto Channel, Inc. v. Speedvision Network, LLC*
144 F. Supp. 2d 784 (W.D. Ky. 2001)

Auto Channel disclosed proprietary programming concepts and marketing strategies to Speedvision during joint venture negotiations. No nondisclosure agreement was signed. When Speedvision later launched a competing network, Auto Channel sued for misappropriation. The court granted summary judgment for the defendant, holding that the information was not protected because it had been disclosed without any formal confidentiality obligation. The court emphasized that even valuable and original information loses trade secret status when shared without safeguards. Caution alone is not enough. Contractual protection is essential.

The lesson from *Auto Channel* is not simply that NDAs matter but that structure matters. A company that shares trade secrets externally must design the relationship to preserve legal protection at every stage: before disclosure, during collaboration, and after termination. The initial agreement should define what is confidential and how it may be used. The working arrangement should control who has access and what records are kept. The exit provisions should require return or destruction and clarify that rights do not survive the deal. Without these constraints, even careful businesses may find that their secrets no longer qualify for legal protection.

The following sections examine these structural vulnerabilities in context, beginning with vendor relationships—which are often the most underestimated source of external exposure.

# 5.2. Vendor Relationships

Vendors are among the most common sources of external vulnerability. From cloud service providers and IT contractors to supply chain partners and outsourced engineering teams, vendors routinely gain access to the internal operations of a business. In many cases, their technical privileges exceed those of most employees. Yet vendors are not subject to company policies, internal training, or managerial oversight. Their obligations are solely contractual. If those contracts are vague, permissive, or silent, the legal structure collapses, and the company's trade secrets may be exposed without remedy.

## 5.2.1. Limiting Vendor Rights

The core problem in vendor relationships is not overt theft. It is misalignment. Vendors may store confidential data in shared systems, retain access credentials beyond the life of the contract, or allow subcontractors to access sensitive environments. These actions may be ordinary in the vendor's operational model but can be catastrophic for trade secret protection. The vulnerability is amplified when the company does not monitor how its information is handled, cannot trace which personnel accessed what, or lacks exit protocols to ensure clean separation.

### DIGITAL CONTROLS STRENGTHEN TRADE SECRET RIGHTS

*7EDU Impact Academy v. Ya You*
2024 U.S. Dist. LEXIS 230110 (N.D. Cal. 2024)

In a dispute between an education company and a former employee, 7EDU alleged misappropriation of proprietary course materials, customer data, and business methods. The court granted a preliminary injunction, finding a likelihood of trade secret protection based in part on the company's efforts to control access through its digital platform. The court noted that login protections, document labeling, and defined user roles contributed to the showing of reasonable efforts even though some information was shared internally and externally. The case underscores that in digital environments, platform architecture and vendor configuration can make or break trade secret status. The court's reasoning applies equally to current employees as well as contractors and vendors who access a company's systems under defined digital permissions.

The *7EDU* case illustrates how technical infrastructure can support legal claims, but only if it is intentional. Vendor contracts must incorporate both confidentiality obligations and operational constraints that ensure proper alignment between access and accountability. A contract that governs vendor use of confidential information must define the scope of access, limit the individuals authorized to receive the information, prohibit downstream disclosure or subcontracting, and impose firm obligations regarding return or deletion at the end of the relationship. These terms are not merely administrative. They form the structure that courts rely on to determine whether a company took reasonable steps to protect its secrets.

The following sample clause shows how companies can structure vendor access obligations to reduce these vulnerabilities.

**VENDOR ACCESS CLAUSES LIMIT SCOPE, PERSONNEL, AND RETENTION**

"Vendor shall access and use Confidential Information solely to perform the services defined in this Agreement. Vendor shall restrict such access to named personnel approved in writing by the Company, and shall maintain records of all such access. Vendor shall not disclose or permit access to any subcontractor or third party without the Company's prior written consent. Upon termination or completion of the services, Vendor shall promptly return or destroy all Confidential Information in its possession, including any copies stored in backup systems or cloud environments."

An effective vendor-relationship confidentiality clause constrains access both technically and organizationally. It reflects a disclosing party's interest in traceability, containment, and post-engagement closure. By specifying who may access information, limiting transfer to other entities, and requiring return or destruction of materials, the clause reinforces secrecy with procedural enforcement. Companies may also supplement this provision with periodic compliance certifications or system-level audits. Some companies go further by requiring vendor personnel to complete internal confidentiality or data-security training before system access is granted, a practice that strengthens the record of "reasonable measures" and ensures policy alignment across organizational boundaries.

Vendor relationships, which are managed by procurement or IT teams rather than legal counsel, often operate in the background of business operations. But when trade secret disputes arise, those relationships move to the center of litigation. Courts will ask what safeguards were in place to prevent misuse, what records exist to reconstruct access, and whether the vendor agreement adequately limited downstream exposure.

## 5.2.2. Audit Rights and Oversight Clauses

Limiting access and logging usage are essential safeguards, but sometimes the disclosing party needs more than technical constraints. In vendor relationships where the information is especially sensitive or the relationship is particularly complex, companies may reserve the right to audit the recipient's practices. An audit right allows the trade secret owner to inspect how information is handled, verify compliance with confidentiality requirements, and investigate possible breaches. This right is not limited to suspicion. It is a tool for ongoing oversight.

Audit clauses serve multiple purposes. They deter misuse by signaling that compliance is not merely expected but also subject to verification. They also provide evidence that the disclosing party took affirmative steps to maintain secrecy—something courts consider when deciding whether legal protection should apply. In some industries, audits are standard for data security or regulatory compliance. But in trade secret protection, they serve a distinct function: they make secrecy enforceable in real time, not just through later litigation.

The effectiveness of an audit clause depends on its specificity. Open-ended rights to inspect "on demand" may be seen as intrusive or vague. A well-drafted provision typically defines the audit scope, timing, notice requirements, and cooperation obligations. Some agreements require periodic compliance certifications instead of full audits. Others limit inspection rights to business hours or restrict access to specific systems or locations. The clause must strike a balance between oversight and operational feasibility.

**AUDIT CLAUSES PROVIDE OVERSIGHT RIGHTS AND CONFIDENTIALITY COMPLIANCE**

"Recipient shall maintain accurate and complete records regarding its handling of the Discloser's Confidential Information. Upon ten (10) business days' written notice, and no more than twice per calendar year, Discloser may audit Recipient's facilities, systems, and relevant records to verify compliance with the confidentiality obligations in this Agreement. Recipient shall cooperate in good faith and provide reasonable access to personnel, records, and systems necessary for the audit. Discloser shall bear the cost of such audits unless material noncompliance is discovered."

This clause gives the disclosing party a practical mechanism for enforcement. It also imposes a recordkeeping obligation that can later support litigation. By framing the audit as a right—not just a reaction—the clause turns vigilance into structure.

Audit rights are especially powerful when paired with technical controls. Together, they create a system of external secrecy that is not only defined by contract but also observable in practice. When companies can monitor their vendors both through platforms and legal inspections, they transform risk into something measurable and, more importantly, governable.

## 5.2.3. Indemnity and Liquidated Damages Clauses

Legal enforcement is often reactive. But in high-risk external relationships, companies can take a more proactive approach by assigning financial responsibility for trade secret loss in advance. Two tools are commonly used for this purpose: indemnification and liquidated damages. They may be included in vendor contracts as well as other third-party relationships.

An indemnity clause shifts liability. If the recipient causes exposure—by failing to comply with confidentiality obligations, permitting unauthorized disclosure, or mishandling trade secrets—the recipient agrees to compensate the disclosing party for resulting losses. These losses may include not only direct damages but also legal fees, regulatory costs, and reputational harm. The clause does not replace trade secret litigation. It supplements it with a contractual promise to make the disclosing party whole.

A liquidated damages clause, by contrast, sets a predetermined financial consequence for breach. This is particularly useful where actual damages would be difficult to prove or where the mere fact of misappropriation could destroy the business's competitive position. Courts will enforce liquidated damages only if the amount is reasonable and was negotiated in good faith. Excessive or punitive figures are likely to be rejected.

These clauses are especially important in distribution, where trade secrets may be exposed to large numbers of end users or incorporated into customer-facing operations. If a distributor fails to protect confidential sales tools, pricing models, or implementation methods, the cost of exposure may exceed the company's direct contractual remedies. Indemnity and liquidated damages provide a second line of defense.

### INDEMNITY AND LIQUIDATED DAMAGES CLAUSES ALLOCATE TRADE SECRET MISAPPROPRIATION RISK

"Recipient shall indemnify, defend, and hold harmless Discloser from and against any and all losses, damages, liabilities, costs, and expenses (including reasonable attorneys' fees) arising out of or related to any unauthorized use or disclosure of Confidential Information by Recipient or its agents, employees, or contractors. In the event of breach of the confidentiality obligations in this Agreement, the parties agree that actual damages would be difficult to determine, and Recipient shall pay Discloser liquidated damages in the amount of $250,000, which the parties acknowledge represents a reasonable estimate of anticipated harm."

This clause combines indemnity and liquidated damages to provide both flexibility and predictability. The indemnity captures unknown downstream costs. The liquidated amount provides a floor for recovery and strengthens the deterrent effect of the agreement.

Courts apply these same principles when evaluating real-world agreements. The next case shows how a liquidated damages clause failed because it resembled a penalty rather than a reasonable estimate of loss.

### LIQUIDATED DAMAGES: PENALTY VERSUS COMPENSATION

*SIS, LLC v. Stoneridge Software, Inc.*,
2023 U.S. App. LEXIS 748 | 2023 WL 164067 (11th Cir. 2023)

A confidentiality agreement required the breaching party to pay "all forms of compensation or benefits" it realized from the breach. Applying Georgia's three-factor test, the Eleventh Circuit held the clause unenforceable because it operated as punishment: it measured the breacher's gains rather than a reasonable pre-estimate of the non-breacher's probable loss. The court affirmed only nominal damages despite proof of breach.

Statutory trade secret claims, however, operate independently of contractual caps, as shown in the next case.

### STATUTORY REMEDIES EXCEED CONTRACTUAL CAPS

*Ingram v. Cantwell-Cleary Co., Inc.*
260 Md. App. 122 (2023)

The court awarded $780,757.32 and $867,335.44 in trade secret damages under Maryland's UTSA despite non-compete agreements that contained $50,000 liquidated-damages caps. The statutory misappropriation claim was independent of the contract claims, so the liquidated-damages ceiling did not limit the trade secret recovery.

The practical point is to draft liquidated-damages clauses to address contract breaches, but do not assume they cap statutory trade secret remedies. Analyze both tracks in pleadings and settlement strategy.

Let's now address the second identified gap: indemnity and liquidated damages provisions in external relationships.

These clauses are not about secrecy per se—they are about consequences. When trade secrets are disclosed to vendors, distributors, or development partners, the disclosing party may want to shift the financial risk of exposure through contract. If the recipient mishandles the information, fails to follow procedures, or causes leakage—whether negligently or through breach—the disclosing party can seek compensation under an indemnification clause or pre-agreed payment under a liquidated damages clause.

These tools are especially useful in settings where actual damages may be hard to quantify or where a dispute could impose costs beyond the trade secret itself, such as regulatory penalties, customer churn, or loss of investor confidence.

# 5.3. Collaborative Development: Blurred Boundaries and Ownership Confusion

When companies work together to develop new technologies, processes, or products, the resulting innovation often reflects the input of both parties. These collaborations can generate enormous value, but they also create deep structural vulnerabilities. The most significant of these is uncertainty about ownership. A company may contribute proprietary know-how to a project under the belief that it remains the exclusive owner while its partner believes the resulting insights are jointly held or freely usable. Without clear contractual delineation, courts may struggle to determine whether any trade secret rights remain intact.

This vulnerability is distinct from theft. The danger in collaborative development is not misappropriation by outsiders but rather ambiguity between partners. That ambiguity can arise at multiple levels: whether the disclosing party retains rights in its background technology, whether new information is considered jointly owned or subject to separate confidentiality obligations, and whether either party may use the information after the collaboration ends. In many cases, courts are forced to reconstruct the parties' expectations from informal communications and vague contracts, with mixed and unpredictable results.

### DEFINING BOUNDARIES PRESERVES TRADE SECRET RIGHTS IN COLLABORATION

*Altavion, Inc. v. Konica Minolta Systems Laboratory, Inc.*
226 Cal. App. 4th 26 (2014)

Altavion developed a method for embedding secure digital barcodes into documents and disclosed it to Konica Minolta for potential integration into Konica's products. Although the parties operated under a confidentiality agreement, no development deal was finalized. Konica Minolta later filed patent applications covering the same concepts. The California Court of Appeal ruled that Altavion had alleged a valid trade secret misappropriation claim, emphasizing that the information was technical in nature, disclosed in confidence, and not generally known. The decision turned in part on the absence of any agreement transferring ownership or permitting such use. The court rejected the argument that technical ideas must be reduced to physical form to be protected, underscoring that early-stage collaboration does not justify appropriation without permission.

The Altavion case illustrates a common scenario. A smaller company shares a technical concept with a larger prospective partner, hoping for a joint venture or integration. No deal is finalized, but the larger company moves forward with a similar product or patent. If the contract does not clearly state that shared information remains the property of the disclosing party and cannot be used absent further agreement, the legal consequences may depend on how courts interpret the relationship. In Altavion, the court sided with the discloser. In other cases, the absence of defined boundaries may lead to the opposite result.

To mitigate these vulnerabilities, companies entering into joint development arrangements must clearly distinguish three categories of intellectual property: background IP (what each party brings to the table), resulting IP (what is developed during the collaboration), and residual or derivative knowledge (what individuals retain or repurpose after the project ends). Each of these must be defined in the contract, along with specific rules governing ownership, use, and post-termination rights.

### OWNERSHIP CLAUSES PRESERVE RIGHTS IN JOINT-DEVELOPMENT PROJECTS

"Each party shall retain all right, title, and interest in and to its Background IP. Except as expressly provided in this Agreement, nothing herein shall be construed to grant any rights or licenses to the other party's Background IP. Any Resulting IP developed in the course of the collaboration shall be jointly owned unless otherwise agreed in writing. The parties shall negotiate in good faith any commercialization terms prior to use of Resulting IP outside the scope of this Agreement."

This clause preserves preexisting rights, allocates shared rights in joint outputs, and flags the need for further negotiation before broader commercialization. More sophisticated versions may assign resulting IP based on contribution or include license-back mechanisms.

Even when ownership is clear, the contract must also address how trade secrets may be used during and after the collaboration. Use restrictions are essential to prevent a partner from taking confidential information, embedding it in a separate project, and claiming independent development or mutual license. The next subsection explores how courts have evaluated such use, particularly in cases where the project ends without a formal agreement or proceeds informally based on goodwill.

## 5.3.1. Use Restrictions in Joint Development

Collaborative projects often begin in a spirit of openness. The parties may share engineering specifications, design concepts, technical drawings, or early-stage code under the assumption that mutual benefit will follow. But when the relationship ends—whether through termination, non-renewal, or a simple lack of progress—the question becomes whether those shared materials may still be used. If the contract does not include enforceable use restrictions, a party may repurpose what it has learned and argue that the disclosing party implicitly authorized that use by participating in the project.

This vulnerability is especially dangerous when a company contributes trade secrets to a collaboration that ultimately benefits the other party more than itself. Without use restrictions, the contributing party may lose control not only over the information but also over its competitive position. Courts are reluctant to imply limitations that were not expressed, even where the facts suggest an imbalance in outcome. That makes express language essential.

**EXPRESS USE RESTRICTIONS PRESERVE TRADE SECRET RIGHTS AFTER COLLABORATION ENDS**

*C3.ai Inc. v. Cummins, Inc.*
2024 Del. Super. LEXIS 622 (2024)

C3.ai entered into a pilot project with Cummins to develop artificial intelligence tools for fuel optimization. After the collaboration ended, Cummins launched a similar product. C3.ai alleged that Cummins had used trade secrets disclosed during the partnership. The court denied Cummins's motion to dismiss, finding that C3.ai had plausibly alleged the information was shared in confidence, subject to use restrictions, and not intended for general application. The case illustrates that courts will enforce use limitations even after a project ends—if the parties structured their relationship with enough specificity.

The *C3.ai* case demonstrates that disclosing parties do not lose their rights when a project ends, although they must be able to prove that the information was subject to continued protection. A general confidentiality clause may be insufficient unless it includes limits on how the information may be used, by whom, and for what purpose. The more valuable and technical the trade secret, the more important it is to restrict derivative use.

**USE RESTRICTION CLAUSES LIMIT APPLICATIONS OUTSIDE THE PROJECT**

"Recipient shall use the Discloser's Confidential Information solely for purposes of performing under this Agreement. Recipient shall not use such information to develop, test, commercialize, or support any product or service outside the scope of the collaboration, either directly or through any affiliate or third party, without Discloser's prior written consent."

This clause limits both commercial and developmental uses, constraining information to the agreed context. It also bars derivative use through related entities. Companies concerned about overreach may further require documentation of all internal recipients and impose deletion requirements post-termination.

When contracts lack such restrictions, courts may look to circumstantial evidence: how the parties behaved, what emails or meeting notes reflect, and whether there was a shared understanding of purpose. But reliance on inference introduces uncertainty. A clearly drafted use clause eliminates that uncertainty and strengthens the disclosing party's position. The next section turns to what happens after a project ends: whether and how the trade secrets shared during the collaboration must be returned, deleted, or otherwise withdrawn from use.

## 5.3.2. Return and Destruction Obligations at Termination

When a collaboration ends, the disclosing party must act to reestablish exclusive control over its trade secrets. If confidential information remains in the possession of a former partner—whether stored on servers, embedded in drafts, or circulating among team members—the risk of unintended use persists. Courts evaluating trade secret claims often focus on whether the disclosing party took steps to secure the information after the relationship ended. A failure to demand return or destruction can suggest abandonment or waiver, even if there was no intent to relinquish protection.

The vulnerability here is temporal. Many agreements include confidentiality obligations that expire after a fixed period. Others require nondisclosure but say nothing about what must happen to the information at the end of the deal. In some cases, a partner continues using information it acquired during the relationship under the assumption that it has some residual license. Courts are unlikely to supply stricter protections than the contract provides. It is the responsibility of the disclosing party to ensure that the exit terms support ongoing secrecy.

### FAILURE TO FORMALIZE RETURN OBLIGATIONS LIMITS TRADE SECRET PROTECTION

*Bianco v. Globus Medical, Inc.*
30 F. Supp. 3d 565 (E.D. Tex. 2014)

Dr. Bianco, a spinal surgeon, disclosed a concept for an intervertebral fusion device to Globus Medical during discussions about potential collaboration. Globus went on to commercialize a similar product without entering into a formal development agreement or returning any of the information provided. The court found that Bianco had disclosed protectable trade secrets in confidence and that Globus had misappropriated them. However, the absence of clear documentation regarding post-engagement handling complicated the assessment of damages and scope. The case shows how failure to establish return or destruction obligations can undermine trade secret enforcement, even when misappropriation is proven.

The *Bianco* case reflects a broader pattern. Informal relationships and early-stage discussions often involve the exchange of valuable information without clear terms about what happens when those discussions end. A company that discloses trade secrets in this context must assume that the default outcome is that the information remains in the recipient's possession unless otherwise stated. To preserve protection, the agreement should include a mandatory exit procedure and require written certification that all materials have been removed or returned.

### RETURN AND DESTRUCTION CLAUSES PROVIDE END-OF-PROJECT PROTOCOLS FOR CONFIDENTIAL INFORMATION

"Upon expiration or termination of this Agreement, Recipient shall promptly return or securely destroy all Confidential Information received from Discloser, including all copies, extracts, and derivative materials. Upon request, Recipient shall certify in writing that it has complied with these obligations. This provision shall survive the termination of the Agreement."

This clause establishes a clear obligation to eliminate retained materials and provides a mechanism for verification. While enforcement may still depend on practical cooperation, the existence of a certification requirement creates a legal hook for demanding compliance and strengthens the disclosing party's position in any later dispute.

Without these mechanisms, companies expose their trade secrets to quiet appropriation. Even a partner acting in good faith may retain materials in backups, internal wikis, or team notes that later influence new projects. Trade secret protection depends not only on initial disclosure discipline but on exit discipline as well. The next section examines a different type of vulnerability: disclosures made to customers, where exposure can occur through reverse engineering or insufficient restriction during product evaluation.

## 5.4. Customer Disclosures: Evaluation, Exposure, and Reverse Engineering

Customer relationships often require companies to reveal the very information they seek to protect. Demonstrations, pilot programs, and evaluation licenses are common features of enterprise sales, especially when the product involves technical complexity or integration with customer systems. In these settings, companies may grant access to source code, design specifications, performance data, or even live environments. But customer-facing disclosures are uniquely dangerous. The company disclosing the information has no control over how the customer stores it, who sees it, or how long it persists in internal systems. Without a carefully designed structure, the trade secret may not survive the sales process.

The vulnerability here is twofold. First, trade secrets can be lost through lawful reverse engineering. If a customer receives a product and there is no contractual restriction on analysis, disassembly, or replication, then reverse engineering is a permitted means of discovery. In that case, even the most valuable design or process loses protection—not because the customer misbehaved, but because the disclosing company failed to impose enforceable limits. Courts routinely uphold reverse engineering as a legitimate pathway to information unless clearly prohibited.

Second, even where reverse engineering does not occur, the absence of clear evaluation terms can create confusion about permissible use. A customer may believe it is free to retain a demo device, continue using sample data, or adapt the disclosed features into its own processes. If the contract does not define the limits of use, these assumptions may go unchallenged. Trade secret law requires affirmative steps to preserve secrecy. It does not shield companies from the consequences of ambiguity.

### NO-REVERSE-ENGINEERING CLAUSES CAN PROTECT TRADE SECRETS

*Accent Packaging, Inc. v. Leggett & Platt, Inc.*
707 F.3d 1318 (Fed. Cir. 2013)

Accent Packaging developed a bale tie machine and alleged that Leggett & Platt acquired a sample product, reverse engineered it, and began selling a similar device. Accent argued that its design constituted a trade secret. The court disagreed, holding that because Leggett & Platt obtained the machine lawfully and no contract restricted analysis, reverse engineering was a permissible means of discovery. The decision reinforces that trade secrets do not shield information that can be acquired through lawful reverse engineering—unless an enforceable agreement says otherwise.

The lesson from *Accent Packaging* and many similar cases is not that reverse engineering is inevitable but rather that companies must act affirmatively to prevent it. Contracts can impose enforceable limits on analysis, but those terms must be written clearly and agreed to before disclosure. Boilerplate confidentiality provisions are unlikely to suffice. Courts generally treat reverse engineering prohibitions as distinct from ordinary nondisclosure terms.

The structure of the evaluation matters just as much as the contract. Companies should consider how information is delivered, whether digital access can be time-limited, and whether logs can verify what was viewed or downloaded. If software is involved, code may be obfuscated or hosted on secure servers with monitored user sessions. If hardware is involved, sample products should be retrieved or disabled after the evaluation ends. These operational details strengthen the argument that secrecy was preserved.

To support these efforts, evaluation agreements should include narrow use restrictions, explicit bans on reverse engineering, and clear obligations to return or delete all materials. The following clause reflects these elements.

### EVALUATION CLAUSES LIMIT USE AND PROHIBIT REVERSE ENGINEERING

"Recipient shall use the Evaluation Materials solely for the purpose of internal evaluation and shall not reverse engineer, decompile, disassemble, or otherwise attempt to derive the underlying structure, function, or design. Recipient shall not use the Evaluation Materials for any commercial, developmental, or comparative purpose. All materials shall be returned or deleted upon completion of the evaluation period."

This clause preserves the ability to engage potential customers while ensuring that the scope of use is limited. By restricting reverse engineering and commercial application, the disclosing party protects against loss of secrecy during a legitimate business process. The return obligation reinforces the temporary nature of the access.

General restrictions, while useful, must be supplemented by documentation and enforcement. A company should track what was shared, for how long, and with whom. It should follow up at the end of the trial period to request return or destruction. If these steps are not taken, a court may later find that the disclosing party failed to maintain secrecy—even if the customer acts in ways the company never intended or foresaw.

Customer access cannot be treated as a casual transaction. When trade secrets are involved, even routine sales activities must be governed by structured agreements and thoughtful delivery mechanisms. Otherwise, the pursuit of new business can become the pathway to irreversible loss. The next section turns to distribution relationships, where the challenge is not evaluation but control over information that passes through intermediaries and into broader markets.

# 5.5. Distribution Relationships and Downstream Risk

Trade secrets often move beyond the original transaction. When companies rely on distributors, licensees, or channel partners to deliver products and services, confidential information can travel further than anticipated. These relationships enable commercial growth, but they also expose trade secrets to indirect loss. The disclosing party may not know how many hands its information passes through, what systems are used to store it, or whether the agreed restrictions are understood by everyone with access. These vulnerabilities must be addressed both contractually and structurally. This section examines three specific risks in distribution: informal relationships without legal protection, uncontrolled downstream propagation, and post-termination retention.

## 5.5.1. Informal Channels and the Absence of Control

Distribution often begins informally. A promising business opportunity emerges, and information is shared to support negotiations or initial rollout. Documentation may come later, if at all. But when trade secrets are disclosed without a signed agreement or with only vague terms in place, protection is rarely available. Courts evaluating misappropriation claims look not only at what was shared but also at how it was shared. If the disclosing party cannot show that it took clear and deliberate steps to impose confidentiality, the information may be treated as forfeited.

This is especially true in joint venture discussions, regional distribution negotiations, or exploratory sales channel arrangements. Companies may provide business plans, marketing strategies, pricing models, or product designs without realizing that, absent a formal structure, these materials become unprotected once disclosed.

**CONTRACT FOR CONFIDENTIALITY TO PROTECT SHARED INFORMATION**

*Auto Channel, Inc. v. Speedvision Network, LLC*
144 F. Supp. 2d 784 (W.D. Ky. 2001)

Auto Channel disclosed business plans, programming strategies, and marketing ideas to Speedvision while discussing a possible joint venture. No nondisclosure agreement was signed. Speedvision later launched a similar network, and Auto Channel sued for trade secret misappropriation. The court rejected the claim, holding that Auto Channel had not taken reasonable steps to maintain secrecy. Without any written agreement or formal controls, the information was not protected. The court did not question the value or originality of the content but instead focused entirely on the lack of structural safeguards.

What makes *Auto Channel* notable is not the facts, which are common, but the clarity with which the court dismissed the claim. Even highly sensitive commercial information cannot qualify as a trade secret if the owner treats it casually. Informal relationships, even with trusted partners, are not an excuse. They are a vulnerability.

## 5.5.2. Downstream Propagation and Sub-Agent Risk

Even where a distribution agreement is in place, problems arise when the contract protects the information only in the hands of the primary recipient. Many distributors operate through agents, subcontractors, or localized partners. These sub-agents often perform customer-facing work and receive access to trade secrets, but they may not be bound by the same contractual terms as the original distributor. If the agreement fails to impose flow-down obligations, the disclosing company has little basis to pursue enforcement when the information leaks beyond the first layer.

The risk is not always malice. In many cases, a distributor shares materials with other actors for operational reasons. A training manual is forwarded to a service partner. A confidential configuration tool is installed by a subcontractor. A support engineer uses internal documentation to answer customer questions. Without clear contractual rules, these actions may fall outside the scope of protection. Courts will not presume that confidentiality extends automatically.

To prevent this kind of exposure, contracts must require the distributor to bind all personnel and sub-entities to equivalent obligations. The language must be specific, enforceable, and durable.

**CHANNEL CONFIDENTIALITY CLAUSES IMPOSE FLOW-DOWN OBLIGATIONS**

"Distributor shall maintain the confidentiality of all Confidential Information provided under this Agreement and shall not disclose such information to any third party without the prior written consent of the Company. Distributor shall ensure that all employees, agents, contractors, and sub-distributors who access Confidential Information are bound by written confidentiality obligations no less restrictive than those set forth herein. These obligations shall survive the termination or expiration of this Agreement."

This clause ensures that the obligations do not end with the primary party. It closes the downstream gap and creates an enforceable framework for holding third-level recipients accountable.

It is common and sensible to pair a channel (flow-down) confidentiality clause with indemnification for downstream breaches and, where appropriate, a liquidated-damages floor. So long as each piece is drafted cleanly and the liquidated damages amount is a reasonable pre-estimate of loss (not a penalty), courts will generally enforce these provisions in tandem.

A flow-down clause is not a formality. It is the only legal tool available to extend protection beyond the initial handshake. In distribution, information moves. The contract must follow it.

## 5.5.3. Termination and Retained Access

One of the most persistent threats in distribution is what happens after the relationship ends. Distributors often retain physical or digital materials containing trade secrets. These may include technical documentation, training resources, implementation tools, or customer data. If the contract does not require return or deletion, and if systems do not enforce revocation, the trade secret remains outside the control of its owner. Over time, that exposure undermines both secrecy and enforceability.

This problem is structural, not behavioral. Even a distributor acting in good faith may retain protected information simply because no one asked for it back. Courts evaluating these situations want to see evidence that the disclosing party took affirmative steps to reclaim or disable access. If nothing in the contract requires it, and if the company cannot prove what was done at the end of the relationship, the trade secret may be deemed abandoned.

The solution is to treat termination as a process, not an event. Agreements should mandate the return or destruction of all materials and require written confirmation. Companies should also implement system-level controls to revoke login credentials, remove shared files, and disable support portals as part of their offboarding process. If these steps are taken promptly and documented, the owner strengthens its legal claim that secrecy was preserved.

Distribution expands a company's reach. But every new hand that touches a trade secret must be governed. When contracts are written with this reality in mind, the risks of indirect disclosure become manageable. When they are not, the legal consequences can be swift and irreversible.

## 5.6. Architectural Safeguards and System-Level Enforcement

Legal agreements define the boundaries of confidentiality, but those boundaries must be reflected in the way information is actually handled. Trade secret law does not protect information in theory. It protects information that is actively and consistently kept secret. System architecture plays a critical role in meeting that standard. When trade secrets are shared with external parties, protection depends not only on what the contract says but also on how access is managed, monitored, and ultimately revoked.

System-level safeguards are not a substitute for legal obligations, but they are often the clearest evidence that a company took its obligations seriously. Courts regularly ask whether the disclosing party limited access, tracked usage, and retained control over who could see what. If a company can answer those questions with documentation and precision, its position is strengthened. If it cannot, no amount of contractual language will rescue the claim.

Access segmentation is one of the most effective tools for external secrecy. Instead of providing full access to a partner or vendor, companies should isolate the specific information necessary for the task and provide access only to that subset. This can be implemented through secure data rooms, password-protected folders, user-specific permissions, or cloud environments that allow time-limited access. Segmentation supports the argument that the company shared the information strategically and did not expose its full knowledge base.

Monitoring is the next layer of protection. A system that records who accessed which files, when they were viewed, and whether they were copied or transferred provides both deterrence and proof. These logs can reveal patterns of overuse, unauthorized behavior, or data exfiltration. They also allow the company to respond in real time if something goes wrong. Without monitoring, a company may be unaware that a trade secret has already left its control.

These architectural elements matter most when the relationship ends. If a system allows the recipient to continue accessing shared information after termination, or if files remain in shared drives with no expiration mechanism, the company has likely failed to maintain secrecy. Revoking access, deleting shared accounts, and requiring confirmation of deletion are essential steps in restoring control.

### CONTROL AND MONITOR ACCESS TO PROTECT TRADE SECRETS

*GlobeRanger Corp. v. Software AG USA, Inc.*
836 F.3d 477 (5th Cir. 2016)

GlobeRanger entered into a reseller relationship with Software AG involving proprietary middleware technology. Although the contract included confidentiality terms, the company failed to implement clear technical safeguards. Employees across both organizations had access to the information, and GlobeRanger did not restrict retention or monitor usage. When Software AG began developing similar technology, GlobeRanger sued for misappropriation. The court allowed the claim to proceed, but it noted that the absence of consistent access controls and monitoring made it harder to show that GlobeRanger had taken reasonable steps to preserve secrecy. The result was a weakened case that might have been stronger if architectural safeguards had been in place.

The court's comments in *GlobeRanger* reflect a broader truth. Reasonable efforts are not measured solely by intention. They are measured by the totality of the system. When companies share information without knowing how it will be used, where it will be stored, or who will have access to it, they place their rights at risk. When they instead build secure channels, define access parameters, and maintain a record of what was done, they convert legal theory into enforceable reality.

These principles can be reinforced through contract, but they are most effective when supported by design. The following clause shows how to align legal commitments with system-level enforcement.

### ACCESS AND MONITORING CLAUSES MANDATE INTEGRATED TECHNICAL CONTROLS

"Recipient shall access Confidential Information only through systems designated by the Discloser. Such systems may include secure data rooms, credentialed portals, or other platforms subject to access logging and usage monitoring. Recipient shall not disable, bypass, or otherwise interfere with these controls. Upon expiration or termination of this Agreement, access credentials shall be revoked and all Confidential Information shall be returned or securely deleted."

This clause does more than impose a legal duty. It anticipates a technical process. By aligning the contract with the platform through which information is delivered, the company creates a defensible record of how secrecy was preserved.

System architecture is not always visible. But when trade secrets are shared externally, it becomes central. A company's ability to track, limit, and withdraw access reflects its commitment to secrecy. Without those capabilities, protection becomes speculative. The final section of this chapter offers a synthesis of these lessons and shows how contract and architecture must work together to support containment and control.

## 5.7. Cybersecurity and Trade Secret Exposure

Trade secret protection increasingly depends on the strength of an organization's digital infrastructure. In a world where confidential information is stored in cloud environments, accessed through vendor portals, and transmitted across global networks, cybersecurity is no longer just a technical issue. It is a legal one. Courts evaluating whether a company took reasonable steps to maintain secrecy do not look only at employment agreements or nondisclosure provisions. They also examine system architecture, access control, encryption practices, and the ability to detect and contain unauthorized use.

This chapter has already shown how contracts, workflows, and technical safeguards can help protect trade secrets when information is shared externally. But even well-drafted agreements can be undone by insecure configurations, poorly monitored integrations, or shared credentials that outlive the relationship. The most disciplined legal framework cannot overcome the failures to revoke access after termination, segment user privileges, or monitor who views sensitive data. In cybersecurity, exposure is not always intentional. Sometimes it results from indifference, legacy systems, or an unclear division of responsibility between parties. But trade secret law does not distinguish between accidental and deliberate failure. The standard is effort. The benchmark is control.

Cybersecurity vulnerabilities also introduce enforcement complexity. A company that cannot prove when information left its control or who had access to it may lose not because it lacks a valid claim but because it lacks evidence. That evidentiary gap becomes a legal failure. The solution is not simply to invest in technology but also to align legal and technical controls. Contracts must reflect how systems are configured. System logs must support contractual claims. Termination procedures must be executed both on paper and in the cloud.

The subsections that follow examine the specific ways in which cybersecurity failures create legal vulnerability. They address persistent access credentials, API integrations, multi-tenant cloud storage, enforceable security obligations, incident response, and containment strategies. Each reflects a simple premise: secrecy cannot survive in ungoverned digital environments. Where systems are porous, the law may presume waiver. Where they are structured, secrecy becomes defensible. The line between technical configuration and legal protection is no longer theoretical. It is the battleground for modern trade secret enforcement.

### 5.7.1. Persistent Access and Credential Mismanagement

One of the most overlooked causes of trade secret exposure is the failure to revoke access. When employees, vendors, or collaborators are given credentials to access confidential information, those credentials often outlive the relationship. A terminated contractor may retain access to a shared folder. A former vendor may still have administrative rights to a cloud platform. An internal user who has shifted roles may continue to hold read-write access to systems that no longer concern them. These gaps are not unusual. But they are dangerous.

Persistent credentials create structural vulnerability. Courts have repeatedly emphasized that trade secrets must be subject to ongoing control. If information remains accessible to individuals who are no longer authorized to receive it, or if the company cannot document who has what level of access, it becomes difficult to claim that the information was kept secret. This failure is not merely technical. It is legal. When companies cannot terminate access promptly and verify that access has in fact been terminated, they compromise their ability to prove reasonable efforts.

The problem often arises in external relationships, where access is shared across organizations. A customer support partner may be given login credentials to a service platform. A development vendor may receive access to a private repository. A sales agent may be issued a device containing preloaded pricing tools. In each case, the disclosing party must retain the ability to revoke access centrally and confirm that it has been revoked. Informal arrangements, shared credentials, and decentralized access management systems all create traceability failures. And without traceability, secrecy cannot be enforced.

The legal response to this risk is twofold. First, companies must treat credential issuance and revocation as legal events, not just IT procedures. User access should be mapped to contractual terms and controlled through account provisioning systems that can generate logs, revoke permissions, and verify deletion. Second, agreements should require the recipient to cooperate in credential revocation and confirm compliance. Where credentials are shared across teams or embedded in workflows, companies may need to demand periodic access audits and deactivation reports.

**CREDENTIAL REVOCATION CLAUSES GOVERN TERMINATION OF ACCESS UPON EMPLOYEE SEPARATION OR PROJECT CONCLUSION**

"Recipient shall ensure that all credentials, login information, and system access rights granted in connection with this Agreement are revoked immediately upon termination of the relationship or the reassignment of personnel no longer requiring access. Recipient shall cooperate in verifying that such revocations have occurred and shall provide written confirmation upon request. Continued access to Confidential Information following termination shall constitute a material breach of this Agreement."

This clause transforms access management into a legal obligation. It also establishes non-revocation as breach—thus ensuring that forgotten credentials carry enforceable consequences.

Credential mismanagement is not a rare failure. It is a daily reality in many organizations, especially where IT functions are siloed from legal operations. But for trade secrets to remain protected, access must be closed when the relationship ends. If not, a door is left open, and the law may treat it as an invitation.

## 5.7.2. API Access and Embedded Data Flows

Modern collaboration often occurs not through shared files but through software integrations. Trade secrets may be accessed, processed, or transmitted via application programming interfaces, or APIs, that link systems across companies. These integrations are often invisible once configured. Data flows continuously, sometimes in real time, from one environment to another. The technical convenience of APIs introduces a legal risk: trade secrets may pass through an external system without adequate documentation, restriction, or monitoring. If that happens, secrecy may be lost even if the information never appears on a screen.

The vulnerability here lies in scope. Many API relationships are structured quickly, especially in pilot projects or customer trials. An engineer may enable access to test data or internal functionality on the assumption that the integration will be limited. But the API may expose more than intended by allowing external users to query, copy, or store protected data without triggering alarms. Worse, if the integration remains active after the project ends, the recipient may continue accessing confidential materials indefinitely. This can occur without new credentials or intentional misconduct. It happens because the information was never clearly fenced.

Trade secret law does not distinguish between visible and invisible disclosures. If a company enables external access to protected information through an API and does not limit that access through contract and configuration, the company may be deemed to have abandoned secrecy. Courts look at whether the disclosing party took steps to control exposure, not whether the exposure was observed in real time. APIs can create persistent, silent leakage.

Companies using API integrations must treat them as legal gateways. The access scope should be documented, limited to necessary data fields, and subject to role-based permissions. Logs should record what queries were made and by whom. Sunset dates or access expiration terms should be imposed to ensure that integrations do not outlive their purpose. Where high-value trade secrets are involved, the company should disable the integration entirely at the conclusion of the project or engagement.

These expectations must also be reflected in contract. The agreement should define the permitted scope of API use, prohibit unauthorized data capture, and require access to be disabled when the relationship ends.

### API USE LIMITATION CLAUSES CONTROL SCOPE AND DURATION OF DATA ACCESS

"Recipient shall access the Discloser's systems or data through API connections only as expressly authorized in writing and solely for the purposes described in this Agreement. Recipient shall not copy, store, analyze, or transfer any data retrieved via API access for purposes beyond the scope of this Agreement. API credentials shall expire upon the conclusion of the project or termination of the Agreement, whichever occurs first, and Recipient shall cooperate in the prompt deactivation of all integrations."

This clause sets legal limits on what technical integrations may do. It anticipates silent overreach and constrains it by contract.

APIs are efficient, flexible, and powerful. But they are also pipelines. If trade secrets pass through them without control, those secrets may be treated as disclosed. Companies that rely on integrations to deliver value must also design those integrations to preserve secrecy. Anything less leaves them vulnerable not just to technical misuse but also to legal failure.

## 5.7.3. Cloud Storage and Multi-Tenant Infrastructure

Cloud environments offer flexibility, scalability, and cost efficiency, but they also introduce significant uncertainty into trade secret protection. When information is stored on a third-party platform, the disclosing company often has limited visibility into how that information is managed. It may not control which personnel at the cloud provider can access the data, how the data is backed up or replicated, or whether deletion procedures are actually followed. These uncertainties matter. In a trade secret dispute, the company must be able to show that the information remained secret and was subject to reasonable efforts to maintain that secrecy. When cloud systems operate as black boxes, that showing becomes more difficult.

One of the central vulnerabilities of cloud storage is multi-tenancy. Many cloud services store data for multiple customers on shared physical infrastructure, relying on logical separation rather than physical segregation. This structure may be secure in practice, but if the company cannot explain how access is restricted or demonstrate that no other party had visibility into its data, courts may question whether secrecy was truly preserved. This problem is exacerbated when the company lacks a detailed understanding of the provider's security controls or has no contractual rights to audit or inquire into data handling practices.

Cloud-based collaboration also creates legal ambiguity. A file stored in a shared cloud folder may be downloaded, copied, or forwarded without trace. Access logs may be incomplete or hard to retrieve. A project that ends informally may leave legacy documents on a cloud drive that is still accessible to former vendors, customers, or partners. If those materials are later misused, the company may have no record of when the exposure occurred or who was responsible. Without that evidence, even a valid trade secret claim may fail.

To address these risks, companies should adopt cloud usage policies that align with their trade secret obligations. This includes selecting providers that offer granular access control, robust logging, and compliance with recognized security standards. It also includes maintaining internal inventories of where trade secrets are stored, who can access them, and how that access is reviewed or revoked over time. Most importantly, companies must treat cloud environments as extensions of their legal obligations, not as neutral platforms.

Cloud service agreements should reflect this approach. The contract should include representations about how data is stored, what security measures are in place, and whether the customer retains ownership and control. It should also allow for inspection, certification, or inquiry when something goes wrong. Where trade secrets are involved, companies should avoid providers that disclaim all responsibility for data loss or access control failures.

**CLOUD SECURITY CLAUSES BOLSTER TRADE SECRET PROTECTIONS IN HOSTED ENVIRONMENTS**

"To the extent that Confidential Information is stored or processed on cloud-based platforms or services, Recipient shall ensure that such platforms implement access controls, data segregation, encryption in transit and at rest, and audit logging consistent with industry standards for protection of sensitive information. Recipient shall not use any cloud service provider that does not permit data ownership to remain with the customer or that prohibits verification of security controls upon request."

This clause imposes minimum expectations and creates a contractual basis for investigating mishandling. It treats cloud hosting as a legally meaningful act, not merely an infrastructure choice.

The decision to store trade secrets in the cloud is not inherently flawed. But it must be accompanied by measures that replicate the control and accountability available in physical or on-premises systems. Without that replication, the trade secret may be lost not through malice but through diffusion. Courts evaluating digital secrecy want to see intentional design. When cloud usage reflects that design, legal protection becomes sustainable. When it does not, the legal consequences may be beyond recovery.

## 5.7.4. Security Standards and Contractual Promises

When companies entrust trade secrets to third parties—especially vendors, service providers, or cloud platforms—they often rely on general contractual language requiring the recipient to "maintain appropriate security." But vague promises are not enough. In a legal dispute, the company must show that its trade secrets were subject to specific, verifiable protections. Courts have increasingly looked to whether the disclosing party demanded compliance with recognized cybersecurity frameworks or industry certifications. These standards serve as proxies for reasonableness and provide a benchmark against which performance can be measured.

The most widely adopted frameworks include ISO 27001, SOC 2, (a widely used U.S. auditing and compliance framework developed by the American Institute of Certified Public Accountants) and the NIST Cybersecurity Framework. Each provides a structured approach to access control, incident response, data integrity, and system monitoring. Requiring adherence to such standards does not guarantee protection, but it demonstrates that the disclosing party demanded a recognized level of care.

This demand matters. When trade secrets are exposed due to poor security practices, courts often ask whether the disclosing party selected its partners carefully and imposed meaningful constraints.

Certifications alone are not enough. Companies should also require third parties to maintain written security policies, perform regular risk assessments, and update their controls in response to evolving threats. These obligations should be written into the agreement. When security is treated as an informal understanding, the resulting protections are rarely enforceable. When it is documented in contract and verified through audits or attestations, it becomes part of the structure of secrecy.

Security standards also function as a form of risk allocation. If a vendor agrees to maintain a certain level of protection and later suffers a breach due to its own failure, the disclosing party has a stronger claim that secrecy was lost due to the vendor's conduct, not its own. This distinction can be critical in litigation. It may determine whether the trade secret owner is entitled to relief or deemed to have failed the reasonable efforts standard.

### SECURITY STANDARDS CLAUSES REQUIRE IMPLEMENTATION OF RECOGNIZED CYBERSECURITY FRAMEWORKS

"Recipient shall implement and maintain administrative, physical, and technical safeguards consistent with the ISO/IEC 27001 standard (or its successor), the SOC 2 Type II framework, or an equivalent cybersecurity standard approved in writing by Discloser. Recipient shall maintain written information security policies, conduct regular security assessments, and certify compliance with these standards on an annual basis or upon request. Failure to maintain such safeguards shall constitute a material breach of this Agreement."

This clause makes cybersecurity expectations explicit. It also creates a mechanism for accountability by tying contractual performance to verifiable frameworks.

Trade secret law is flexible. It does not mandate a particular security architecture or standard. But it does require intentionality. When a company demands compliance with recognized standards and confirms that those standards are being met, it builds a record of care. That record may later be the difference between a viable claim and a finding that secrecy was never truly protected. In external relationships, contracts are not just about access. They are about expectation. And when expectations are framed in the language of security, they carry legal weight.

## 5.7.5. Incident Response and Notification Obligations

No cybersecurity system is perfect. Even companies that implement strong technical controls and require their vendors to follow industry standards must plan for failure. When trade secrets are exposed—whether through a system breach, misdirected transmission, or internal misuse—the response can determine whether protection is preserved or lost. Courts examining trade secret claims routinely ask how the company reacted when something went wrong. Silence, delay, or lack of follow-up may suggest that secrecy was not treated as a serious obligation.

This responsibility does not fall solely on the trade secret holder. In external relationships, the risk of exposure often originates with the other party. A vendor may suffer a ransomware attack. A customer may forward confidential materials to an unsecured system. A third-party service provider may accidentally grant access to an unauthorized user. In each case, the damage may be difficult to detect without cooperation. That is why trade secret protection requires not only preventive security measures but also affirmative duties to notify, coordinate, and investigate.

Notification obligations are essential. If a breach occurs or is suspected, the recipient of the trade secret should be required to alert the disclosing party promptly and share all relevant information, including when the incident occurred, what systems were involved, which data may have been exposed, and what steps are being taken to contain the event. These details matter. They allow the disclosing party to assess legal exposure, notify regulators if required, and take its own protective steps. Without a contractual obligation to disclose this information, the disclosing party may be left unaware until it is too late.

Timeliness is also critical. Many companies set notification windows of 24 or 48 hours for cybersecurity incidents. Courts do not require a specific number of hours, but they do look at whether the response was prompt and whether the delay contributed to further harm. Contracts that define clear timelines and content requirements help establish that the company took reasonable steps to preserve secrecy, even in moments of vulnerability. Courts do not require proof that the parties negotiated exact notification windows; acceptance of a clear and commercially reasonable standard (e.g., 24 hours, 48 hours, or "promptly upon discovery") is generally sufficient.

Coordination is the third leg of response. A company that receives notice of an incident should have the right to participate in the investigation, request updates, and receive access logs or forensic findings. These rights can be built into the agreement and tied to audit clauses or certification requirements. When a breach occurs, the right to information becomes a structural necessity.

**INCIDENT RESPONSE CLAUSES REQUIRE BREACH NOTIFICATION AND INVESTIGATION COOPERATION**

"Recipient shall notify Discloser in writing within forty-eight (48) hours of becoming aware of any actual or suspected unauthorized access, use, or disclosure of Confidential Information. Such notice shall include the date and time of the incident (if known), the nature and scope of the incident, the systems affected, the identity of any individuals involved, and the corrective actions taken or planned. Recipient shall cooperate fully with Discloser in investigating the incident and mitigating its effects, including by providing access to relevant logs, personnel, and third-party investigators upon request."

This clause ensures that the disclosing party is not left in the dark when secrecy is threatened. It establishes a timeline, defines the content of the notice, and imposes an affirmative duty to cooperate.

A trade secret claim often hinges not on whether information was exposed but rather on how the owner responded. If the disclosing party acted quickly, demanded documentation, and took steps to minimize harm, courts are more likely to find that secrecy was preserved. If it ignored warning signs, failed to investigate, or relied on informal channels, its claim may collapse. In a networked environment, incident response is no longer just an IT function. It is a legal obligation, and one that must be shared across the contractual relationship.

## 5.7.6. Designing Digital Containment Systems

The legal standard for trade secret protection is not perfection. It is reasonableness. But in digital environments, reasonableness cannot be improvised. It must be designed. This is especially true in external relationships, where information flows across organizational boundaries and into systems the trade secret holder does not control. In these cases, containment becomes the central challenge. The goal is not to eliminate exposure entirely but to ensure that exposure remains knowable, limited, and correctable.

Digital containment means structuring systems so that trade secrets do not travel further than intended. It means limiting access based on role, segregating sensitive data from other materials, and ensuring that every interaction with confidential information is recorded, reviewable, and reversible. It also means building expiration into access, so that time-limited projects or evaluations do not create open-ended vulnerability.

Containment also requires alignment between technical systems and legal structures. Contracts should mirror the way systems are configured, and systems should reflect what the contract demands. If a contract limits use to a particular team or timeframe, the system should enforce those limits. If the contract requires return or destruction, the system should allow for verification. Mismatches between law and infrastructure weaken both. When systems are not designed to support the legal framework, the legal framework becomes theoretical.

Many companies assume that monitoring is enough. But monitoring without segmentation is like recording who walks through an open door. To protect trade secrets, the door must be closed—or at least visible, controlled, and time-limited. Containment strategies should include revocable links, session timeouts, geo-fencing, encryption, and forensic watermarking. These tools are not just technical features. They are evidence. They allow the company to show that it took secrecy seriously.

The most effective containment systems are those that prevent misuse without impeding productivity. Trade secrets often need to be shared to generate value. The task is not to lock them away but rather to create environments where they can be used safely. This requires thoughtful design, coordinated policy, and cross-functional cooperation among legal, engineering, security, and business teams. Containment is not a security protocol. It is a cultural and architectural commitment.

Digital containment does not guarantee that trade secrets will remain secret. But it creates a record of diligence, and that record is what courts rely on when determining whether legal protection should survive. When the structure supports the claim, the law has something to enforce. When it does not, the best intentions fall away. In external relationships, structure is not optional. It is the condition of secrecy itself.

## 5.8. Conclusion

Trade secret law rewards structure. Nowhere is that more apparent than in the context of external relationships. When information is shared beyond the boundaries of the organization, the strength of legal protection depends entirely on the systems built to contain it. This chapter has shown that external risk is not a single problem. It is a composite of legal ambiguity, technical integration, misaligned incentives, and diffuse accountability. The common thread is that secrecy cannot survive where responsibility is unclear.

Every external interaction—whether with a vendor, collaborator, customer, or distributor—introduces its own form of vulnerability. Vendors may retain system-level access after a project ends. Collaborators may misunderstand who owns the results. Customers may reverse engineer a product or continue using information after a trial expires. Distributors may share materials downstream without proper constraints. And in each of these cases, it is the disclosing party who bears the burden of foresight.

What this chapter offers is not a checklist of protections but rather a method of thinking. It urges companies to treat trade secrets not just as legal assets but as operational responsibilities. Agreements must do more than prohibit disclosure. They must define scope, limit use, impose termination procedures, and extend obligations to every recipient in the chain. Systems must do more than provide access. They must restrict it, monitor it, and allow it to be withdrawn. And organizations must do more than hope that others will behave. They must build relationships that are constrained by design.

The underlying principle is containment. In external environments, secrecy cannot be enforced unless it has been architected in advance. That architecture is legal, technical, and cultural. It is expressed through audit rights, credential management, reverse engineering clauses, and cloud security protocols. It is tested when something goes wrong. And it is judged in hindsight, when the company must explain how its trade secrets were protected—not in theory, but in fact.

The next chapter turns from prevention to enforcement. It asks what happens when secrecy fails or someone crosses the line. But the strength of that enforcement depends on what came before. Courts cannot enforce what was never defined. They cannot restore what was never controlled. And they cannot protect secrets that were not kept. External protection begins long before any dispute arises. It begins with the decision to build a structure where secrecy is not only preserved but also provable.

# Chapter 6

# Enforcing Trade Secret Rights

Trade secret law protects the use of secrecy in commerce, not secrecy in isolation. It does not demand that information be hidden away or stripped of its economic potential. Instead, it expects that those who use trade secrets in business take reasonable steps to preserve their confidentiality. The law fills the space between privacy and exchange. It allows secrets to move through the economy—to be shared with employees, vendors, partners, and customers—without being lost along the way.

Enforcement is what makes that structure meaningful. A trade secret becomes legally enforceable only when the information is both protected and misappropriated. There is no cause of action simply for possession. The law intervenes only when something has gone wrong: when a competitor acquires information improperly, when a former employee misuses confidential knowledge, or when a recipient violates a promise to keep certain data secure. These moments of breach transform secrecy from an internal discipline into a legal claim.

This chapter addresses how those claims are asserted, proven, and resolved. The two primary statutes are the UTSA, adopted in some form by nearly every state, and the federal DTSA, enacted in 2016. While the two laws are closely aligned, the DTSA provides access to federal courts and includes certain remedies and procedural tools unavailable under state law. In practice, many trade secret lawsuits assert claims under both statutes in parallel.

The sections that follow walk through the major components of trade secret enforcement. They begin with the legal definition of misappropriation and proceed to the core evidentiary requirement: proving that the information at issue qualifies as a trade secret. From there, the chapter turns to remedies—injunctions, damages, seizure orders, and attorneys' fees—and concludes with a discussion of criminal liability and procedural strategy. Along the way, the doctrine is grounded in real cases: disputes where courts had to decide whether secrecy had been preserved, whether conduct was improper, and whether enforcement was justified.

Trade secret enforcement is not just about recovering losses. It is about validating the company's protection system. Courts ask whether the plaintiff treated the information as secret, whether it communicated those expectations to others, and whether it took action when those expectations were breached. A lawsuit is not the beginning of trade secret protection. It is the final test. Everything that came before—contracts, controls, culture, and communication—will be judged in the cold light of litigation. This chapter explains how that process works.

# 6.1. The Statutory Definition of Misappropriation

Every trade secret case begins with the allegation of misappropriation. This is not a general claim that valuable information was misused. It is a specific legal assertion that the defendant acquired, disclosed, or used a trade secret by improper means or in breach of a legal duty. The UTSA and the DTSA use nearly identical language to define misappropriation, and courts interpreting both statutes have developed a shared body of doctrine. That doctrine draws a clear distinction between ordinary competition and wrongful appropriation.

Under both statutes, misappropriation includes three distinct acts: improper acquisition, improper disclosure, and improper use. A single case may involve more than one. For example, a departing employee may take trade secrets when resigning (acquisition), send them to a competitor (disclosure), and help that competitor launch a new product based on the information (use). But each form of misappropriation is independently actionable. A plaintiff does not need to prove all three.

The statutes also impose liability on recipients who acquire a trade secret from someone else but knew or should have known that it was misappropriated. This provision expands liability to downstream actors and prevents companies from turning a blind eye to suspicious disclosures. Courts do not require actual knowledge, but they do examine what the defendant should have understood from the circumstances. That standard can be satisfied by timing, relationship history, or the nature of the information involved. Courts apply a totality-of-the-circumstances test, weighing these factors together to decide whether the recipient had reason to know the disclosure was improper.

What these definitions share is the requirement that the defendant crossed a legal line. The conduct must have involved deception, breach of duty, or some form of improper access. Trade secret law does not prohibit independent development. It does not punish observation of publicly available products. It does not block reverse engineering so long as the product was lawfully acquired. The focus is on fairness and trust. Misappropriation occurs when those expectations are violated.

The sections that follow examine each type of misappropriation in turn—starting with improper acquisition, the most direct and visible form of trade secret theft.

## 6.1.1. Acquisition by Improper Means

The most straightforward form of misappropriation is improper acquisition. When a person or entity obtains a trade secret through theft, deception, or some other wrongful act, the violation occurs at the moment of acquisition, regardless of whether the information is later used or shared. Courts have little difficulty recognizing this form of misappropriation. It is the clearest violation of both legal duties and commercial ethics.

The UTSA and the DTSA both define "improper means" to include theft, bribery, misrepresentation, breach or inducement of a duty to maintain secrecy, and espionage through electronic or other means. These examples are illustrative, not exhaustive. Courts have extended the definition to cover creative or indirect tactics, including surveillance, trickery, and deliberate circumvention of access restrictions. The essential idea is that the information was acquired in a way that violated the rules governing its confidentiality.

The case of *E.I. du Pont de Nemours v. Christopher* is one of the most iconic early examples. DuPont was constructing a chemical plant designed to produce methanol using proprietary processes. The plant was open to the air for construction purposes but otherwise shielded from public view. The defendants, acting on behalf of a competitor, hired a pilot to take aerial photographs of the site. DuPont sued for trade secret misappropriation, arguing that the photography revealed confidential design information.

### VIOLATING COMMERCIAL NORMS CAN ESTABLISH "IMPROPER MEANS"

*E.I. du Pont de Nemours & Co. v. Christopher*
431 F.2d 1012 (5th Cir. 1970)

Defendants hired a pilot to fly over DuPont's methanol plant construction site and take photographs revealing structural features of a proprietary process. Although the site was visible from the air and not physically secured against aerial observation, the court held that such surveillance constituted improper means. It emphasized that trade secret law requires companies to guard against only those intrusions that violate reasonable commercial norms, not all possible intrusions. A competitor cannot claim innocence merely because the information was obtained without trespassing. Although decided before widespread state adoption of the UTSA or enactment of the DTSA, the Fifth Circuit's reasoning in remains cited as good law for its articulation of the common-law duty to refrain from improper means of acquisition.

The Fifth Circuit's opinion in *DuPont* has remained influential. It illustrates that improper means is not limited to physical theft or direct misrepresentation. It also includes conduct that, while technically legal in another context, becomes unlawful when used to acquire confidential information. The test is not whether the method was creative—rather, it is whether it respected the norms of confidentiality that make trade secret protection possible.

Improper acquisition also occurs in more conventional settings. Employees who download confidential files before resigning, vendors who copy proprietary materials outside the scope of a project, and researchers who smuggle internal data to a competitor all fall within the statute. In many of these cases, the act of acquisition itself is a breach of contract or fiduciary duty. But even where no formal relationship exists, the circumstances may impose a duty not to seek access through trickery or coercion.

One of the challenges in modern litigation is distinguishing improper acquisition from passive receipt. A person who stumbles upon a confidential document without seeking it out may not be liable unless they had reason to know it was protected. But a person who solicits, extracts, or manipulates their way into access—especially if the information is marked confidential or clearly sensitive—takes on legal risk. The more deliberate the conduct, the stronger the inference of impropriety.

The next section turns to a different kind of violation: improper use of trade secrets that were lawfully acquired. While acquisition often defines the front end of misappropriation, many cases are built on what the defendant did with the information once they had it.

## 6.1.2. Improper Use

A person who lawfully acquires a trade secret may still be liable for misappropriation if they use it in violation of a duty. This form of liability does not depend on theft, deception, or surveillance. It depends on how the information is used once it is in the defendant's hands. The core idea is that trade secret protection follows the information—not just how it is obtained, but how it is exploited.

Improper use occurs when a person leverages a trade secret for their own benefit or for the benefit of a third party in a way that violates an obligation of confidentiality or breaches the expectations under which the information was shared. This includes using the secret to develop a competing product, inform internal strategy, accelerate timelines, or bypass costly research and development. The use need not be visible to the public or result in a final product. Even internal application can trigger liability if it confers a commercial advantage and violates the terms under which the information was received.

Improper use claims often arise in collaborative settings. A company shares a prototype, process, or dataset with a partner under the terms of a joint project or evaluation agreement. The partner then applies that knowledge in another context, sometimes unintentionally, sometimes deliberately. The legal question is not whether the information was helpful but whether its use exceeded the scope of the agreed purpose.

**IMPROPER USE OF PROPERLY ACQUIRED INFORMATION CAN BE MISAPPROPRIATION**

*Altavion, Inc. v. Konica Minolta Systems Laboratory, Inc.*
226 Cal. App. 4th 26 (Cal. Ct. App. 2014)

Altavion disclosed a digital authentication concept to Konica Minolta for evaluation in connection with possible collaboration. Konica Minolta later filed patent applications incorporating the core ideas. Altavion sued for trade secret misappropriation. The court held that the disclosed information, while not a finished product, qualified as a trade secret and that Konica's use in patent filings was actionable. The case confirmed that misuse of confidential ideas—even when received under a business relationship—can constitute improper use.

*Altavion* is illustrative of a broader principle. Companies do not lose trade secret protection simply because they share information in the hope of collaboration. But when that information is used outside the bounds of the relationship, especially in ways that confer exclusive control or public recognition, the law treats that as misappropriation.

Improper use also arises within employment. Employees may take knowledge acquired on the job and apply it in a new role for a competitor. Courts do not prohibit the use of general experience or publicly known practices. But when the employee draws on specific, nonpublic information that provided a competitive edge, and does so in a way that violates a contractual or implied duty of confidentiality, liability may follow.

**INTERNAL USE OF CONFIDENTIAL INFORMATION CAN BE MISAPPROPRIATION**

*3M v. Pribyl*
259 F.3d 587 (7th Cir. 2001)

An employee left 3M and joined a competitor, taking with him knowledge of internal manufacturing processes that were not publicly disclosed. He used these insights to improve production at the new company. The court held that the use of the confidential process information gained during prior employment and subject to ongoing confidentiality obligations constituted misappropriation. The fact that the employee did not take physical documents did not alter the outcome.

The *3M* case makes clear that trade secrets do not need to be copied or disclosed to be misused. If the defendant internalizes the information and applies it in a way that substitutes for independent development, the law may impose liability. Courts typically infer use of internalized information from circumstantial evidence—such as temporal proximity, similarity of results, or absence of an independent development record—rather than requiring direct proof of copying.

Improper use can be subtle. It often occurs without fanfare or direct communication. But where the facts show that a defendant derived value from confidential information in breach of an expectation, the law treats that conduct as a form of theft. The next section turns to improper disclosure—where the secret is not used by the defendant but rather passed to others in violation of the duty to maintain confidentiality.

## 6.1.3. Improper Disclosure

Disclosure of a trade secret without authorization is a standalone basis for liability. It does not require that the defendant benefit personally or use the information for competitive purposes. The legal wrong lies in breaking the expectation that the information would remain confidential. Disclosure often causes greater harm than use because it multiplies the number of actors who now possess the secret. Once information is shared without control, legal remedies may still exist, but practical containment is far more difficult.

Improper disclosure occurs when someone entrusted with a trade secret provides access to another person or entity who is not authorized to receive it. This can happen through an intentional leak, a negligent communication, or an indirect handoff—such as uploading a confidential file to a public folder or forwarding an email without redacting sensitive material. In each case, the key issue is whether the defendant had a duty to keep the information secret and whether that duty was breached.

Employees and former employees are the most common defendants in disclosure cases. If a person learns a trade secret in the course of their work and then shares it with a competitor, colleague, or new employer without permission, they have likely committed misappropriation. The same is true for contractors, vendors, or consultants who receive confidential information under a nondisclosure agreement or implied duty of confidentiality. Disclosure in violation of those obligations breaches both legal norms and commercial trust.

In *Airfacts v. Amezaga*, the plaintiff, an aviation data firm, alleged that a departing employee had emailed proprietary flight records and analysis tools to his personal account before leaving the company. The court found that the information was not adequately protected (there was no nondisclosure agreement and access was not clearly limited), but it still addressed the question of disclosure. The employee's act of transferring data outside the company's systems constituted potential misappropriation through improper disclosure, even if the information was not further disseminated.

**IMPROPER DISCLOSURE (WITHOUT USE) CAN CONSTITUTE MISAPPROPRIATION**

*Airfacts, Inc. v. Amezaga*
909 F.3d 84 (4th Cir. 2018)

An employee emailed internal aviation data to himself before resigning. The company alleged misappropriation, and the court acknowledged that even without later use, the act of removing confidential information from the company's control could be actionable as improper disclosure. However, the court ultimately denied relief due to insufficient evidence that the company had taken reasonable steps to protect the information as a trade secret.

The *Airfacts* case illustrates how closely courts link disclosure with secrecy. Even when the act of disclosure is clear, a plaintiff cannot prevail unless it also shows that the information was treated as confidential. Disclosure alone is not enough. The law protects secrets—not merely data.

Other cases involve more public forms of dissemination. In *Allstate v. Fougere*, a departing insurance agent was accused of providing business strategy documents and customer data to a rival firm. The court evaluated whether the materials were shared in violation of contract and whether the disclosures rendered the information no longer secret. Improper disclosure is a double injury: it violates the duty of confidentiality and may destroy the very trade secret status the plaintiff seeks to protect.

Improper disclosure is often harder to prove than improper use. Documents may be shared through private channels, and the plaintiff may only discover the leak after damage has occurred. Courts look at circumstantial evidence, such as email logs, overlapping timelines, and parallel product features, to assess whether the defendant likely disclosed the information to others. Where the evidence is strong, relief may include not just damages but also injunctions barring further dissemination.

Trade secrets are often shared internally under assumptions of trust. But when those assumptions break down, improper disclosure becomes a gateway to irreversible harm.

## 6.1.4. Liability for Knowing Receipt

Trade secret law does not limit liability to those who originally misappropriate information. It also imposes liability on recipients who acquire trade secrets from others and who knew or had reason to know that the information was obtained through improper means. This provision serves a critical role in modern business contexts, where confidential information is often passed between entities, across transactions, or through intermediaries. It prevents companies from insulating themselves by claiming that they were not the original wrongdoer, even as they benefit from the misappropriation.

The key element is knowledge. The statute requires that the recipient "knew or had reason to know" that the information was misappropriated. Courts interpret this standard objectively. It does not require that the recipient be told explicitly that the trade secret was stolen. Instead, it asks whether a reasonable person in the same position would have understood that the information came with baggage. Factors such as the timing of disclosure, the nature of the parties' relationship, the level of detail involved, and the presence of protective markings are illustrative rather than exhaustive. Courts assess the totality of the circumstances to determine whether a reasonable recipient should have recognized that the information was improperly obtained.

Cases involving departing employees frequently raise this issue. A new employer who receives valuable information from a recent hire may face liability if the context suggests that the knowledge was obtained from the former employer in violation of a duty. Courts expect companies to perform diligence, especially when hiring from competitors in sensitive roles. Failing to ask questions or choosing not to know can be treated as willful blindness.

### CONSTRUCTIVE KNOWLEDGE OF INSIDER INFORMATION CAN BE "THREATENED" MISAPPROPRIATION

*PepsiCo, Inc. v. Redmond*
54 F.3d 1262 (7th Cir. 1995)

Redmond, a former PepsiCo executive, accepted a position with Quaker, a direct competitor. PepsiCo sought an injunction on the grounds that Redmond would inevitably use trade secrets in his new role. The court found that Redmond had knowledge of PepsiCo's confidential pricing and marketing strategies and that Quaker had hired him into a role that would benefit from those secrets. The court held that Quaker either knew or should have known that it would receive and use the information improperly, even if no documents were taken or disclosures made.

*PepsiCo* illustrates that courts do not require direct evidence of misappropriation when the circumstances strongly suggest that trade secrets will be used or disclosed. When a new employer places a former competitor's insider in a position to exploit that knowledge, the law may impute liability. Knowledge can be inferred from context.

Liability for knowing receipt of confidential information also arises in joint ventures, licensing discussions, and mergers and acquisitions. A company reviewing another party's confidential materials under a nondisclosure agreement may later be accused of misuse even if it believed the materials were not protected. If the information was clearly marked as confidential and shared in a structured way, the recipient has little excuse. Courts are skeptical of claims that the recipient did not understand the material's status, particularly when the parties had negotiated access under specific legal terms.

### KNOWING RECEIPT OF CONFIDENTIAL INFORMATION CAN ESTABLISH MISAPPROPRIATION LIABILITY

*Bimbo Bakeries USA, Inc. v. Botticella*
613 F.3d 102 (3d Cir. 2010)

Botticella, a senior executive at Bimbo Bakeries, accepted an offer from a competitor while still employed. He continued to access confidential product development files after accepting the new role. The court held that the new employer had reason to know that the information Botticella possessed had been obtained in violation of his duties to Bimbo. The risk of disclosure was inherent in the role, and the circumstances surrounding Botticella's departure raised red flags that the recipient company failed to address.

A takeaway from *Bimbo Bakeries* is that recipients cannot ignore obvious warning signs. When someone departs from a position with access to sensitive materials and immediately moves to a competitor, courts expect the recipient to investigate. A failure to do so may convert the recipient into a participant in the misappropriation—even without active solicitation.

However, an employer is not automatically liability for its new employee's misappropriation. Of that employee's prior employer's trade secrets. A hiring company's liability for trade secret misappropriation depends on its own knowledge and intent, not merely the actions of the employee. Even when misappropriation occurs, the absence of corporate scienter (knowing wrongdoing) can preclude punitive damages and fee awards, which is a critical factor for both damages assessment and settlement strategy.

### CORPORATE LIABILITY AND WILLFULNESS

*Allied Erecting & Dismantling Co. v. Genesis Equip. & Mfg., Inc.*
511 F. App'x 398 (6th Cir. 2013)

Mark Ramun, a former manager at Allied Erecting, retained approximately 15,000 pages of confidential design documents, including information relating to Allied's patented demolition attachment, the Allied MT, when he left Allied in 2001. In 2003, Genesis—a direct competitor—hired Ramun for sales and later promoted him to director of development. The jury found that Ramun misappropriated Allied's trade secrets in developing Genesis's competing LXP and Versi-Pro products, but it declined to find Genesis liable for willful or malicious conduct. The Sixth Circuit affirmed, holding that a company hiring a former competitor's employee is not automatically liable for the employee's misconduct absent evidence that the company knowingly exploited misappropriated information.

A company hiring from a competitor should require written certifications of non-use, audit incoming devices, assign clean teams, and document independent design steps. Courts view such compliance records as persuasive evidence of good faith and a barrier to secondary liability.

The legal theory behind knowing receipt is simple. Trade secret protection depends on reinforcing commercial ethics. If companies could benefit from stolen or misused information simply by not asking questions, the doctrine would collapse. By imposing liability on those who should have known, the law promotes diligence, fairness, and structural accountability.

## 6.1.5. Limits of the Statutory Scope

Trade secret law does not protect everything a business prefers to keep private. The statutes impose rigorous limits on what qualifies as a trade secret, requiring plaintiffs to demonstrate that the information at issue is specific, nonpublic, and subject to reasonable protection efforts. The cases in this section define the outer boundaries of the doctrine and serve to reinforce the principle that protection is earned through discipline, not presumed by law.

Some claims fail because the alleged trade secret is too vague. Courts require a reasonably specific description of the information at issue—enough to distinguish it from general business practices or publicly available materials.

**TRADE SECRET CLAIMS REQUIRE SPECIFICITY**

*Aday v. Westfield Ins. Co.*
2021 WL 1173003 (W.D. Ky. Mar. 29, 2021)

The plaintiff alleged that Westfield Insurance misappropriated his "claims handling process," which he claimed was confidential. The court dismissed the claim, holding that the process was described only in general terms and lacked the specificity needed to qualify as a trade secret. The court emphasized that business acumen or professional judgment is not protectable unless tied to concrete, identifiable information.

A common pitfall for plaintiffs is the failure to precisely articulate what they believe is a trade secret. In *Aday*, the plaintiff accused an insurer of misappropriating a "claims handling process" yet never described that process in specific detail. The court dismissed the case on the pleadings, emphasizing that trade secret law can only protect information when it is clearly defined and distinguishable from general business practices or a professional's "know-how." Abstract references, conclusory labels, or vague allusions are not enough. Trade secret statutes do not provide retroactive protection for instructional materials, processes, or systems that are already widely used in an industry. For content or processes to qualify as a "trade secret," the plaintiff must demonstrate genuine secrecy and originality, not just commercial value or effort expended.

### PUBLIC DISCLOSURE DESTROYS TRADE SECRET PROTECTION

*Religious Technology Center v. Lerma*
908 F. Supp. 1362 (E.D. Va. 1995)

The plaintiff alleged that movie industry information posted online by a former employee constituted a trade secret. The court disagreed, holding that once the content had been published to the internet and circulated publicly, it no longer satisfied the secrecy requirement. The court declined to impose liability for use of information that was already in the public domain.

Even where a trade secret once existed, its protection is not permanent. In *Lerma*, proprietary information was posted online and rapidly circulated in the public domain. The court held that the moment information becomes widely accessible, it instantaneously loses its status as a protectable secret. The law does not permit a trade secret owner to "recapture" confidentiality after allowing public access. Relentless discipline in controlling access, use, and distribution is mandatory; once lost, trade secret protection cannot be restored.

These decisions underscore the structural nature of trade secret law. To be protected, the information must be clearly defined, objectively secret, and actively treated as confidential. Courts do not stretch the statute to cover business grievances that arise from weak protections, broad generalizations, or post hoc claims of confidentiality. At the boundary of the doctrine, the law insists on discipline—and denies protection to those who fail to impose it.

# 6.2. Limits of Liability and Early Dismissal

The substantive limits discussed above have direct procedural consequences. Unlike patent or copyright suits, which begin with a registered right, trade secret litigation requires the plaintiff to prove at the outset that a protectable secret existed. If the complaint fails to plausibly allege the foundational elements—a specific secret, reasonable security measures, and improper conduct—the case is vulnerable to early dismissal.

This section reviews these common failure modes in early-stage litigation. Courts apply the law with discipline, not to deny protection but rather to ensure that it applies only where the statutory requirements are met. The following subsections group early dismissal cases according to the specific legal deficiency alleged by the defendant.

## 6.2.1. Failure to Allege a Cognizable Trade Secret

A trade secret plaintiff must describe the secret it seeks to protect with enough specificity to give the defendant fair notice and allow the court to assess whether the information qualifies for protection. While a plaintiff is not expected to reveal the entire secret in a public filing, the complaint must contain more than vague references to "proprietary processes" or "confidential strategies." Claims that fail this standard are often dismissed before discovery begins, as courts are skeptical of complaints that rely on conclusory language to protect general business concepts.

**VAGUE ALLEGATIONS OF SECRETS ARE SUBJECT TO EARLY DISMISSAL**

*Aday v. Westfield Ins. Co.*
2021 WL 1173003 (W.D. Ky. Mar. 29, 2021)

The plaintiff alleged that Westfield Insurance misappropriated his "claims handling process," but he did not describe the process in concrete terms. The court dismissed the case on the pleadings, holding that the plaintiff's description was too general to support a trade secret claim. Without more detail, the court could not determine whether the process was novel, valuable, or non-obvious to others in the industry.

The procedural consequences of failing to meet the specificity requirement are illustrated clearly in *Aday*. The plaintiff's claim that Westfield Insurance misappropriated his "claims handling process" was dismissed on the pleadings because the description was too abstract. The court could not determine whether the process was novel, valuable, or non-obvious to others in the industry. This outcome serves as a critical lesson for litigators: If the court cannot distinguish the alleged secret from general business acumen or publicly available information based on the complaint's allegations, the claim will not survive a motion to dismiss pursuant to FRCP 12(b)(6). A plaintiff must be prepared to articulate the specific boundaries of their secret from day one.

## 6.2.2. Failure to Show Reasonable Efforts to Maintain Secrecy

The most frequently misunderstood requirement in trade secret litigation is the obligation to take reasonable efforts to maintain secrecy. Plaintiffs often assume that the importance of the information speaks for itself or that its confidential nature is obvious within the organization. But trade secret law does not rely on assumption. It requires evidence—evidence that the information was treated as a secret in policy, in practice, and in communication.

Courts do not demand perfection. The standard is not absolute security but rather reasonable conduct under the circumstances. What counts as reasonable will vary depending on the sensitivity of the information, the structure of the business, the size of the team, and the nature of the relationship between the parties. But certain basic expectations apply across industries: the use of nondisclosure agreements, access limitations, document labeling, employee training, and termination procedures. Where these are absent or inconsistently applied, courts are quick to find that the secrecy element has not been met.

The following case shows how the complete absence of these controls can be fatal to the plaintiff's claim.

### REASONABLE EFFORTS REQUIRE FOUNDATIONAL SAFEGUARDS

*Airfacts, Inc. v. Amezaga*
909 F.3d 84 (4th Cir. 2018)

A former employee allegedly disclosed proprietary airline data after leaving the company. The court found that Airfacts had not taken reasonable steps to protect the information. There were no signed nondisclosure agreements, no documented access restrictions, and no internal protocols indicating that the information was treated as confidential. Because the company had failed to impose even minimal protections, the court ruled that the information was not a trade secret under the statute.

This case illustrates the structural nature of the secrecy requirement. It is not enough for information to be internal or useful. If the company has not documented its protections, defined its expectations, or limited access to those with a need to know, courts are likely to conclude that it forfeited any claim to secrecy, whether intentionally or not.

Some cases present closer questions. The company may have some protections in place but fail to apply them uniformly. Courts are especially wary of inconsistency: when a company treats similar materials differently or allows exceptions to its own rules, it undermines its position in litigation. The next case demonstrates how these internal contradictions can unravel a trade secret claim.

**REASONABLE EFFORTS MUST BE CONSISTENTLY APPLIED**

*Allstate Ins. Co. v. Fougere*
2021 WL 4441348 (D. Mass. Sept. 28, 2021)

Allstate alleged that a former insurance agent took confidential customer information and internal training materials to a competitor. The court found that Allstate had not applied its secrecy policies consistently. Some materials were shared widely without restriction, while others were protected. Because the company had not made a clear and uniform effort to designate the information as confidential, the court dismissed the trade secret claim in part.

*Fougere* reflects a broader judicial concern: If the company itself was unclear about what was confidential, how could a third party be expected to understand the boundaries? Trade secret law assumes that secrets must be signaled. It is not enough that they are understood internally; rather, they must be actively communicated and enforced. Lapses, ambiguity, or silence create vulnerability not just to misuse but also to legal failure.

These cases also reflect the evidentiary posture of early-stage litigation. Courts do not wait for discovery to test the secrecy element. They look for concrete allegations in the complaint that show reasonable efforts were made, i.e., that the plaintiff had a plan, that the plan was followed, and that the secret was protected accordingly. When those details are missing, the claim may not proceed.

Reasonable efforts are not a matter of checklists or boilerplate. They require alignment between what the company values and how it behaves. Courts reward that alignment. They do not supply it after the fact.

## 6.2.3. Failure to Allege Improper Conduct

The final category of early dismissal involves claims where the defendant's conduct, even if commercially aggressive, does not qualify as misappropriation. Trade secret law does not prohibit competition, independent development, or the use of general industry knowledge. It prohibits the acquisition, use, or disclosure of trade secrets through improper means or in breach of a duty. If the complaint fails to allege that kind of conduct, the case is likely to be dismissed, even if the outcome feels unfair to the plaintiff.

Improper means must involve some form of deception, breach of trust, or circumvention of access restrictions. This includes theft, misrepresentation, violation of nondisclosure agreements, or leveraging insider knowledge obtained under a duty of confidentiality. But many plaintiffs allege only that the defendant developed a competing product or benefited from access to ideas discussed in a business meeting. Without more, those facts do not establish liability. The law is designed to protect secrets, not to preserve advantage indefinitely after the information is shared.

The case below illustrates a common mistake: pleading commercial harm without showing a breach of legal obligation.

**MISAPPROPRIATION CLAIMS MUST ALLEGE IMPROPER CONDUCT**

*American Registry, LLC v. Hanaw*
2013 WL 6332971 (M.D. Fla. Dec. 5, 2013)

The plaintiff alleged that a former business associate used customer data and business methods to start a competing service. The court dismissed the trade secret claim, holding that the complaint failed to describe how the information was protected or how the defendant's conduct qualified as improper. Even assuming the data had value, there was no allegation of breach, deception, or contractual duty. The court found that the plaintiff's claims amounted to a complaint about competition, not misappropriation.

*Hanaw* demonstrates that trade secret claims must be rooted in clear legal theory. Courts expect plaintiffs to identify the duty that was breached, whether contractual, fiduciary, or circumstantial, and to show how the defendant's conduct crossed the line. If the complaint does not allege improper acquisition, unauthorized disclosure, or misuse of confidential information, it will not survive.

This limitation also protects legitimate reverse engineering and independent development. A company that creates a similar product based on public materials or its own research does not commit misappropriation, even if the final result resembles that of a competitor. The statutes are not designed to punish similarity. They punish breach.

Courts apply this boundary with increasing discipline. As trade secret claims have become more common in business disputes, judges have grown wary of plaintiffs attempting to use trade secret law to block fair competition or to dress up failed business negotiations as torts. To avoid early dismissal, the complaint must identify specific conduct that qualifies as wrongful under the statute and connect that conduct to a protectable secret. Anything less, and the claim will not proceed.

## 6.3. Proving the Trade Secret at the Time of Suit

Trade secret status is not established by allegation alone. Even if a plaintiff survives a motion to dismiss, it must eventually prove that the information at issue qualifies for protection under the law. This proof must be made with evidence. It is not sufficient that the information was secret at some point in the past; rather, it must have been a trade secret at the time of the alleged misappropriation. This requirement imposes a continuing obligation on trade secret holders to maintain control, to monitor access, and to treat the information as confidential over time.

Courts apply a three-part standard derived from the statutory definition. The plaintiff must prove that the information (1) is a form of knowledge or expression covered by the statute; (2) has (a) independent economic value from being (b) not generally known and (c) not readily ascertainable by proper means; and (3) was subject to reasonable efforts to keep it secret. This standard applies at every stage of litigation—from preliminary injunction to summary judgment to final verdict. Plaintiffs who fail to meet it cannot prevail, no matter how egregious the defendant's conduct may appear.

Proving secrecy is often the most demanding element. It requires both internal and external evidence. Internally, the plaintiff must show that access was limited, that recipients were trained or bound by agreement, and that controls were in place to prevent leakage. Externally, the plaintiff must show that the information was not available through public sources or independent research. General statements that the information was "confidential" or "valuable" are not enough. Courts expect specificity and structure.

### TRADE SECRET PROTECTION EXTENDS TO EARLY-STAGE CONCEPTS

*Altavion, Inc. v. Konica Minolta Systems Laboratory, Inc.*
226 Cal. App. 4th 26 (2014)

Altavion disclosed a digital stamping method to Konica Minolta during discussions about collaboration. Konica later filed patent applications covering the disclosed ideas. Altavion sued for misappropriation. The court held that the information qualified as a trade secret even though it was not embodied in a commercial product. It emphasized that trade secret status depends not on the stage of development but rather on secrecy, value, and control. Altavion had documented the concept, disclosed it under a confidentiality agreement, and kept it out of the public domain. That was enough.

*Altavion* confirms that trade secrets do not need to be market-ready to be protectable. What matters is whether the information was treated as confidential and whether it conferred a potential advantage because it was not known to others. Early-stage technical concepts, internal algorithms, and business strategies may all qualify if handled with care.

Secrecy must also be maintained through the life of the dispute. Information that leaks during litigation or was already disclosed before the defendant's alleged misconduct may lose protection. Courts focus on what was happening at the moment of the alleged misappropriation. Plaintiffs who fail to monitor access or who allow secrets to spread uncontrolled may find that the legal claim evaporates—even if the information still feels proprietary.

### INDIVIDUAL DISCIPLINE CAN SATISFY REASONABLE SECRECY EFFORTS

*Bianco v. Globus Medical, Inc.*
30 F. Supp. 3d 565 (E.D. Tex. 2014)

Dr. Bianco disclosed a spinal implant concept to Globus Medical during discussions about possible collaboration. No agreement was reached, but Globus later commercialized a similar design. The court held that the disclosed concept qualified as a trade secret. Although Bianco did not patent or manufacture the device himself, he had developed detailed documentation, shared it only under confidentiality, and kept it out of the public sphere. The court awarded damages based on lost licensing value.

*Bianco* demonstrates that even solo inventors and individual contributors can prevail if they take formal steps to preserve secrecy. Courts do not require corporate infrastructure. They require discipline. When the evidence shows that the information was economically valuable, closely held, and improperly used, protection follows.

What emerges from these cases is a picture of trade secret litigation as an evidentiary challenge. The plaintiff must show not just what the information is but how it was treated and why it matters. That showing must be made with precision. A trade secret cannot be proven by assertion. It must be demonstrated through documentation, access logs, contractual structure, and commercial context. That burden—proving the secret—is the first true test of every plaintiff's case.

## 6.3.1. Secrecy, Value, and Control

Trade secret status rests on three interrelated pillars: secrecy, economic value, and control. These elements must be proven together. Information that is secret but trivial will not be protected. Information that is valuable but widely known is not a secret. And information that is both secret and valuable but handled carelessly may be treated by the court as abandoned. Trade secret law protects only what the owner has chosen to protect and has taken steps to keep protected over time.

Secrecy does not mean absolute invisibility. Courts recognize that trade secrets are often shared within organizations and disclosed to business partners. What matters is that the information is not generally known or readily ascertainable and that its circulation is controlled. Access must be limited. Sharing must be governed by contract or clear expectation. Courts frequently ask: Who had access, under what conditions, and what obligations were imposed?

Value is assessed by how the information functions in the marketplace. Does it provide a competitive edge? Could a rival replicate it easily without access to the secret? Is it the result of substantial investment, insight, or iteration? These questions help distinguish trade secrets from professional knowledge or public information assembled with effort. Trade secret law protects commercial advantage derived from confidentiality—not effort alone.

Control is about conduct. Plaintiffs must demonstrate that they took reasonable measures to prevent loss of secrecy. This includes both formal steps, like nondisclosure agreements and system restrictions, and informal norms, such as access discipline and employee training. Courts are not interested in theoretical controls. They want to see what was actually done. A well-drafted policy that was never implemented carries little weight. A pattern of confidential treatment that can be corroborated by witnesses and records carries much more.

These factors often rise and fall together. Weak controls cast doubt on whether the information was secret. Ambiguous documentation casts doubt on value. The plaintiff must weave a coherent narrative showing that the information was distinctive, closely held, and significant. That narrative must be supported by evidence, and it must hold up when challenged under oath.

## 6.3.2. Evidentiary Burdens and Typical Defenses

Once litigation begins, the burden shifts from pleading to proof. The plaintiff must not only describe the trade secret with specificity but also support each element with admissible evidence. This includes showing what the trade secret is, how it was protected, when it was misappropriated, and by whom. These are not abstract questions.

Courts require concrete, fact-specific answers, and defendants often mount aggressive challenges to each part of the claim.

At summary judgment, the plaintiff must present evidence sufficient to create a triable issue of fact. That includes documents, sworn testimony, internal records, and expert analysis. Vague statements that the information was "confidential" or "important to the business" are not enough. Courts look for specificity: the exact nature of the secret, the mechanisms of protection, the ways in which it was used, and how it provided a competitive advantage. Plaintiffs who fail to provide that detail may lose without reaching trial.

Defendants often attack trade secret claims by arguing that the information was not actually secret or that it was already known in the industry. They may introduce evidence from public websites, academic publications, prior patents, or testimony from industry professionals to show that the information could have been obtained through proper means. If the trade secret is functionally available to others, the claim fails, regardless of whether the defendant actually used those sources.

Another common defense is that the plaintiff failed to take reasonable steps to protect the information. This is often supported by pointing to gaps in documentation, inconsistent enforcement of policies, or informal practices that allowed broad access. For example, a company that stores all files on an open-access server or fails to revoke credentials for former employees may struggle to show control. Courts weigh these facts heavily when deciding whether the plaintiff met its burden.

A related defense is that the defendant developed the information independently. If the defendant can show that its work was derived from public sources, internal expertise, or a development timeline that preceded any alleged disclosure, that can defeat the claim. Courts do not presume misappropriation merely because the end product is similar. They require proof that the secret was taken and that it made a difference.

These defenses underscore the central reality of trade secret litigation: plaintiffs bear the burden not only to claim secrecy but also to prove it—under conditions where the defendant is free to deny, distinguish, and reinterpret the facts. That burden is significant. It can be met, but only with careful preparation, detailed records, and internal discipline that existed long before the lawsuit began.

## 6.3.3. Litigation-Stage Reasonableness Analysis

The question of whether reasonable efforts were taken to maintain secrecy is not assessed in the abstract. Courts evaluate it based on what the plaintiff actually did before and during the alleged misappropriation. This includes how the information was stored, labeled, transmitted, and accessed; what policies were in place; and whether those policies were followed in practice. Crucially, courts examine whether secrecy was preserved at the time of the alleged breach, not just at some earlier stage when the information may have first been developed.

This litigation-stage assessment often reveals weaknesses in trade secret protection systems that went unnoticed internally. For example, a company may have required employees to sign nondisclosure agreements but never trained them on how to handle confidential files. Or a system may have had theoretical access controls, but the password was shared among teams or never changed. These kinds of implementation failures matter. Courts do not enforce good intentions. They enforce what actually happened.

Timing also plays a key role. Trade secrets can be lost by exposure. If a plaintiff allowed information to circulate without restrictions or failed to notice that a third party had published or leaked it, protection may be lost before the case even begins. Courts ask whether the information was still a trade secret at the time of the alleged misappropriation. If secrecy had already lapsed, there is nothing left to enforce.

Litigation also puts internal consistency under a microscope. Plaintiffs who describe the same information differently in different contexts, such as telling regulators one story and courts another, risk undercutting their claim. So do plaintiffs who try to reclassify information as confidential after the fact. Courts look for contemporaneous evidence that the information was understood to be sensitive and that appropriate steps were taken to protect it in real time.

Reasonableness is also judged relative to industry norms. Courts often ask whether companies of similar size and sophistication would have done more to protect similar information. This is especially true in technology, finance, healthcare, and other fields where expectations around data protection are evolving rapidly. A plaintiff that lags behind its peers may struggle to show that its practices were reasonable, particularly if the defendant followed stronger protocols or acted based on different assumptions about what was protected.

Ultimately, this stage of litigation reveals whether the company's protection efforts were built to withstand scrutiny. Trade secret law rewards structure and foresight. The plaintiff must not only convince the court that a trade secret exists but also that it was preserved through deliberate, consistent, and timely action. That is the foundation on which every remedy depends.

## 6.4. Injunctive Relief

Injunctive relief plays a significant role in trade secret litigation, but it is not always the primary remedy. The decision to grant an injunction depends on the facts of each case, the harm caused by the alleged misappropriation, and the nature of the trade secret itself. Injunctive relief is most commonly sought when the plaintiff can demonstrate that monetary damages will not be sufficient to remedy the harm caused by continued use or disclosure of the trade secret. However, courts weigh the interests of both the plaintiff and the defendant, balancing the need for protection against the defendant's business interests.

Temporary Restraining Orders (TROs) and preliminary injunctions are typically sought in the early stages of litigation to prevent further harm before a full trial can take place. These forms of relief serve to stop the defendant's actions while the case is ongoing, but they are not permanent solutions. Permanent injunctions, issued after a trial, provide more lasting protection. The following subsections examine the requirements and considerations for granting TROs, preliminary injunctions, and permanent injunctions.

## 6.4.1. Temporary Restraining Orders

A Temporary Restraining Order (TRO) is a short-term emergency remedy that can be granted without notice to the defendant in certain situations. A TRO is typically issued to preserve the status quo and prevent immediate harm to the plaintiff, such as the continued use or disclosure of a trade secret. Because TROs are generally granted ex parte—meaning the defendant is not present to contest the order—courts apply a heightened standard. The plaintiff must show that they will suffer irreparable harm if the TRO is not granted and that the balance of hardships favors the plaintiff.

The primary purpose of a TRO is to stop immediate harm before a full hearing can be held. It is a temporary measure that usually lasts only a few days to a few weeks, enough to give the plaintiff time to prepare for a more comprehensive hearing on a preliminary injunction. Courts will grant a TRO only if the plaintiff demonstrates that they are likely to succeed on the merits of their case and that there is no adequate remedy at law.

TROs are powerful tools, but they are short-lived. If the plaintiff cannot convert the TRO into a preliminary injunction, the relief is temporary and may not provide the long-term protection the plaintiff seeks. Courts exercise discretion in granting TROs, recognizing that they may disrupt the defendant's business operations and impose burdens even before the allegations are fully tested.

## 6.4.2. Preliminary Injunctions

A preliminary injunction is another form of interim relief granted before trial, but unlike a TRO, it is issued after a hearing in which both parties have the opportunity to present evidence. A preliminary injunction is intended to prevent further harm while the case is pending and is generally more comprehensive than a TRO. Courts issue preliminary injunctions when the plaintiff demonstrates that there is a likelihood of success on the merits, that irreparable harm will occur if the injunction is not granted, and that the balance of hardships favors the plaintiff.

A preliminary injunction serves to protect the plaintiff's interests while the full case is litigated. The plaintiff must show that they have a strong case on the underlying merits of the trade secret claim: they must show not just that they may eventually win, but that the harm to their trade secret cannot be remedied by money damages alone. In addition, the court will consider whether the defendant will suffer undue harm from the injunction and whether the public interest would be served by granting the order.

In many trade secret cases, the harm caused by the unauthorized use or disclosure of the trade secret cannot be adequately measured in monetary terms. In these cases, the plaintiff is likely to succeed in obtaining a preliminary injunction, particularly if they can demonstrate that the continued use of the trade secret will undermine their competitive advantage and cause ongoing damage.

**"INEVITABLE DISCLOSURE" CAN JUSTIFY A PRELIMINARY INJUNCTION**

*PepsiCo, Inc. v. Redmond*
54 F.3d 1262 (7th Cir. 1995)

PepsiCo sought an injunction to prevent a former employee, Redmond, from working for Quaker Oats. The company argued that Redmond would inevitably use PepsiCo's confidential pricing strategies and marketing plans at Quaker. The court held that PepsiCo had shown a reasonable likelihood of success on the merits of its claim and granted the injunction. The court's decision was rooted in the inevitable disclosure doctrine, which allows for injunctive relief when it is shown that the defendant's new employment would almost certainly lead to the use of the plaintiff's trade secrets, even without direct disclosure.

### 6.4.3. Permanent Injunctions and Post-Trial Remedies

Once a court has fully adjudicated a trade secret misappropriation claim, it may issue a permanent injunction to stop further harm caused by the defendant's actions. A permanent injunction is typically issued after a trial and is meant to provide long-term protection to the plaintiff. Unlike temporary or preliminary injunctions, which are interim measures, a permanent injunction is intended to provide final relief after the court has determined that the defendant's conduct constitutes trade secret misappropriation.

A permanent injunction can include a range of remedies, including prohibiting the defendant from continuing to use or disclose the trade secret, requiring the return of confidential information, and barring the defendant from engaging in specific competitive activities for a designated period of time. The scope of the permanent injunction will depend on the facts of the case, including the nature of the trade secret, the extent of the defendant's misuse, and the potential harm to the plaintiff.

**AN ONGOING THREAT OF MISUSE CAN JUSTIFY A PERMANENT INJUNCTION**

*Bimbo Bakeries USA, Inc. v. Botticella*
613 F.3d 102 (3d Cir. 2010)

Bimbo Bakeries sought a permanent injunction to prevent Botticella, a former employee, from using or disclosing trade secrets related to the company's product formulations. The court granted the injunction, finding that the company had demonstrated that the former employee would use the confidential information in his new employment with a competitor. The court reasoned that the information was essential to Bimbo's success and that allowing the defendant to use it would cause irreparable harm to the company's competitive position.

In granting permanent injunctions, courts take into account both the defendant's role in the misappropriation and the potential ongoing harm to the plaintiff. A permanent injunction serves as a long-term safeguard, ensuring that the trade secrets are not further exploited. Courts also consider the public interest in preventing trade secret theft and promoting fair competition, particularly in cases where the defendant's actions have broader implications for the industry.

## 6.5. Monetary Remedies

While injunctive relief is often the most immediate remedy in trade secret litigation, monetary damages are central to any case involving misappropriation. Courts award damages to compensate the plaintiff for the harm caused by the misappropriation, to deter future misconduct, and, in some cases, to punish egregious behavior. Monetary remedies in trade secret cases are generally divided into three categories: actual loss, unjust enrichment, and reasonable royalty. Each category addresses a different aspect of the harm caused by the misappropriation and can be awarded independently or in combination, depending on the facts of the case.

The goal of damages is not just to compensate the plaintiff but also to ensure that the defendant does not benefit from its wrongful actions. Courts often look at the full extent of the defendant's misconduct and the economic advantage gained through misappropriation. In some cases, the plaintiff may not know the full extent of the loss, especially if the defendant has used the trade secrets to develop products that have already been marketed or sold. In such cases, courts may rely on expert testimony or other evidence to estimate the damages.

## 6.5.1. Actual Loss

Actual loss damages aim to compensate the plaintiff for the actual harm caused by the defendant's wrongful actions. This category of damages includes lost profits, damage to business relationships, and any other direct financial losses resulting from the misappropriation. In determining actual loss, courts look at how the misappropriation has harmed the plaintiff's competitive position, whether it has caused a loss of market share, and how the defendant's use of the trade secret has affected the plaintiff's ability to compete.

The plaintiff must prove the extent of its losses by presenting evidence of the economic value of the trade secret, the market conditions, and the amount of business or profit that was lost due to the misappropriation. In some cases, the plaintiff may need to show how the defendant's use of the trade secret allowed them to achieve a competitive advantage or to develop a competing product or service.

**LOST LICENSING VALUE CAN ESTABLISH ACTUAL LOSS DAMAGES**

*Bianco v. Globus Medical, Inc.*
30 F. Supp. 3d 565 (E.D. Tex. 2014)

Dr. Bianco disclosed a spinal implant concept to Globus Medical during discussions about possible collaboration. No agreement was reached, but Globus later commercialized a similar design. The court awarded damages based on the licensing value of the concept, recognizing that Dr. Bianco had lost the opportunity to license his idea to a competitor. The award was based on the potential economic benefit Bianco had lost due to Globus's use of his trade secret.

In *Bianco*, the court calculated actual loss damages by focusing on the licensing potential of the trade secret. This case demonstrates that when the harm caused by misappropriation is quantifiable—such as lost licensing opportunities or lost sales—actual loss damages can be substantial.

## 6.5.2. Unjust Enrichment

Unjust enrichment damages are intended to strip the defendant of any profits gained through the misappropriation of trade secrets. Unlike actual loss, which compensates the plaintiff for their direct harm, unjust enrichment seeks to eliminate any benefit the defendant gained from the wrongful use of the trade secret. This form of damages is meant to ensure that the defendant does not profit from their illegal actions.

In calculating unjust enrichment, courts look at the profits the defendant made as a result of using the trade secret, such as the value of products sold or services provided using the misappropriated information. The key question is whether the defendant's profits were directly tied to the use of the trade secret and whether those profits would have been earned without it.

**DEFENDANT'S PROFITS FROM MISAPPROPRIATION CAN BE AWARDED AS UNJUST ENRICHMENT**

*3M v. Pribyl*
259 F.3d 587 (7th Cir. 2001)

3M alleged that former employees had misappropriated proprietary trade secrets regarding manufacturing processes. The court awarded damages based on the defendant's unjust enrichment, recognizing that the defendant's sales of products developed using 3M's trade secrets represented an unfair profit gained through wrongful conduct. The court emphasized that the defendant should not benefit from the misappropriation.

In *3M v. Pribyl*, the court awarded unjust enrichment damages to 3M, focusing on the defendant's profits earned from the use of proprietary manufacturing processes. This case shows how courts calculate unjust enrichment damages: by looking at the benefit the defendant gained from the trade secrets and then determining a damages award sufficient to ensure that the defendant does not profit from its unlawful conduct.

## 6.5.3. Reasonable Royalty

In cases where actual loss and unjust enrichment are difficult to quantify, courts may award damages based on a reasonable royalty. A reasonable royalty is an amount that represents what the plaintiff would have received if the defendant had negotiated for the right to use the trade secret. This approach is often used when the plaintiff cannot establish actual loss or the defendant's profits; it provides a way to compensate the plaintiff based on the value of the trade secret.

Reasonable royalty damages are typically calculated based on expert testimony, industry standards, and hypothetical licensing negotiations. Courts may look at factors such as the plaintiff's actual licensing history, the market value of similar trade secrets, and the defendant's use of the trade secret in its products or services.

**MISAPPROPRIATION DAMAGES CAN BE ESTIMATED BY A "REASONABLE" ROYALTY**

*Mattel, Inc. v. MGA Entertainment, Inc.*
616 F.3d 904 (9th Cir. 2010)

In a battle over the Bratz dolls, Mattel alleged that MGA had used its trade secrets in the development of a competing line of dolls. The court awarded a reasonable royalty reflecting the licensing value of the trade secrets that Mattel would have earned had it licensed the information to MGA. The court relied on expert testimony to determine the value of the trade secrets in the context of the doll market.

In *Mattel v. MGA Entertainment*, the court awarded a reasonable royalty to Mattel for the misappropriation of trade secrets related to the development of dolls. This case illustrates how reasonable royalty damages can be applied when actual loss or unjust enrichment is difficult to measure, and it shows how courts use expert testimony to determine the value of the trade secret.

This section illustrates how courts determine the appropriate monetary remedy depending on the facts and circumstances of the case. Actual loss compensates the plaintiff for the harm caused by the defendant's actions, unjust enrichment removes the defendant's ill-gotten gains, and reasonable royalty damages fill the gap when other remedies are difficult to calculate.

## 6.6. Ex Parte Seizure

The UTSA provides a unique and powerful remedy for trade secret holders: the right to seek ex parte seizure of misappropriated trade secrets. This remedy allows the plaintiff to seize the defendant's property—such as documents, files, or electronic devices—before the defendant has an opportunity to contest the action. It is an extraordinary remedy, available only in specific and urgent circumstances. Ex parte seizure is typically sought when there is a risk that the defendant will destroy or conceal the trade secrets, or when immediate relief is necessary to prevent irreparable harm to the plaintiff's competitive position.

The DTSA sets out an eight-part test that must be satisfied before a court can grant ex parte seizure. These requirements are strict because of the severe nature of the remedy. Courts will only grant such orders if the plaintiff demonstrates that:

1. Immediate and irreparable harm would result from the misappropriation of the trade secret.
2. The plaintiff is likely to succeed on the merits of the trade secret claim.
3. The defendant would destroy or move the trade secrets unless the court intervenes immediately.
4. The seizure is necessary to prevent further misuse of the trade secrets.
5. The plaintiff has made reasonable efforts to preserve the confidentiality of the trade secret.
6. The plaintiff has provided sufficient information about the trade secret and the misappropriation.
7. The harm to the defendant from the seizure does not outweigh the harm to the plaintiff.
8. The plaintiff has provided an adequate bond to cover potential damages to the defendant.

These criteria reflect the exceptional nature of the seizure remedy. It is a drastic measure, which is why the law requires plaintiffs to prove an immediate need for relief that is backed by strong evidence of misappropriation and the likelihood of harm. Ex parte seizure is not typically used for routine trade secret disputes but for cases where the defendant's conduct has been egregious and time is of the essence.

### AN EX PARTE SEIZURE REQUIRES A STRONG SHOWING OF EXTRAORDINARY URGENCY

*Janssen Prods. L.P. v. Evenus Pharms. Labs. Inc.*
85 F.4th 147 (3d Cir. 2023)

Janssen Pharmaceuticals sought an ex parte seizure order to recover misappropriated trade secrets from Evenus Pharmaceuticals, alleging that Evenus was using confidential data related to drug formulations. The court denied the seizure, finding that Janssen had not shown the urgency or imminent risk required for such an extraordinary remedy. The decision reinforced the narrow application of ex parte seizure under the DTSA, emphasizing that it is available only in situations where the defendant's actions pose an immediate and irreparable threat to the plaintiff's business interests.

A court's decision to grant an ex parte seizure order is based on rigorous standards that plaintiffs must meet to obtain the remedy. While Janssen presented a strong case of misappropriation, the court found that the evidence did not meet the high threshold required for such drastic action. This case demonstrates how courts weigh the urgency of the situation and the potential harm to both the plaintiff and defendant before granting such an intrusive remedy.

Ex parte seizure is a powerful tool, but its application is limited. Plaintiffs who seek seizure orders must demonstrate not just that they have a valid claim but also that the defendant's actions are likely to cause immediate and irreparable harm. This remedy is used sparingly and is generally reserved for cases where there is clear evidence of concealment or destruction of trade secrets.

Even when the seizure order is granted, it is not a comprehensive solution. Once the information is seized, the plaintiff must still go through the normal litigation process to prove the existence of the trade secret, misappropriation, and the appropriate remedy. The seizure order serves as an emergency intervention, not as a final judgment in the case.

## 6.7. Attorneys' Fees and Enhanced Damages

In addition to compensating plaintiffs for their actual loss or unjust enrichment, trade secret law provides for the recovery of attorneys' fees and, in some cases, enhanced damages. These remedies are particularly relevant when the defendant's conduct is found to be willful, malicious, or otherwise egregious. The goal is to deter wrongful conduct and to ensure that trade secret owners are not penalized for having to bring a lawsuit to protect their secrets.

The UTSA and the DTSA both allow for the award of attorneys' fees in cases where the defendant's misappropriation is deemed willful and malicious. Courts are generally reluctant to award fees in trade secret cases, but when they do, it is often because the defendant's conduct has been particularly egregious or has involved bad-faith litigation tactics. Attorneys' fees serve as a deterrent and as a means of compensating the plaintiff for the expense of defending its rights.

In cases where the misappropriation was willful, courts may also award enhanced damages. Under the UTSA and the DTSA, enhanced damages can be awarded up to two times the amount of actual damages, provided the defendant's conduct was egregious. This means that if the defendant acted with knowledge that their actions were wrongful or with deliberate disregard for the plaintiff's rights, the court may increase the damages award to provide a stronger deterrent.

One example of a case where enhanced damages were awarded for willful conduct is *Amnet v. CrossCountry Mortgage*. In that case, the defendant was found to have knowingly misappropriated the plaintiff's trade secrets and to have engaged in bad-faith litigation tactics. As a result, the court awarded attorneys' fees and enhanced damages to the plaintiff. This case highlights how courts will use these remedies to punish defendants who act with disregard for the law and to prevent them from profiting from wrongful conduct.

**WILLFUL AND MALICIOUS MISAPPROPRIATION CAN TRIGGER ENHANCED DAMAGES**

*Amnet v. CrossCountry Mortgage*
2020 WL 3489317 (N.D. Ill. June 26, 2020)

Amnet accused CrossCountry Mortgage of misappropriating its proprietary mortgage underwriting software. The court found that CrossCountry had willfully misappropriated the software, and it awarded Amnet both attorneys' fees and enhanced damages. The court noted that CrossCountry had engaged in bad-faith litigation by attempting to delay the proceedings and avoid producing key evidence. The award of enhanced damages was aimed at punishing this conduct and deterring similar behavior in the future.

The award of attorneys' fees and enhanced damages emphasizes that trade secret law is not just about compensating the plaintiff for losses. It is also about ensuring that the defendant is not allowed to benefit from wrongdoing and to deter future violations. These remedies are particularly important in cases where the defendant's actions were not merely negligent but involved willful misconduct.

If the court finds that the defendant's behavior was particularly egregious or malicious, it may impose additional penalties as part of its judgment. This serves as a warning to potential defendants that misappropriating trade secrets or engaging in bad-faith litigation will have significant legal consequences beyond the standard damages award.

# 6.8. Criminal Enforcement

While trade secret misappropriation is primarily a civil matter, there are circumstances where the theft of trade secrets can lead to criminal prosecution under the Economic Espionage Act (EEA). The EEA criminalizes the theft or misappropriation of trade secrets with the intent to benefit a foreign government or to gain a competitive advantage. The law provides for significant penalties, including fines and imprisonment, for those found guilty of trade secret theft under criminal statutes.

The key difference between civil and criminal enforcement is the burden of proof. In criminal cases, the government must prove its case beyond a reasonable doubt, which is a higher standard than the "preponderance of the evidence" standard used in civil cases. This makes criminal enforcement more difficult to pursue. Criminal prosecution is typically reserved for cases involving large-scale theft, industrial espionage, or theft with foreign connections.

Under the EEA, penalties for criminal misappropriation can be severe. Individuals convicted under the Act can face up to 10 years in prison and fines up to $5 million. Organizations found guilty of violating the Act may face even larger penalties, including fines of up to $10 million or three times the value of the stolen trade secrets, whichever is greater. The EEA's criminal provisions are designed to serve as a deterrent, particularly in cases of economic espionage, where the theft of trade secrets can undermine national security or economic interests.

Although criminal enforcement is less common in trade secret cases, it plays an important role in deterring high-level theft, particularly when the defendant's conduct involves foreign governments or actors. The government may initiate a criminal investigation and prosecution independently of any civil case, or criminal charges may be brought alongside a civil claim.

### THE ECONOMIC ESPIONAGE ACT IMPOSES CRIMINAL LIABILITY FOR TRADE SECRET "THEFT"

*United States v. Aleynikov*
676 F.3d 71 (2d Cir. 2012)

In this case, Sergey Aleynikov, a former employee of Goldman Sachs, was convicted under the Economic Espionage Act for stealing proprietary computer code related to high-frequency trading algorithms. Aleynikov had downloaded the code to his personal computer before leaving the company, intending to use it for a future employer. The court found that the trade secrets in question were valuable to Goldman Sachs, and Aleynikov's actions were in violation of the EEA. His conviction was overturned on appeal due to technical issues in how the law was applied, but the case demonstrated the reach of criminal enforcement for trade secret theft.

The *Aleynikov* case illustrates the broad scope of the Economic Espionage Act and how it applies to high-level theft in the financial industry. It shows that criminal liability can attach even when the misappropriation is not immediately damaging to the original company, especially when the trade secret involved has substantial value in the industry or national security context.

The key advantage of criminal prosecution is the severity of the penalties. Criminal defendants face not only financial penalties but also the threat of imprisonment. This makes criminal enforcement an important tool for deterring large-scale theft and espionage. However, because the burden of proof in criminal cases is so high, the government typically only pursues criminal prosecution in cases of clear and egregious misconduct.

Criminal enforcement also intersects with civil trade secret claims in certain cases. It is not uncommon for a defendant who is facing civil litigation for trade secret misappropriation to also be prosecuted criminally, especially if the case involves foreign espionage or the theft of highly sensitive information. In these cases, the civil case may proceed independently of the criminal prosecution, but the potential for criminal penalties adds an additional layer of deterrence and consequence.

# 6.9. Strategic and Procedural Dynamics

In trade secret litigation, the legal arguments are only part of the story. The strategy behind the case—how and when to file, how to manage discovery, and how to present the evidence—can determine the outcome just as much as the substance of the claims. Trade secret cases often involve highly confidential and technical information, and the parties will battle not just over legal definitions but also over how the facts are framed and how the law is applied to the evidence.

One of the first strategic decisions involves venue and jurisdiction. This decision can affect the entire course of the case, from how quickly it moves through the court system to what rules govern the litigation. After filing, the litigation strategy continues with critical decisions about discovery—what evidence to pursue and how to protect confidential materials during the process. This section breaks down these strategic considerations and explains how to navigate them.

## 6.9.1. Venue and Jurisdiction

Choosing the right venue is critical in trade secret litigation. The rules that apply to trade secret claims can vary depending on the jurisdiction, and where a case is filed can significantly impact both procedural and substantive outcomes. For federal claims brought under the DTSA, venue is governed by the general federal venue statute, 28 USC § 1391. This means a DTSA claim may be brought in any federal district where a defendant resides or where a substantial part of the events giving rise to the claim occurred. While plaintiffs do not have unfettered discretion to choose any district court, they may still have some strategic flexibility in selecting among proper venues, for example, by favoring jurisdictions with experience in complex intellectual property litigation or those where the defendant has a business presence.

However, when a trade secret claim is brought under state law—such as under a state's adoption of UTSA—venue is determined by the relevant state's venue statutes and rules of civil procedure. Typically, venue is proper in the county or judicial district where the defendant resides, where the misappropriation occurred, or where the injury was sustained. However, trade secret owners should carefully evaluate not only the substantive law but also the local court's experience and receptivity to complex commercial or intellectual property cases, as some jurisdictions are more familiar with the nuances of trade secret law and may administer the litigation more effectively.

For example, in a case involving multiple jurisdictions—such as when the misappropriation took place in one state but the defendant operates nationally or internationally—the plaintiff may need to assess the convenience of the venue for their witnesses, the location of the evidence, and whether the chosen court has experience handling multijurisdictional litigation.

**STRATEGIC VENUE SELECTION CAN PROVIDE PROCEDURAL ADVANTAGES**

*Amgen, Inc. v. Sandoz Inc.*
791 F.3d 1313 (Fed. Cir. 2015)

In this case, Amgen sued Sandoz for trade secret misappropriation in relation to a biologic drug. The court found that Amgen had selected an appropriate venue for its case, emphasizing that the venue chosen had the proper jurisdiction and experience in handling complex intellectual property claims. The court's analysis demonstrated the strategic value of venue selection in IP litigation.

This case highlights the importance of making careful venue decisions early on. Strategic venue choices can impact procedural advantages, such as access to specialized judges or the speed with which the case progresses.

## 6.9.2. Discovery, Protective Orders, and Evidence Management

Discovery is a critical phase in trade secret litigation. Plaintiffs and defendants alike must be prepared to handle highly sensitive and confidential information, and the management of this data can determine whether the case proceeds smoothly or becomes bogged down in disputes over access and secrecy. Trade secret owners often face the challenge of ensuring that their confidential materials remain protected during discovery, particularly when they are shared with experts, consultants, or opposing counsel.

A protective order is essential in these cases. Courts routinely issue protective orders to ensure that confidential information disclosed during discovery is not misused or disclosed outside the bounds of the litigation. Protective orders pursuant to FRCP 26(c) can limit access to specific individuals (such as attorneys or experts) and establish protocols for how confidential documents should be handled, stored, and destroyed. Plaintiffs seeking a protective order must typically demonstrate that the information qualifies as a trade secret and that its disclosure would cause harm to their business.

Defendants may seek to limit the plaintiff's ability to review certain documents or restrict the plaintiff's access to specific confidential information, arguing that the documents are irrelevant or not properly protected under the trade secret claim. Courts are often tasked with balancing the need for full disclosure with the protection of sensitive materials. This makes effective evidence management a crucial aspect of trade secret litigation. Plaintiffs must ensure that they can prove their trade secret status with admissible evidence while minimizing the risk of improper disclosure.

### PROTECTIVE ORDERS CAN LIMIT DISCLOSURE DURING DISCOVERY

*Bimbo Bakeries USA, Inc. v. Botticella*
613 F.3d 102 (3d Cir. 2010)

In this case, Bimbo Bakeries sought to protect its trade secrets during discovery in a case involving former employees who disclosed confidential business plans. The court issued a protective order to limit the distribution of confidential documents to a select group of experts and attorneys. The decision reinforced the importance of managing sensitive materials during litigation to prevent further harm or misuse.

*Bimbo Bakeries*, an oft-cited case in trade secret law, highlights the practical necessity of securing protective orders during discovery. A well-managed discovery process helps ensure that confidential materials are not disclosed beyond the litigation team, and it reduces the likelihood of inadvertent disclosure.

## 6.9.3. Summary Judgment and Early Disposition

Trade secret cases are complex and often heavily reliant on factual disputes. However, there are instances where a case can be resolved before trial through summary judgment. In trade secret litigation, summary judgment motions typically arise when one party argues that the plaintiff has not met its burden of proof or that the defendant's actions do not qualify as misappropriation under the law.

Summary judgment motions are particularly important when the evidence is clear or when one party's claims fail to meet the necessary legal standards. For example, a plaintiff may fail to identify a protectable trade secret, or a defendant may demonstrate that they independently developed the alleged trade secret. In such cases, summary judgment can be used to eliminate claims that are factually unsupported.

**PLAINTIFFS MUST PROVE SECRECY-IN-FACT TO SURVIVE SUMMARY JUDGMENT**

*Airfacts, Inc. v. Amezaga*
909 F.3d 84 (4th Cir. 2018)

In this case, the court granted summary judgment in favor of the defendant because the plaintiff had not demonstrated that its data qualified as a trade secret. The court emphasized that without adequate evidence showing that the data was treated as confidential, the case could not proceed to trial. This decision illustrates the importance of strong factual evidence in trade secret litigation.

The *Airfacts* case highlights how summary judgment can serve as a tool for defendants in trade secret litigation. When plaintiffs fail to prove the basic elements of trade secret protection, including secrecy and reasonable efforts to protect the information, courts may dismiss the claim before trial.

## 6.9.4. Litigation Timing and Investigative Coordination

In trade secret litigation, timing is crucial. Once a trade secret is misappropriated, time is of the essence. The longer the defendant uses or discloses the trade secret, the greater the harm to the plaintiff's competitive position. Plaintiffs must act quickly to preserve evidence and secure injunctions. Courts are more likely to grant injunctive relief when the plaintiff can show that they acted swiftly upon discovering the misappropriation.

Timing is also important in managing the investigative process. Trade secret claims often involve complex technical details, and both sides may rely on expert testimony to explain the value of the trade secret and how it was misappropriated. Ensuring that investigations are thorough but not overly prolonged is critical to maintaining momentum in the litigation. Coordination among legal teams, forensic experts, and internal stakeholders helps ensure that all relevant evidence is gathered and preserved in a timely manner.

**UNREASONABLE DELAY CAN JEOPARDIZE INJUNCTIVE RELIEF**

*Janssen Prods. L.P. v. Evenus Pharms. Labs. Inc.*
85 F.4th 147 (3d Cir. 2023)

Janssen sought to recover misappropriated trade secrets related to drug formulation methods. However, the court found that Janssen had delayed its response and failed to take action quickly enough to mitigate the harm. This delay weakened its case for immediate injunctive relief. The court's decision highlighted the importance of timely litigation and investigation in protecting trade secrets.

The *Janssen* case underscores the critical role that timing plays in trade secret litigation. Delays in taking action, especially in seeking protective relief or notifying the court of misappropriation, can significantly damage the plaintiff's chances of success.

## 6.10. Enforcement Plans as Reasonable Steps

Trade secret enforcement is a dynamic process that hinges on both legal principles and practical realities. Unlike intellectual property rights that are granted automatically, trade secrets are only protected when the owner takes reasonable steps to preserve their confidentiality. The protection provided by the law is not absolute, and the measures required to keep secrets safe are not static—they evolve with the nature of the information, the business environment, and the relationships through which the secrets flow. Enforcement of trade secret rights reflects not only the value of the information at issue but also the strength of the systems in place to safeguard it.

In this chapter, we have explored the core tools for enforcing trade secrets: proving the existence of a trade secret, understanding the legal definitions of misappropriation, securing remedies through injunctive relief and damages, and managing the strategic dynamics of the litigation process. We have also examined the procedural hurdles that plaintiffs face in ensuring that their claims survive early dismissal, including the necessity of proving secrecy, value, and reasonable efforts to maintain confidentiality.

One key takeaway from this chapter is that enforcement does not exist in a vacuum. The effectiveness of a trade secret lawsuit is deeply connected to the protection efforts that precede it. The ability to prove a trade secret claim rests not just on legal arguments but also on the robustness of the company's protection system. Courts will evaluate whether the trade secret was treated as such at every stage, from internal policies to contractual agreements to the technical systems used to restrict access. When those protections are weak or inconsistent, even the most valid claim of misappropriation can falter.

As we transition to the next chapter, it is important to consider that trade secret protection is not just a legal issue. It is a strategic one—a combination of legal frameworks, technical infrastructure, business policies, and company culture. Building a robust Trade Secret Protection Plan (TSPP) requires a multidisciplinary approach. The TSPP is not merely a set of legal documents. It is a blueprint for how a company treats its confidential information. It involves clear communication across departments; coordination among legal, technical, and business teams; and a commitment to upholding confidentiality at every level of the organization.

# Chapter 7

# The Living TSPP: Sustaining and Adapting Trade Secret Protection

Throughout this book, you have been building a house for your trade secrets: laying a foundation, erecting walls, and installing systems to keep your most valuable knowledge secure. You have learned how to identify secrets, assess risks, and implement safeguards. You have drafted policies, trained employees, and operationalized a TSPP that works in practice. In short, you have acted as the builder and the technician by making sure each circuit connects and every door locks.

Now, this chapter invites you to become the architect and the structural engineer. It asks not just how trade secret protection works but also why it works. Why does the law require "reasonable efforts"? Why do courts favor injunctions in some cases and damages in others? Why do some NDAs enforce secrecy, while others collapse under scrutiny? These are not just philosophical questions. They define the outer limits of what your TSPP can do.

Legal protection for trade secrets does not come from formality alone. It comes from courts' seeing genuine, continuous effort—and that standard is rooted in theory as much as practice. The "reasonable efforts" requirement, for instance, reflects policy tradeoffs between innovation and competition, flexibility and fairness. Likewise, enforcement strategy draws on foundational debates about property rules and liability rules, while organizational design raises questions about whether secrecy is a control mechanism or a learned routine.

This chapter introduces those debates, not as abstract theory but rather as the scaffolding behind the legal rules and business strategies you have already encountered. Each section surfaces a core tension and then explores how courts, scholars, and organizations have tried to resolve it. You will meet influential voices in the field, from economists to doctrinal theorists, and see how their work shapes (and complicates) everyday decisions about NDAs, training, audits, and AI governance.

By the end of this chapter, you will not just know how to protect secrets—you will understand why some strategies work, why others backfire, and how to craft a TSPP that evolves with both law and context. You will be ready to lead the conversation, not just follow the checklist.

# 7.1. The Lifecycle of a TSPP: Why Static Plans Fail

A Trade Secret Protection Plan (TSPP) is not a checklist to complete and file away. It is a living system that must evolve with your organization and adapt to new risks, technologies, and business realities. The law recognizes this by requiring "reasonable efforts" to maintain secrecy—not just at the outset, but continuously over time. To understand why, we must look beyond black-letter law to the legal doctrines, economic incentives, and policy debates that shape trade secret protection across its lifecycle.

At the heart of trade secret law is the principle that protection is not automatic. Courts require companies to take visible, active steps to safeguard their secrets—not as a formality but instead as a core doctrinal requirement. This emphasis on ongoing effort is grounded in economic theory. Brian Love argues that trade secret law's primary function is not simply to reward innovation but also to prevent firms from relying on socially harmful self-help measures. Without legal recourse, companies might over-invest in secrecy or impose sweeping contractual restrictions that chill mobility and stifle competition. The "reasonable efforts" standard encourages systematic, transparent protection strategies that balance the interests of innovators, competitors, and the public.

**THEORY IN TENSION**

*Does Trade Secret Law Incentivize or Chill Innovation?*

Trade secret law is often defended on incentive grounds: by allowing firms to keep valuable know-how confidential, the law encourages investment in innovation and knowledge creation. This logic is well-articulated in Landes and Posner's The Economic Structure of Intellectual Property Law, where they describe trade secrets as a "second-best" mechanism for capturing returns on innovation without the disclosure costs of patenting.

But that same logic has critics. David Levine and Joshua Sarnoff argue that overbroad trade secret protection can create an "information paradox": firms may assert secrecy over information that should be disclosed, such as public health data or algorithmic bias, thereby undermining transparency, competition, and accountability. In their view, trade secrecy can function as a regulatory shield impeding disclosure obligations that serve the public interest.

This tension has real implications for TSPP design. Should a firm treat all business knowledge as protectable or reserve that label for genuinely proprietary innovations? The more aggressive the claim, the greater the legal risk, especially if disclosure becomes necessary or compelled. A living TSPP must walk this line: strong enough to protect valuable assets but mindful of the public-facing risks of overreach.

Levine and Sarnoff's work regards how trade secret law can undermine public interests, and it highlights the complexity of the "information paradox": it is often impossible to determine whether information should be protected or disclosed without revealing it first. This dilemma sits at the heart of many contemporary disputes, from biased algorithms to toxic spills. Courts and policymakers are more sensitive than ever to the risks of overprotection, making vigilance and adaptability essential.

Empirical work reinforces these insights. Ivan Png's study of UTSA adoption finds that stronger trade secret protections correlate with increased R&D investment in secrecy-intensive sectors. This evidence supports the view that robust TSPPs do more than check a box. They fuel innovation and reinforce competitive advantage.

To remain effective, TSPPs must be treated as adaptive systems. They should be revisited after business pivots, technology shifts, or leadership changes. Training must continue beyond onboarding, and organizations must establish feedback channels to learn from incidents and near-misses. These are not "nice to haves." They're part of what makes a TSPP legally credible.

Consider a fast-growing startup. At first, the founders implement NDAs, restrict access to code, and manage everything themselves. But as they scale, new hires arrive, access spreads, and the original protocols fray. When litigation arises, a court finds no consistent pattern of reasonable effort, and the company loses protection. This scenario is not uncommon. It shows that even strong initial controls will fail without follow-through.

By rooting your TSPP in both doctrine and economic logic, you move from rote compliance to strategic stewardship. You are not just enforcing secrecy. You are building an adaptive, defensible system that evolves with your organization.

## 7.2. Property Rules, Liability Rules, and Enforcement Strategy

Trade secret law is distinguished not only by its requirement for ongoing protection but also by the nature of the remedies it provides. A foundational distinction, first articulated by Guido Calabresi and A. Douglas Melamed, divides legal entitlements into property rules and liability rules. This framework is essential for understanding how courts enforce trade secret rights and how companies should design enforcement strategies.

Property rules allow the owner to prevent unauthorized use through injunctive relief. In trade secret law, this means that courts will often issue injunctions to stop misappropriation, recognizing that once a secret is disclosed, its value may be irretrievably lost. The law's preference for property rules reflects its concern with preserving exclusivity and the irreparable harm that can result from disclosure.

Liability rules, by contrast, permit unauthorized use so long as the user pays compensation. While trade secret doctrine generally defaults to property rules, liability rules emerge in certain contexts: compulsory licensing during emergencies, strategic business resolutions, or government-imposed access mandates. In such cases, courts may award damages instead of blocking use altogether.

**REMEDY DESIGN**

*Should Misappropriation Be Stopped or Just Compensated?*

Trade secret remedies operate on a spectrum between property rules (injunctions barring use) and liability rules (damages for unauthorized use). Calabresi and Melamed's foundational framework explains this dichotomy: property rules protect exclusivity, while liability rules permit use with compensation. In trade secret law, courts traditionally favor property rules—issuing injunctions to prevent irreversible harm from disclosure.

But this preference faces modern challenges. Levine and Sarnoff argue that in public health crises (e.g., vaccine production shortages), liability rules should temporarily override secrecy to allow compulsory licensing of trade secrets. Similarly, Mark Lemley notes that in fast-moving tech markets, injunctions can stifle follow-on innovation by locking competitors out of foundational knowledge.

For TSPP designers, the implication is strategic: anticipate when to seek exclusion and when to seek compensation. Property rules remain the default for core secrets—but liability rules may better serve the firm when public interest demands access, when litigation lags behind market cycles, or when secrecy is only partially breached. In each case, enforcement planning must reflect both doctrinal realities and ethical considerations.

This distinction has direct implications for TSPP enforcement. Companies should plan for swift action to stop unauthorized use—knowing that courts generally favor injunctions—but also prepare for liability-based outcomes in exceptional cases. Effective strategy requires documenting misappropriation clearly and early, selecting forums that align with enforcement goals, and evaluating whether monetary remedies may sometimes serve business or public needs better than exclusion.

Recent scholarship has explored the boundaries of this framework. Levine and Sarnoff, for example, argue for broader use of liability rules in cases where secrecy thwarts urgent public needs—like access to pharmaceutical know-how or environmental disclosures. Their work underscores the need for flexibility and ethical sensitivity in trade secret enforcement.

By grounding enforcement in this property/liability framework, TSPPs become not only more doctrinally sound but also more responsive to real-world risks and opportunities. The goal is not simply to protect secrets at all costs but to deploy legal tools strategically, in ways that align with both legal trends and market realities.

## 7.3. The Contract–Trade Secret Interface

Trade secret protection is deeply intertwined with the use of contracts, which serve as both evidence of protection efforts and substantive tools for defining rights and obligations. Deepa Varadarajan's scholarship provides a foundational framework for understanding this complex relationship by showing how contracts shape and are shaped by trade secret doctrine. Unlike patents, which are publicly registered, trade secrets gain legal recognition in part through contractual signals that demarcate confidential information. Well-drafted contracts identify specific secrets, establish clear duties for recipients, and create an evidentiary trail that proves reasonable protection efforts. Courts increasingly rely on such contracts as objective proof that information was treated as secret and thus satisfies the "reasonable efforts" requirement under the UTSA.

Recent empirical work by Camilla Hrdy and Christopher Seaman highlights a troubling trend: many nondisclosure agreements (NDAs) function as *de facto* noncompetes by prohibiting the use or disclosure of information far beyond what is legally protectable as a trade secret. Their analysis of federal cases reveals that a substantial majority of NDAs contain no temporal or geographic limits, cover "any information disclosed" rather than genuine secrets, and impose injunctive relief and attorneys' fees for breaches. Such overbroad contracts risk invalidation under emerging legal standards, and the Federal Trade Commission's 2023 rule banning noncompetes explicitly warns that NDAs may be scrutinized as unlawful restraints on trade if they effectively prevent workers from seeking employment.

### PRIVATE AGREEMENTS

#### *Tools for Trade Secret Protection or Unlawful Restraints on Trade?*

Contracts play a pivotal role in trade secret protection, but what exactly do they do? Deepa Varadarajan argues that confidentiality agreements serve a critical notice function: they define what counts as a trade secret, establish expectations of confidentiality, and provide objective evidence that the information was treated as valuable and secret. On this view, contracts help satisfy the "reasonable efforts" requirement under the Uniform Trade Secrets Act not by replacing the statute but rather by reinforcing it.

But what happens when contracts go too far? Camilla Hrdy and Christopher Seaman's empirical analysis of over 100 federal NDA cases reveals widespread overreach. Many agreements prohibit the use or disclosure of any information, lack temporal or geographic limits, and automatically impose injunctive relief—even when the information would not qualify as a trade secret under law. Such terms, they argue, risk transforming NDAs into *de facto* noncompetes that chill employee mobility and undermine the legitimacy of trade secret enforcement.

TSPP implication: The contract–trade secret interface must be tight but not taut. Strong NDAs support trade secret claims, but overbroad ones invite legal challenges, regulatory scrutiny, and employee resistance. Practitioners should ensure that agreements track real secrets, use defensible language, and evolve with doctrine and enforcement trends.

These contractual tensions are especially acute when secrecy claims intersect with employee mobility—a flashpoint for courts, policymakers, and practitioners alike.

**SECRECY AND MOBILITY**

*Where Do a Company's Rights End and an Employee's Rights Begin?*

Trade secret law protects firms. But what about the people who power them? The tension between secrecy and labor mobility lies at the heart of modern innovation policy. Camilla Hrdy argues that secrecy creates value by enabling firms to commercialize ideas without disclosure, but it can also chill mobility and stifle knowledge spillovers that drive innovation ecosystems.

Deepa Varadarajan similarly warns that overreliance on secrecy, especially when coupled with broad NDAs and noncompetes, can morph into a tool for employee lock-in. Courts have long struggled with the inevitable disclosure doctrine, where employers seek to block former employees from working for competitors on the theory that they'll "inevitably" use trade secrets. While some courts accept this logic, others see it as an end-run around employment freedom.

For TSPP design, the message is clear: trade secret enforcement should not become a proxy for unlawful labor restrictions. NDAs should be narrowly tailored to actual secrets, not to generalized experience, and should avoid language that implies permanent information ownership. Managers must be trained to distinguish between lawful protection and anti-competitive constraints. The best defense is often clarity—firms must define what is protectable, document what is disclosed, and respect what employees legitimately carry with them: their skills, memories, and know-how.

In practice, organizations must carefully navigate the contract–trade secret interface to ensure their protection strategies are both legally defensible and operationally effective. This means drafting contracts that are precise in their definitions, tailored to genuine trade secrets, and regularly reviewed to avoid overreach. It also means educating employees about their obligations and the limits of confidentiality, and maintaining clear documentation of all protection efforts. The goal is to reinforce statutory trade secret boundaries rather than attempt to expand them beyond what the law will support.

Consider, for example, a software company protecting its AI training methodologies. Rather than relying on blanket NDAs, it implements a tiered approach to confidentiality agreements, with different levels of restriction based on the sensitivity and business value of the information. Public algorithms might be unrestricted, proprietary datasets subject to limited use prohibitions, and core architecture protected by permanent nondisclosure provisions. Dynamic annexes listing current secrets and sunset provisions for expiring restrictions help ensure that contracts remain aligned with both legal requirements and business needs. This approach exemplifies Varadarajan's ideal of contracts that "reinforce rather than replace" statutory trade secret boundaries.

Key TSPP contract practices include drafting contracts with precise definitions of trade secrets and clear duties for recipients, regularly auditing and updating confidentiality agreements to avoid overreach, educating employees on their obligations and the limits of confidentiality, and maintaining documentation of all protection efforts to satisfy evidentiary requirements.

## 7.4. Organizational Culture and Continuous Improvement

Trade secret protection cannot be sustained by legal doctrine and contracts alone. The most robust Trade Secret Protection Plans (TSPPs) are those that are embedded within the organizational culture, supported by leadership, and continuously improved through feedback and adaptation. Recent scholarship in management science and organizational behavior underscores the importance of culture, routines, and incentives in making secrecy a living process rather than a static set of rules.

Leadership plays a pivotal role in setting the tone for trade secret protection. When executives and managers consistently signal the importance of confidentiality—through their words, actions, and resource allocation—employees are more likely to internalize the value of secrecy and adhere to established protocols. This cultural reinforcement is often more effective than formal policies alone, as it creates a shared understanding and collective responsibility for protecting sensitive information.

Continuous improvement is another hallmark of effective TSPPs. Organizations must create feedback loops that allow employees to report concerns, suggest improvements, and learn from incidents or near-misses. Regular audits, training sessions, and "after-action" reviews of breaches or vulnerabilities help ensure that protection strategies remain current and responsive to changing circumstances. Ionela Andreicovici, Sara Bormann, and Katharina Hombach's research demonstrates that strong trade secret enforcement can actually facilitate internal information sharing by reducing the perceived risk of leaks, thus leading to greater integration and better decision-making within the firm. This finding challenges the assumption that secrecy necessarily leads to organizational silos; instead, it suggests that a well-designed TSPP can balance confidentiality with the need for collaboration and innovation.

### ORGANIZATIONAL CULTURE OF SECRECY

*Legal Shield or Dynamic Capability?*

What makes a Trade Secret Protection Plan (TSPP) stick? Many companies treat secrecy as a compliance matter—write the NDA, limit access, check the box. But organizational scholars argue that lasting protection comes not from static controls but from secrecy-as-capability: a routinized, adaptive practice woven into the fabric of how firms operate.

Oleksandra Ozcan and colleagues argue that trade secret protection should be understood as a form of dynamic capability—a firm's ability to sense risks, seize opportunities, and reconfigure internal processes in response to change. On this view, secrecy is not a static shield; it is an organizational routine that evolves through training, reflection, and learning from incidents.

A related study by Ionela Andreicovici, Sara Bormann, and Katharina Hombach challenges the assumption that secrecy stifles collaboration. Their empirical research shows that robust trade secret enforcement can enhance internal information sharing by reducing fear of leaks, thereby enabling greater integration across departments. Instead of fostering silos, a well-designed TSPP builds trust, clarifies expectations, and supports knowledge flow.

For TSPP implementation, the implication is clear: Secrecy must be lived, not just documented. This means investing in onboarding, recurring training, incident debriefs, and leadership modeling. It also means designing systems that support transparency within the firm while keeping sensitive material insulated from external threats. In short: to protect secrets, build habits.

Yet strong culture alone is not enough. As organizations grow, routines that once ensured secrecy can erode, thus raising the stakes for scale-conscious design.

### SECRECY AT SCALE

*Can Trade Secret Protection Plans Survive Organizational Growth?*

Building a TSPP is hard. Scaling it is harder. As firms grow—especially through hiring, acquisitions, remote work, or international expansion—systems that once worked can quietly fail. Trade secrets may be documented but not updated, or disclosed to vendors without proper controls, or forgotten by new managers focused on speed over structure.

Organizational research shows that rapid growth increases the likelihood of "protection gaps": inconsistencies in training, contract enforcement, or access controls that undermine legal protection. Even companies with strong startup protocols often see these systems degrade under the pressure of scaling, especially when legal teams lag behind hiring or product expansion.

Andreicovici, Bormann, and Hombach's empirical study reveals that secrecy enforcement can actually foster internal information sharing—but only when firms proactively manage integration. This supports a key insight from Ozcan et al.: secrecy routines must evolve alongside the firm's dynamic capabilities. What worked with 20 engineers and 1 founder-lawyer may collapse at 200 employees across 3 countries.

The lesson for TSPPs is simple but vital: growth is a vulnerability. Trade secret protection must scale with systems, not individuals. That means updating contracts during onboarding surges, refreshing access protocols after reorgs, and auditing cultural gaps between legacy teams and new hires. The best secrecy plans are modular, adaptable, and built for institutional—not just founder-level—memory.

In short, leaders must model confidentiality, organizations must invest in continual feedback and training, and protection plans must balance secrecy with collaboration. When these principles are embedded into organizational routines, trade secret protection becomes more than just a legal obligation. It becomes a durable source of competitive advantage.

# 7.5. Technology, Globalization, and Emerging Challenges

The landscape of trade secret protection is being reshaped by rapid advances in technology and the increasing globalization of business. These developments introduce new risks, complicate enforcement, and require organizations to continuously adapt their Trade Secret Protection Plans (TSPPs) to remain effective. Camilla Hrdy's recent work on generative AI illustrates how digital transformation is creating novel challenges for trade secret law and practice. Companies are now grappling with the risks of inadvertent disclosure through AI tools, the need to protect AI-generated outputs that may not qualify for other forms of intellectual property protection, and the use of restrictive contracts to safeguard technology even when traditional legal protections fall short. This evolving environment demands that TSPPs include robust technical controls, such as encryption, access logs, and closed-source architectures, alongside clear contractual terms that define permissible and impermissible uses of sensitive information.

### SECRECY WITH ARTIFICIAL INTELLIGENCE

#### *Can Firms Leverage Innovative Technologies Without Giving Up Intellectual Property Rights?*

Can you keep a secret—when your algorithm cannot? As generative AI transforms business operations, it also exposes fault lines in trade secret doctrine. Camilla Hrdy warns that AI systems both rely on and produce trade secrets, but their opacity raises hard questions: How do we protect the data that trains the model, the model itself, and its outputs, especially when disclosure is integral to their use?

Hrdy identifies a doctrinal gap: Trade secret law demands reasonable efforts to maintain secrecy, yet AI tools are often integrated into cloud-based workflows or accessed through third-party APIs, especially when tools are embedded in external platforms or accessed via cloud vendors outside the firm's control. This makes traditional confidentiality measures fragile, if not impossible. When models "leak" outputs or training data, courts may conclude that no secret was effectively kept. In response, companies increasingly turn to restrictive licenses or end-user agreements to compensate for legal gaps—which raises concerns that private governance may override democratic accountability.

This doctrinal uncertainty echoes broader policy debates. Mark Lemley cautions that courts should be skeptical of "secrecy through obscurity"—particularly when AI systems produce outputs with significant social consequences, such as hiring recommendations or predictive policing. In such contexts, transparency and accountability may outweigh the interests of secrecy.

For TSPP designers, the implication is clear: secrecy strategies must now account for technical realities, legal ambiguities, and growing public demand for explainability. Rather than treating AI-generated assets as wholly private and controllable, firms should clarify what information is genuinely protectable, adopt safeguards that match deployment environments, and be prepared to justify their secrecy claims when systems affect rights, markets, or reputations.

Globalization further complicates the picture. As firms expand across borders, they must navigate a patchwork of legal regimes with differing standards for trade secret protection, enforcement mechanisms, and cultural attitudes toward secrecy.

Marta Arroyabe and colleagues' empirical research on mergers and acquisitions shows that while strong trade secret protection can make companies more attractive to domestic buyers, it may also create information asymmetries that deter foreign acquirers, who may prefer minority investments or additional safeguards to mitigate risk. These findings highlight the importance of tailoring TSPPs to the specific legal and business environments in which a firm operates, and of ensuring that protection strategies are communicated clearly to partners, suppliers, and employees across jurisdictions.

### GLOBALIZATION AND RISK

*Can International Firms Protect Trade Secrets Across Legal Borders?*

In a global economy, trade secrets do not stay put. They cross borders with employees, contractors, suppliers, and servers—often faster than legal protections can follow. For companies operating internationally, the biggest challenge is legal asymmetry: what counts as a protectable secret and how it is enforced varies dramatically across jurisdictions.

Empirical research by Marta Arroyabe and colleagues illustrates this challenge in the M&A context. Their findings show that stronger trade secret regimes can both attract and deter investment: domestic buyers value secrecy enforcement, but foreign acquirers may avoid deals if legal uncertainty or disclosure risks create asymmetries in bargaining power or integration. Secrecy, in other words, affects deal structure.

Comparative scholars, like Tanya Aplin and Jorge Contreras, also highlight diverging approaches. The US model, especially post-DTSA, emphasizes aggressive enforcement and broad injunctions. In contrast, EU regimes often weigh secrecy against transparency, competition, and labor rights. China's recent reforms increase penalties for theft but still lack procedural parity, which raises due process concerns for foreign firms.

Implication for TSPPs: Global firms must design protection plans that travel well. This means mapping legal environments in every country of operation, tailoring controls and contracts to local norms and enforceability, and centralizing enforcement readiness. A strong home jurisdiction strategy can serve as a legal anchor, even when misappropriation occurs abroad.

Internal information integration is another area where technology and globalization intersect. Andreicovici, Bormann, and Hombach's work demonstrates that robust trade secret enforcement can actually enhance internal collaboration by reducing the perceived risk of leaks, thus allowing employees to share knowledge more freely within the organization. Modern IT systems, such as enterprise management platforms with secure access controls, enable firms to balance the need for secrecy with the benefits of internal transparency and innovation. This approach is particularly valuable for multinational companies, where information must flow efficiently across geographically dispersed teams while remaining protected from external threats.

In summary, the combined forces of digital transformation and legal asymmetry demand that TSPPs be not only secure but also portable and explainable. They must be able to withstand both technical disruption and global legal complexity. By designing protection plans that anticipate new risks, accommodate diverse legal environments, and leverage technological solutions, firms can ensure that their most valuable assets remain protected in an increasingly complex and interconnected world.

## 7.6. Synthesis: The Living TSPP

The preceding sections have demonstrated that sustaining a Trade Secret Protection Plan (TSPP) is not a matter of drafting a single document or implementing a set of static controls. Instead, it is a dynamic, living process that must evolve with the organization, its environment, and the broader legal and technological landscape. This synthesis weaves together the doctrinal, economic, organizational, and operational insights that make a TSPP not just legally defensible but also strategically essential.

At the core of trade secret law is the requirement for "reasonable efforts" to maintain secrecy—a standard that is inherently dynamic and context-dependent. As Sharon Sandeen and others have shown, this requirement reflects a deliberate policy choice: trade secrets are not protected in the abstract but rather only when the owner demonstrates ongoing vigilance and adaptation. The law does not reward mere intent; it requires visible, consistent action. Yet what counts as "reasonable" is far from settled. See Box.

### THE "REASONABLE EFFORTS" DOCTRINE

*Flexible Standard or Unpredictable Risk?*

What counts as "reasonable efforts" to protect trade secrets? The statute is famously vague, leaving courts significant discretion to decide whether a company's safeguards are sufficient to trigger legal protection. Traditionally, courts looked for evidence of access controls, NDAs, and training programs. But recent cases show a growing divergence: some courts apply the standard flexibly, adapting to modern business realities, while others demand rigorous formalities, creating uncertainty for firms.

Sharon Sandeen argues that this ambiguity is not a bug but a feature. The "reasonable efforts" standard is context-sensitive by design, meant to balance flexibility for innovators with fairness to third parties. Yet that very flexibility creates risk. As Camilla Hrdy notes, what qualifies as "reasonable" may shift as norms evolve or high-profile breaches raise judicial expectations. Courts have become more skeptical of boilerplate policies and more attentive to implementation: a pristine NDA is no substitute for sloppy onboarding or ignored training.

Meanwhile, AI-driven compliance systems and data-loss prevention tools are reshaping what courts might expect. If technical safeguards are widely available but not used, is that still "reasonable"? As expectations rise, what was defensible yesterday may be deficient tomorrow.

Implication for TSPP design: The "reasonable efforts" threshold is a moving target. Protection plans must be tailored, documented, and—above all—lived. Judges are increasingly asking not just what rules were written but also how they were applied. To future-proof your secrets, treat compliance as an evolving conversation, not a checklist.

Economically, trade secret protection is justified as a means of encouraging innovation by allowing companies to capture the value of their investments in knowledge and know-how. Landes and Posner's analysis underscores that trade secrecy is a "second-best" mechanism for innovation, one that balances the need for disclosure and competition with the value of secrecy. Further supporting this view is recent empirical work by Ivan Png demonstrating that stronger trade secret protection leads to increased R&D investment in sectors where secrecy is most valuable. This feedback loop—where robust protection encourages innovation, and innovation in turn increases the value of protection—reinforces the importance of a living, evolving TSPP.

From an organizational perspective, the effectiveness of a TSPP depends on its integration into the daily rhythms and culture of the company. Oleksandra Ozcan and colleagues emphasize that trade secret strategies must be treated as part of a firm's dynamic capabilities because they require continuous sensing of threats, seizing of opportunities, and reconfiguring of resources. Ionela Andreicovici, Sara Bormann, and Katharina Hombach's research adds that strong trade secret enforcement can actually facilitate internal information sharing by reducing the perceived risk of leaks, which can lead to greater integration and better decision-making within the firm. This challenges the assumption that secrecy necessarily leads to silos; instead, it suggests that a well-designed TSPP can balance confidentiality with the need for collaboration and innovation.

The contract–trade secret interface further illustrates the importance of ongoing adaptation. Deepa Varadarajan's work highlights how contracts serve both evidentiary and substantive roles in trade secret law and create a web of obligations that courts scrutinize when assessing whether secrecy was maintained. Camilla Hrdy and Christopher Seaman's empirical analysis warns against the overuse of nondisclosure agreements that function as de facto noncompetes, underscoring the need for contracts that are precise, tailored, and regularly reviewed to avoid overreach.

Technological change and globalization add further layers of complexity. Camilla Hrdy's analysis of generative AI and digital transformation shows how new technologies introduce novel risks and require updated protection strategies. Marta Arroyabe and colleagues' research on mergers and acquisitions demonstrates that strong trade secret protection can make companies more attractive to domestic buyers but also may create information asymmetries that deter foreign acquirers, highlighting the need for tailored, context-sensitive protection strategies.

In practice, these insights mean that a TSPP must be both robust and flexible. It must be grounded in a clear understanding of what information is valuable and why and be implemented through a combination of technical, legal, and cultural controls. It must be regularly reviewed and updated to reflect changes in the business, the legal environment, and the threat landscape. And it must be embedded in the culture of the organization so that protection is not just a compliance exercise but a shared responsibility.

Across the literature and doctrine, a set of recurring tensions emerges: the need to balance secrecy and disclosure, to align statutory baselines with contractual safeguards, to promote innovation without chilling competition, and to protect employer interests without restricting employee mobility. These tensions are not flaws in the system—they are the design. They reflect the policy tradeoffs and institutional judgments that give trade secret law its shape. They also reflect the real-world complexity faced by organizations that operate across borders, integrate new technologies, and rely on intangible knowledge as a core asset.

Ultimately, a living TSPP is not a checklist or a formality. It is a strategic response to the law's demand for visible, continuous effort. It is a system that evolves with the organization, learns from experience, and is sustained by the people who live it. By grounding your protection plan in these legal, economic, organizational, and ethical principles, you move beyond compliance and into stewardship, where you can build a trade secret strategy that is not only defensible but also durable.

## *Conclusion: The Partner-Level Mindset*

As you reach the end of this chapter, reflect on the path you have taken—from the concrete work of building a Trade Secret Protection Plan to the exploration of deeper foundations of law, economics, organizational design, and strategic foresight. The shift from practice to theory is not just academic. It marks the difference between executing instructions and leading with purpose.

A living TSPP is not a static document or compliance checklist. It is a dynamic system that evolves with your business, anticipates new risks, and withstands legal scrutiny. Its strength lies in continuous attention and adaptation. It is grounded in the law's demand for "reasonable efforts," shaped by policy choices and incentive structures, and sustained by culture, governance, and technical systems.

This chapter has invited you to step into the role of architect—where you are not just wiring the circuits but designing the structure. You now understand why the foundation matters, what pressures it must bear, and how its integrity affects everything above it. With this knowledge, you are prepared to engage in partner-level conversations that shape not simply policies, compliance, and protection but also strategy, leadership, and stewardship.

## References

Sharon K. Sandeen, *The Evolution of Trade Secret Law and Why Courts Commit Error When They Do Not Follow the Uniform Trade Secrets Act*, 33 Hamline L. Rev. 493 (2010).

Guido Calabresi & A. Douglas Melamed, *Property Rules, Liability Rules, and Inalienability: One View of the Cathedral*, 85 Harv. L. Rev. 1089 (1972).

Oleksandra Ozcan, David Pickernell, & Paul Trott, *A Trade Secrets Framework and Strategic Approaches*, IEEE Transactions on Eng'g Mgmt. (2023), https://doi.org/10.1109/TEM.2023.3285292.

Ionela Andreicovici, Sara Bormann, & Katharina Hombach, *Trade Secret Protection and the Integration of Information Within Firms*, TRR 266 Working Paper No. 78 (2023), https://dx.doi.org/10.2139/ssrn.3881395.

Tun-Jen Chiang, *The Economic Structure of Trade Secret Law*, George Mason L. & Econ. Res. Paper No. 25-03 (2024), https://dx.doi.org/10.2139/ssrn.4942344.

William M. Landes & Richard A. Posner, The Economic Structure of Intellectual Property Law (Harv. Univ. Press 2003).

David S. Levine & Joshua D. Sarnoff, *Compelling Trade Secret Sharing*, 74 Hastings L. J. 987 (2023).

I. P. L. Png, *Secrecy and Patents: Theory and Evidence from the Uniform Trade Secrets Act*, 2(3) Strategy Science 176–93, https://doi.org/10.1287/stsc.2017.0035.

Mark A. Lemley, *The Surprising Virtues of Treating Trade Secrets as IP Rights*, 61 Stan. L. Rev. 311 (2010).

Deepa Varadarajan, *The Trade Secret–Contract Interface*, 103 Iowa L. Rev. 1543 (2018).

Camilla A. Hrdy & Christopher B. Seaman, *Beyond Trade Secrecy: Confidentiality Agreements That Act Like Noncompetes*, 133 Yale L.J. 669 (2024).

Camilla A. Hrdy, *The Value in Secrecy*, 91 FORDHAM L. REV. 129 (2022).

Charles Tait Graves, *Intentionality in Trade Secret Law*, 39 BERKELEY TECH. L. J. 721 (2024), https://doi.org/10.15779/Z38000018N.

Camilla A. Hrdy, *Keeping ChatGPT a Trade Secret While Selling It Too*, 40 BERKELEY TECH. L.J. 75 (2025), https://doi.org/10.15779/Z38FT8DM21.

Christopher Buccafusco, Jonathan S. Masur, & Deepa Varadarajan, *Trade Secrecy's Information Paradox*, 100 NOTRE DAME L. REV ___ (forthcoming 2025), https://dx.doi.org/10.2139/ssrn.4909857.

Camilla A. Hrdy, Christopher Buccafusco, Jonathan S. Masur, & Deepa Varadarajan, *Does Trade Secrecy Have an "Information Paradox"?*, RUTGERS INST. FOR INFO. POL'Y & L. (2025), https://perma.cc/PRN9-2ENV.

Marta F. Arroyabe, Christopher Grimpe, & Katrin Hussinger, *Safeguarding Secrets, Shaping Acquisitions: Trade Secret Protection and the Role of Distance Between Acquirer and Target*, ZEW—Ctr. for European Econ. Res. Discussion Paper No. 25-007 (2025), https://dx.doi.org/10.2139/ssrn.5116418.

Tanya Aplin, *The Interface Between Trade Secrets and Freedom of Expression: A Comparative Perspective*, *in* THE LAW OF TRADE SECRETS (Rochelle C. Dreyfuss & Katherine J. Strandburg eds., Edward Elgar Publ'g 2d ed. 2020).

Jorge L. Contreras, *Trade Secret*, CONCURRENCES GLOBAL DICTIONARY OF COMPETITION LAW (2023).

# Epilogue

Trade secret law is easy to underestimate. It lacks the dramatic disclosures of patent prosecution, the public visibility of trademarks, or the rhetorical force of copyright infringement. It rarely commands headlines. And yet, in practice, it governs some of the most critical and contested knowledge in the modern economy.

What makes trade secret law powerful is also what makes it quiet. It protects not what is made public but rather what is kept back. It rewards diligence over disclosure, continuity over formality. And it reflects a core insight about innovation in real life: that many of the most valuable ideas are not made in the lab or filed in the PTO. Rather, they are developed informally, iterated privately, and safeguarded through shared effort and institutional design.

This book aims to bridge two domains: the legal doctrine that defines trade secret misappropriation and the organizational realities that shape how secrecy is maintained. The result is a body of law that demands both theoretical precision and practical engagement. It is doctrinally rich, culturally contingent, and deeply embedded in the structures of trust, discretion, and control that govern economic life.

Students of trade secret law must learn to think in multiple registers. They must read cases with care but also ask how those disputes arose: what broke down inside the company, what assumptions were unexamined, what controls failed, and what stories convinced the court. They must learn to advise clients not just on litigation risk but also on information architecture. They must see law as a living constraint—and a framework for proactive design.

The future of trade secret law will not be determined solely in courtrooms. It will be shaped in boardrooms, design studios, codebases, supply chains, and Zoom calls. It will depend on how companies manage internal knowledge, how they govern external collaborations, and how they adapt to emerging threats that legal doctrine may not yet fully anticipate.

What this area of law demands, more than anything, is judgment. Judgment about what is worth protecting. Judgment about how to protect it. And judgment about what trade secret law is truly trying to preserve—not secrecy for its own sake but rather the integrity of innovation in a world where trust is scarce and knowledge moves fast.

That is the work. And that is the invitation.

# Appendix A

# [New Hampshire] Uniform Trade Secrets Act

## 1. Definitions

As used in this chapter, unless the context requires otherwise:

I. "Improper means" includes theft, bribery, misrepresentation, breach or inducement of a breach of a duty to maintain secrecy, or espionage through electronic or other means.

II. "Misappropriation" means:

(a) Acquisition of a trade secret of another by a person who knows or has reason to know that the trade secret was acquired by improper means; or

(b) Disclosure or use of a trade secret of another without express or implied consent by a person who:

(1) Used improper means to acquire knowledge of the trade secret; or

(2) At the time of disclosure or use, knew or had reason to know that his knowledge of the trade secret was derived from or through a person who had utilized improper means to acquire it; or acquired under circumstances giving rise to a duty to maintain its secrecy or limit its use; or derived from or through a person who owed a duty to the person seeking relief to maintain its secrecy or limit its use; or

(3) Before a material change of his position, knew or had reason to know that it was a trade secret and that knowledge of it had been acquired by accident or mistake.

III. "Person" means a natural person, corporation, business trust, estate, trust, partnership, association, joint venture, government, governmental subdivision or agency, or any other legal or commercial entity.

IV. "Trade secret" means information, including a formula, pattern, compilation, program, device, method, technique, or process, that:

(a) Derives independent economic value, actual or potential, from not being generally known to, and not being readily ascertainable by proper means by, other persons who can obtain economic value from its disclosure or use; and

(b) Is the subject of efforts that are reasonable under the circumstances to maintain its secrecy.

## 2. Injunctive Relief

I. Actual or threatened misappropriation may be enjoined. Upon application to the court, an injunction shall be terminated when the trade secret has ceased to exist, but the injunction may be continued for an additional reasonable period of time in order to eliminate commercial advantage that otherwise would be derived from the misappropriation.

II. In exceptional circumstances, an injunction may condition future use upon payment of a reasonable royalty for no longer than the period of time for which use could have been prohibited. Exceptional circumstances include, but are not limited to, a material and prejudicial change of position prior to acquiring knowledge or reason to know of misappropriation that renders a prohibitive injunction inequitable.

III. In appropriate circumstances, affirmative acts to protect a trade secret may be compelled by court order.

## 3. Damages

I. Except to the extent that a material and prejudicial change of position prior to acquiring knowledge or reason to know of misappropriation renders a monetary recovery inequitable, a complainant is entitled to recover damages for misappropriation. Damages can include both the actual loss caused by misappropriation and the unjust enrichment caused by misappropriation that is not taken into account in computing actual loss. In lieu of damages measured by any other methods, the damages caused by misappropriation may be measured by imposition of liability for a reasonable royalty for a misappropriator's unauthorized disclosure or use of a trade secret.

II. If willful and malicious misappropriation exists, the court may award exemplary damages in an amount not exceeding twice any award made under paragraph I.

## 4. Attorneys' Fees

The court may award reasonable attorneys' fees to the prevailing party when:

I. A claim of misappropriation is made in bad faith;

II. A motion to terminate an injunction is made or resisted in bad faith; or

III. Willful and malicious misappropriation exists.

## 5. Preservation of Secrecy

In an action under this chapter, a court shall preserve the secrecy of an alleged trade secret by reasonable means, which may include granting protective orders in connection with discovery proceedings, holding in-camera hearings, sealing the records of the action, and ordering any person involved in the litigation not to disclose an alleged trade secret without prior court approval.

## 6. Statute of Limitations

An action for misappropriation shall be brought within 3 years after the misappropriation is discovered or by the exercise of reasonable diligence should have been discovered. For the purposes of this section, a continuing misappropriation constitutes a single claim.

## 7. Effect on Other Law

I. Except as provided in paragraph II, this chapter displaces conflicting tort, restitutionary, and other law of this state providing civil remedies for misappropriation of a trade secret.

II. This chapter shall not affect:

(a) Contractual remedies, whether or not based upon misappropriation of a trade secret;

(b) Other civil remedies that are not based upon misappropriation of a trade secret; or

(c) Criminal remedies, whether or not based upon misappropriation of a trade secret.

## 8. Uniformity of Application and Construction

This chapter shall be applied and construed to effectuate its general purpose to make uniform the law with respect to the subject of this chapter among states enacting it.

## 9. Short Title

This chapter may be cited as the New Hampshire [Uniform] Trade Secrets Act.

# Appendix B

# Defend Trade Secrets Act (DTSA, 18 USC § 1836 et seq.)

(a) The Attorney General may, in a civil action, obtain appropriate injunctive relief against any violation of this chapter 18 USCS §§ 1831 et seq.

(b) Private civil actions.

(1) In general. An owner of a trade secret that is misappropriated may bring a civil action under this subsection if the trade secret is related to a product or service used in, or intended for use in, interstate or foreign commerce.

(2) Civil seizure.

(A) In general.

(i) Application. Based on an affidavit or verified complaint satisfying the requirements of this paragraph, the court may, upon ex parte application but only in extraordinary circumstances, issue an order providing for the seizure of property necessary to prevent the propagation or dissemination of the trade secret that is the subject of the action.

(ii) Requirements for issuing order. The court may not grant an application under clause (i) unless the court finds that it clearly appears from specific facts that—

(I) an order issued pursuant to Rule 65 of the Federal Rules of Civil Procedure or another form of equitable relief would be inadequate to achieve the purpose of this paragraph because the party to which the order would be issued would evade, avoid, or otherwise not comply with such an order;

(II) an immediate and irreparable injury will occur if such seizure is not ordered;

(III) the harm to the applicant of denying the application outweighs the harm to the legitimate interests of the person against whom seizure would be ordered of granting the application and substantially outweighs the harm to any third parties who may be harmed by such seizure;

(IV) the applicant is likely to succeed in showing that—

(aa) the information is a trade secret; and

(bb) the person against whom seizure would be ordered—

(AA) misappropriated the trade secret of the applicant by improper means; or

(BB) conspired to use improper means to misappropriate the trade secret of the applicant;

(V) the person against whom seizure would be ordered has actual possession of—

(aa) the trade secret; and

(bb) any property to be seized;

(VI) the application describes with reasonable particularity the matter to be seized and, to the extent reasonable under the circumstances, identifies the location where the matter is to be seized;

(VII) the person against whom seizure would be ordered, or persons acting in concert with such person, would destroy, move, hide, or otherwise make such matter inaccessible to the court, if the applicant were to proceed on notice to such person; and

(VIII) the applicant has not publicized the requested seizure.

(B) Elements of order. If an order is issued under subparagraph (A), it shall—

(i) set forth findings of fact and conclusions of law required for the order;

(ii) provide for the narrowest seizure of property necessary to achieve the purpose of this paragraph and direct that the seizure be conducted in a manner that minimizes any interruption of the business operations of third parties and, to the extent possible, does not interrupt the legitimate business operations of the person accused of misappropriating the trade secret;

(iii)

(I) be accompanied by an order protecting the seized property from disclosure by prohibiting access by the applicant or the person against whom the order is directed, and prohibiting any copies, in whole or in part, of the seized property, to prevent undue damage to the party against whom the order has issued or others, until such parties have an opportunity to be heard in court; and

(II) provide that if access is granted by the court to the applicant or the person against whom the order is directed, the access shall be consistent with subparagraph (D);

(iv) provide guidance to the law enforcement officials executing the seizure that clearly delineates the scope of the authority of the officials, including—

(I) the hours during which the seizure may be executed; and

(II) whether force may be used to access locked areas;

(v) set a date for a hearing described in subparagraph (F) at the earliest possible time, and not later than 7 days after the order has issued, unless the party against whom the order is directed and others harmed by the order consent to another date for the hearing, except that a party against whom the order has issued or any person harmed by the order may move the court at any time to dissolve or modify the order after giving notice to the applicant who obtained the order; and

(vi) require the person obtaining the order to provide the security determined adequate by the court for the payment of the damages that any person may be entitled to recover as a result of a wrongful or excessive seizure or wrongful or excessive attempted seizure under this paragraph.

(C) Protection from publicity. The court shall take appropriate action to protect the person against whom an order under this paragraph is directed from publicity, by or at the behest of the person obtaining the order, about such order and any seizure under such order.

(D) Materials in custody of court.

(i) In general. Any materials seized under this paragraph shall be taken into the custody of the court. The court shall secure the seized material from physical and electronic access during the seizure and while in the custody of the court.

(ii) Storage medium. If the seized material includes a storage medium, or if the seized material is stored on a storage medium, the court shall prohibit the medium from being connected to a network or the Internet without the consent of both parties, until the hearing required under subparagraph (B)(v) and described in subparagraph (F).

(iii) Protection of confidentiality. The court shall take appropriate measures to protect the confidentiality of seized materials that are unrelated to the trade secret information ordered seized pursuant to this paragraph unless the person against whom the order is entered consents to disclosure of the material.

(iv) Appointment of special master. The court may appoint a special master to locate and isolate all misappropriated trade secret information and to facilitate the return of unrelated property and data to the person from whom the property was seized. The special master appointed by the court shall agree to be bound by a non-disclosure agreement approved by the court.

(E) Service of order. The court shall order that service of a copy of the order under this paragraph, and the submissions of the applicant to obtain the order, shall be made by a Federal law enforcement officer who, upon making service, shall carry out the seizure under the order. The court may allow State or local law enforcement officials to participate, but may not permit the applicant or any agent of the applicant to participate in the seizure. At the request of law enforcement officials, the court may allow a technical expert who is unaffiliated with the applicant and who is bound by a court-approved non-disclosure agreement to participate in the seizure if the court determines that the participation of the expert will aid the efficient execution of and minimize the burden of the seizure.

(F) Seizure hearing.

(i) Date. A court that issues a seizure order shall hold a hearing on the date set by the court under subparagraph (B)(v).

(ii) Burden of proof. At a hearing held under this subparagraph, the party who obtained the order under subparagraph (A) shall have the burden to prove the facts supporting the findings of fact and conclusions of law necessary to support the order. If the party fails to meet that burden, the seizure order shall be dissolved or modified appropriately.

(iii) Dissolution or modification of order. A party against whom the order has been issued or any person harmed by the order may move the court at any time to dissolve or modify the order after giving notice to the party who obtained the order.

(iv) Discovery time limits. The court may make such orders modifying the time limits for discovery under the Federal Rules of Civil Procedure as may be necessary to prevent the frustration of the purposes of a hearing under this subparagraph.

(G) Action for damage caused by wrongful seizure. A person who suffers damage by reason of a wrongful or excessive seizure under this paragraph has a cause of action against the applicant for the order under which such seizure was made, and shall be entitled to the same relief as is provided under section 34(d)(11) of the Trademark Act of 1946 (15 U.S.C. 1116(d)(11)). The security posted with the court under subparagraph (B)(vi) shall not limit the recovery of third parties for damages.

(H) Motion for encryption. A party or a person who claims to have an interest in the subject matter seized may make a motion at any time, which may be heard ex parte, to encrypt any material seized or to be seized under this paragraph that is stored on a storage medium. The motion shall include, when possible, the desired encryption method.

(3) Remedies. In a civil action brought under this subsection with respect to the misappropriation of a trade secret, a court may—

(A) grant an injunction—

(i) to prevent any actual or threatened misappropriation described in paragraph (1) on such terms as the court deems reasonable, provided the order does not—

(I) prevent a person from entering into an employment relationship, and that conditions placed on such employment shall be based on evidence of threatened misappropriation and not merely on the information the person knows; or

(II) otherwise conflict with an applicable State law prohibiting restraints on the practice of a lawful profession, trade, or business;

(ii) if determined appropriate by the court, requiring affirmative actions to be taken to protect the trade secret; and

(iii) in exceptional circumstances that render an injunction inequitable, that conditions future use of the trade secret upon payment of a reasonable royalty for no longer than the period of time for which such use could have been prohibited;

(B) award—

(i)

(I) damages for actual loss caused by the misappropriation of the trade secret; and

(II) damages for any unjust enrichment caused by the misappropriation of the trade secret that is not addressed in computing damages for actual loss; or

(ii) in lieu of damages measured by any other methods, the damages caused by the misappropriation measured by imposition of liability for a reasonable royalty for the misappropriator's unauthorized disclosure or use of the trade secret;

(C) if the trade secret is willfully and maliciously misappropriated, award exemplary damages in an amount not more than 2 times the amount of the damages awarded under subparagraph (B); and

(D) if a claim of the misappropriation is made in bad faith, which may be established by circumstantial evidence, a motion to terminate an injunction is made or opposed in bad faith, or the trade secret was willfully and maliciously misappropriated, award reasonable attorney's fees to the prevailing party.

(c) Jurisdiction. The district courts of the United States shall have original jurisdiction of civil actions brought under this section.

(d) Period of limitations. A civil action under subsection (b) may not be commenced later than 3 years after the date on which the misappropriation with respect to which the action would relate is discovered or by the exercise of reasonable diligence should have been discovered. For purposes of this subsection, a continuing misappropriation constitutes a single claim of misappropriation.

# Appendix C

# Economic Espionage Act (EEA, including § 1831 and § 1832)

(a) In general. Whoever, intending or knowing that the offense will benefit any foreign government, foreign instrumentality, or foreign agent, knowingly—

(1) steals, or without authorization appropriates, takes, carries away, or conceals, or by fraud, artifice, or deception obtains a trade secret;

(2) without authorization copies, duplicates, sketches, draws, photographs, downloads, uploads, alters, destroys, photocopies, replicates, transmits, delivers, sends, mails, communicates, or conveys a trade secret;

(3) receives, buys, or possesses a trade secret, knowing the same to have been stolen or appropriated, obtained, or converted without authorization;

(4) attempts to commit any offense described in any of paragraphs (1) through (3); or

(5) conspires with one or more other persons to commit any offense described in any of paragraphs (1) through (3), and one or more of such persons do any act to effect the object of the conspiracy,

shall, except as provided in subsection (b), be fined not more than $5,000,000 or imprisoned not more than 15 years, or both.

(b) Organizations. Any organization that commits any offense described in subsection (a) shall be fined not more than the greater of $10,000,000 or 3 times the value of the stolen trade secret to the organization, including expenses for research and design and other costs of reproducing the trade secret that the organization has thereby avoided.

## 18 USC § 1832.
## Theft of trade secrets

(a) Whoever, with intent to convert a trade secret, that is related to a product or service used in or intended for use in interstate or foreign commerce, to the economic benefit of anyone other than the owner thereof, and intending or knowing that the offense will, injure any owner of that trade secret, knowingly—

(1) steals, or without authorization appropriates, takes, carries away, or conceals, or by fraud, artifice, or deception obtains such information;

(2) without authorization copies, duplicates, sketches, draws, photographs, downloads, uploads, alters, destroys, photocopies, replicates, transmits, delivers, sends, mails, communicates, or conveys such information;

(3) receives, buys, or possesses such information, knowing the same to have been stolen or appropriated, obtained, or converted without authorization;

(4) attempts to commit any offense described in paragraphs (1) through (3); or

(5) conspires with one or more other persons to commit any offense described in paragraphs (1) through (3), and one or more of such persons do any act to effect the object of the conspiracy,

shall, except as provided in subsection (b), be fined under this title or imprisoned not more than 10 years, or both.

(b) Any organization that commits any offense described in subsection (a) shall be fined not more than the greater of $5,000,000 or 3 times the value of the stolen trade secret to the organization, including expenses for research and design and other costs of reproducing the trade secret that the organization has thereby avoided.

## 18 USC § 1833. Exceptions to prohibitions

(a) In general. This chapter [18 USCS §§ 1831 et seq.] does not prohibit or create a private right of action for—

(1) any otherwise lawful activity conducted by a governmental entity of the United States, a State, or a political subdivision of a State; or

(2) the disclosure of a trade secret in accordance with subsection (b).

(b) Immunity from liability for confidential disclosure of a trade secret to the government or in a court filing.

(1) Immunity. An individual shall not be held criminally or civilly liable under any Federal or State trade secret law for the disclosure of a trade secret that—

(A) is made—

(i) in confidence to a Federal, State, or local government official, either directly or indirectly, or to an attorney; and

(ii) solely for the purpose of reporting or investigating a suspected violation of law; or

(B) is made in a complaint or other document filed in a lawsuit or other proceeding, if such filing is made under seal.

(2) Use of trade secret information in anti-retaliation lawsuit. An individual who files a lawsuit for retaliation by an employer for reporting a suspected violation of law may disclose the trade secret to the attorney of the individual and use the trade secret information in the court proceeding, if the individual—

(A) files any document containing the trade secret under seal; and

(B) does not disclose the trade secret, except pursuant to court order.

(3) Notice.

(A) In general. An employer shall provide notice of the immunity set forth in this subsection in any contract or agreement with an employee that governs the use of a trade secret or other confidential information.

(B) Policy document. An employer shall be considered to be in compliance with the notice requirement in subparagraph (A) if the employer provides a cross-reference to a policy document provided to the employee that sets forth the employer's reporting policy for a suspected violation of law.

(C) Non-compliance. If an employer does not comply with the notice requirement in subparagraph (A), the employer may not be awarded exemplary damages or attorney fees under subparagraph (C) or (D) of section 1836(b)(3) [18 USCS § 1836(b)(3)] in an action against an employee to whom notice was not provided.

(D) Applicability. This paragraph shall apply to contracts and agreements that are entered into or updated after the date of enactment of this subsection [enacted May 11, 2016].

(4) Employee defined. For purposes of this subsection, the term "employee" includes any individual performing work as a contractor or consultant for an employer.

(5) Rule of construction. Except as expressly provided for under this subsection, nothing in this subsection shall be construed to authorize, or limit liability for, an act that is otherwise prohibited by law, such as the unlawful access of material by unauthorized means.

# 18 USC § 1834. Criminal forfeiture

Forfeiture, destruction, and restitution relating to this chapter [18 USCS §§ 1831 et seq.] shall be subject to section 2323 [18 USCS § 2323], to the extent provided in that section, in addition to any other similar remedies provided by law.

# 18 USC § 1835.
# Orders to preserve confidentiality

(a) In general. In any prosecution or other proceeding under this chapter [18 USCS §§ 1831 et seq.], the court shall enter such orders and take such other action as may be necessary and appropriate to preserve the confidentiality of trade secrets, consistent with the requirements of the Federal Rules of Criminal and Civil Procedure, the Federal Rules of Evidence, and all other applicable laws. An interlocutory appeal by the United States shall lie from a decision or order of a district court authorizing or directing the disclosure of any trade secret.

(b) Rights of trade secret owners. The court may not authorize or direct the disclosure of any information the owner asserts to be a trade secret unless the court allows the owner the opportunity to file a submission under seal that describes the interest of the owner in keeping the information confidential. No submission under seal made under this subsection may be used in a prosecution under this chapter [18 USCS §§ 1831 et seq.] for any purpose other than those set forth in this section, or otherwise required by law. The provision of information relating to a trade secret to the United States or the court in connection with a prosecution under this chapter [18 USCS §§ 1831 et seq.] shall not constitute a waiver of trade secret protection, and the disclosure of information relating to a trade secret in connection with a prosecution under this chapter [18 USCS §§ 1831 et seq.] shall not constitute a waiver of trade secret protection unless the trade secret owner expressly consents to such waiver.

# 18 USC § 1837.
# Applicability to conduct outside the United States

This chapter [18 USCS §§ 1831 et seq.] also applies to conduct occurring outside the United States if—

(1) the offender is a natural person who is a citizen or permanent resident alien of the United States, or an organization organized under the laws of the United States or a State or political subdivision thereof; or

(2) an act in furtherance of the offense was committed in the United States.

# 18 USC § 1838.
# Construction with other laws

Except as provided in section 1833(b) [18 USCS § 1833(b)], this chapter [18 USCS §§ 1831 et seq.] shall not be construed to preempt or displace any other remedies, whether civil or criminal, provided by United States Federal, State, commonwealth, possession, or territory law for the misappropriation of a trade secret, or to affect the otherwise lawful disclosure of information by any Government employee under section 552 of title 5 (commonly known as the Freedom of Information Act).

# 18 USC § 1839.
# Definitions

As used in this chapter [18 USCS §§ 1831 et seq.]—

(1) the term "**foreign instrumentality**" means any agency, bureau, ministry, component, institution, association, or any legal, commercial, or business organization, corporation, firm, or entity that is substantially owned, controlled, sponsored, commanded, managed, or dominated by a foreign government;

(2) the term "**foreign agent**" means any officer, employee, proxy, servant, delegate, or representative of a foreign government;

(3) the term "**trade secret**" means all forms and types of financial, business, scientific, technical, economic, or engineering information, including patterns, plans, compilations, program devices, formulas, designs, prototypes, methods, techniques, processes, procedures, programs, or codes, whether tangible or intangible, and whether or how stored, compiled, or memorialized physically, electronically, graphically, photographically, or in writing if—

(A) the owner thereof has taken reasonable measures to keep such information secret; and

(B) the information derives independent economic value, actual or potential, from not being generally known to, and not being readily ascertainable through proper means by, another person who can obtain economic value from the disclosure or use of the information;

(4) the term "**owner**", with respect to a trade secret, means the person or entity in whom or in which rightful legal or equitable title to, or license in, the trade secret is reposed;

(5) the term "**misappropriation**" means—

(A) acquisition of a trade secret of another by a person who knows or has reason to know that the trade secret was acquired by improper means; or

(B) disclosure or use of a trade secret of another without express or implied consent by a person who—

(i) used improper means to acquire knowledge of the trade secret;

(ii) at the time of disclosure or use, knew or had reason to know that the knowledge of the trade secret was—

(I) derived from or through a person who had used improper means to acquire the trade secret;

(II) acquired under circumstances giving rise to a duty to maintain the secrecy of the trade secret or limit the use of the trade secret; or

(III) derived from or through a person who owed a duty to the person seeking relief to maintain the secrecy of the trade secret or limit the use of the trade secret; or

(iii) before a material change of the position of the person, knew or had reason to know that—

(I) the trade secret was a trade secret; and

(II) knowledge of the trade secret had been acquired by accident or mistake;

(6) the term "**improper means**"—

(A) includes theft, bribery, misrepresentation, breach or inducement of a breach of a duty to maintain secrecy, or espionage through electronic or other means; and

(B) does not include reverse engineering, independent derivation, or any other lawful means of acquisition; and

(7) the term "**Trademark Act of 1946**" means the Act entitled "An Act to provide for the registration and protection of trademarks used in commerce, to carry out the provisions of certain international conventions, and for other purposes, approved July 5, 1946 (15 U.S.C. 1051 et seq.) (commonly referred to as the 'Trademark Act of 1946' or the 'Lanham Act')".

# Appendix D
# Glossary

This comprehensive taxonomy organizes key concepts related to trade secrets into structured categories and provides a concise hashtag for each concept. It prioritizes US trade secret law (covering statutes like the UTSA and DTSA, case law, and enforcement) while also including important international frameworks (e.g., WIPO guidelines, the EU Trade Secrets Directive, GDPR impacts, Chinese trade secret laws). Beyond legal doctrines, it encompasses business strategies (like licensing and M&A), operational practices (security measures and employee training), technical threats (cybersecurity and AI risks), and policy issues (compliance and competition law). Each hashtag is defined with its meaning, importance, and context, and cross-references to related hashtags are provided to show how these concepts intersect.

## General Concepts and Importance

This category lays the groundwork by defining what trade secrets are, why confidentiality is critical, and how these concepts drive competitive advantage and innovation.

**#TS**—Trade secrets: Confidential business information (such as formulas, processes, customer lists, or strategies) that derives its economic value from not being generally known and is maintained through active, reasonable measures. A company's trade secrets are the cornerstone of its competitive edge, as they enable innovation and cost leadership. To preserve this protection, businesses must implement security protocols, train employees, and use legal tools like #NDA. This term connects closely with #FactualSecrecy and #ConfidentialInfo, ensuring that information remains exclusive and supports the firm's overall #CompetitiveAdvantage.

**#FactualSecrecy**—Information claimed as a trade secret is genuinely unknown or not easily accessible to others. Even if some components derive from public sources, the specific combination or details must remain hidden. This concept reinforces trade secrets (#TS) by emphasizing that true secrecy is essential for maintaining competitive advantage and is directly linked to #ConfidentialInfo.

**#IP**—Intellectual property: The broad legal category encompassing patents, copyrights, trademarks, and trade secrets. Within this framework, trade secrets (#TS) do not require registration but depend on maintaining confidentiality. Each method of protection offers distinct advantages and limitations, and #IP connects all these forms under one umbrella for an organization's innovation strategy.

**#ConfidentialInfo**—Confidential information: Refers to any nonpublic data that a business actively protects to preserve its competitive edge. Proper handling—e.g., using #NDAs, access restrictions, and secure systems—is essential to maintain information as a trade secret (#TS) and uphold a #CompetitiveAdvantage.

**#CompetitiveAdvantage**—Competitive advantage is the benefit a company gains when it outperforms its rivals, often by leveraging exclusive or confidential information. Trade secrets (#TS) and confidential information (#ConfidentialInfo) are key drivers of this advantage because they prevent competitors from easily replicating successful methods.

**#InfoMosaic**—Information mosaic: Describes the concept that a unique combination or arrangement of data points can form a protectable trade secret even if individual elements are public. This unique compilation supports a company's #CompetitiveAdvantage by creating value that remains confidential.

**#IntangibleAssets**—These are non-physical resources—like trade secrets, patents, and goodwill—that hold significant economic value. For trade secrets (#TS), their value lies in the exclusive knowledge they represent and is maintained through continuous protection efforts and secrecy.

**#Innovation**—Refers to the creation of new products, processes, or ideas that are often safeguarded as trade secrets. By protecting innovative concepts as #TS rather than immediately disclosing them (e.g. via patents), companies maintain an edge over competitors and reinforce their #CompetitiveAdvantage through a culture of proactive confidentiality.

# Legal Frameworks and Statutes

This category covers the statutory and doctrinal foundations for trade secret protection, detailing US and international laws that govern trade secrets and the legal tools available for enforcement.

## US Doctrines

Key statutes and legal principles in US law define trade secrets and provide remedies for misappropriation.

**#UTSA**—Uniform Trade Secrets Act: A model statute adopted by most US states that clearly defines trade secrets and misappropriation and requires information to be protected by #ReasonableMeasures. The UTSA is foundational for establishing legal rights over #TS at the state level and guides private enforcement (it also provides standard remedies, like damages and #Injunctions).

**#DTSA**—Defend Trade Secrets Act: A federal law that provides a nationwide cause of action for trade secret misappropriation and that aligns with the UTSA while offering unique remedies such as #ExParteSeizure. Enacted in 2016, it enhances protection of #TS by facilitating access to federal courts and ensuring consistency across state lines. The #DTSA also explicitly does not preempt state law, so plaintiffs can pursue both federal and state trade secret claims.

**#EEA**—Economic Espionage Act: A federal law that criminalizes the theft of trade secrets, especially when such misappropriation benefits foreign entities. The EEA targets deliberate acts of industrial or economic espionage and theft, reinforcing protection through criminal penalties for #CriminalTSTheft and complementing civil remedies under the #DTSA.

**#Misappropriation**—The wrongful acquisition, disclosure, or use of trade secrets without authorization. This core wrongful act underlies all trade secret disputes, giving rise to claims for both civil damages and, in some cases, criminal penalties (under statutes like the #EEA).

**#ImproperMeans**—Refers to illegal or unethical methods—such as theft, bribery, fraud, or espionage—used to obtain trade secrets. Demonstrating that a defendant used improper means is critical to a misappropriation claim, and it underscores the need for companies to take #ReasonableMeasures to safeguard their secrets (since proper means like independent discovery or #ReverseEngineering are legal).

**#IndependentDevelopment**—A defense whereby a defendant claims they created the information on their own, without relying on the plaintiff's trade secrets. It distinguishes genuine innovation from wrongful copying of #TS, and a showing of independent development will defeat a misappropriation claim.

**#InevitableDisclosure**—A doctrine suggesting that an employee with deep knowledge of trade secrets will unavoidably reveal or rely on them when joining a competitor. This principle has been used to justify #NonCompete agreements or injunctions preventing an employee from certain employment, and it directly impacts #EmployeeMobility in jurisdictions that recognize the doctrine.

**#Whistleblower**—Whistleblower protections (in the trade secret context) apply to employees who disclose a company's confidential information for the sole purpose of reporting legal violations (e.g., reporting fraud or wrongdoing to authorities or attorneys). Under the DTSA, such whistleblowers have immunity in certain circumstances, ensuring they are not penalized under trade secret laws if their disclosure was made in confidence and solely to report misconduct. This concept distinguishes legitimate whistleblowing from misappropriation and is linked to proper #EmployeeMobility (employees changing jobs should not take secrets, but they can report illegality).

**#EmployeeMobility**—Addresses the tension between an employee's right to change jobs and an employer's need to protect trade secrets (#TS). It is directly influenced by the doctrine of #InevitableDisclosure and the enforceability of agreements like #Non-Compete clauses. Law and public policy seek to balance free labor mobility with reasonable restrictions to prevent trade secret theft when employees move to competitors.

## International and Regional Frameworks

Statutory and treaty instruments that harmonize trade secret protection globally, establishing common minimum standards across jurisdictions.

**#EUTradeSecrets**—EU Trade Secrets Directive: An EU-wide directive (Directive (EU) 2016/943) that harmonizes trade secret laws among member states, ensuring consistent protection and enforcement practices for #TS across the European Union. It requires all EU countries to provide measures against unlawful acquisition, use, or disclosure of trade secrets, raising the baseline protection in regions that previously relied on disparate laws (such as the UK's breach of confidence or varying national statutes).

**#TRIPS**—Trade-Related Aspects of Intellectual Property Rights: A WTO agreement that sets minimum global standards for intellectual property protection, including trade secrets. TRIPS (particularly Article 39) influenced many countries' domestic laws (including guiding the principles in #UTSA and #DTSA) by requiring protection for "undisclosed information" that is secret, has commercial value because it is secret, and is subject to reasonable protective measures.

**#ParisConvention**—An international treaty (1883, as revised) providing baseline intellectual property protections and addressing unfair competition. While it primarily deals with patents, trademarks, etc., it indirectly supports the protection of trade secrets as part of the broader #IP framework through its general provisions against unfair competition (which member countries interpret to include trade secret misappropriation).

**#WIPO**—World Intellectual Property Organization: An international body that coordinates intellectual property policies worldwide and promotes best practices. WIPO provides guidance and resources that support trade secret protection principles (even though no single WIPO treaty focuses solely on trade secrets). It helps countries develop laws consistent with international standards and facilitates cooperation on IP issues, trade secrets included.

**#TradeSecretsDirective**—The formal EU mandate (another term for the EU Trade Secrets Directive) requiring member states to align their national trade secret laws. It ensures uniform definitions of trade secrets and remedies for misappropriation across Europe, reducing country-by-country discrepancies in protecting confidential information. (See also #EUTradeSecrets, which refers to this harmonized EU framework.)

**#USMCA**—United States–Mexico–Canada Agreement: A North American trade pact that includes strong provisions for protecting trade secrets, reinforcing domestic standards, and ensuring cross-border enforcement. The USMCA requires all three countries to provide civil and criminal penalties for trade secret theft (including cyber-theft and state-sponsored misappropriation) and prohibits forced disclosure of source code or algorithms as a condition of doing business, thus bolstering #TS protection in international trade.

**#GDPR**—General Data Protection Regulation: Although primarily focused on personal data privacy in the EU, the GDPR influences how companies handle all sensitive information. It intersects with trade secret protection because stringent data handling and security requirements apply to confidential business data as well. GDPR compliance (e.g., on data access or deletion requests) may sometimes conflict with maintaining #ConfidentialInfo secrecy, posing compliance challenges (#GDPRRisk) for trade secret holders.

**#ChinaTradeSecrets**—Chinese trade secret law: China's trade secret protection is governed largely by the Anti-Unfair Competition Law. Recent amendments (2018 and 2019) significantly strengthened the law's definitions and remedies for trade secret infringement by expanding who can be held liable (including third-party recipients of misappropriated secrets), shifting certain burdens of proof to alleged infringers, and increasing potential damages. These changes signal China's growing commitment to curbing trade secret theft and aligning with international standards under #TRIPS. (They were partly spurred by obligations in US–China trade agreements and aim to improve cross-border enforcement cooperation.)

**#TradeAgreements**—Refers broadly to other bilateral or multilateral accords that incorporate trade secret provisions and support a cohesive global framework for #TS protection. Examples include treaties like NAFTA (and its successor #USMCA), the Comprehensive and Progressive Agreement for Trans-Pacific Partnership (CPTPP), and various US–EU or regional agreements that commit parties to safeguard trade secrets. These agreements often require countries to adopt or enforce certain trade secret laws and facilitate cooperation against cross-border theft.

## Other Legal Frameworks

Additional legal doctrines and regulatory measures interact with trade secret law to enhance protection and enforcement.

**#ReverseEngineering**—The lawful process of analyzing a publicly available product to deduce its design, formula, or functionality (which may include discovering trade secrets), provided no contractual restrictions (such as an #NDA) are violated. Trade secret law permits reverse engineering as a legitimate means of discovery, meaning a company's #TS will not be protected if a competitor figures it out on their own through analysis of a lawfully obtained product.

**#ExportControls**—Regulatory measures that restrict the international transfer of sensitive technologies and information. They help protect trade secrets by preventing certain technical data or products (which may embody trade secrets) from being shared with or exported to unauthorized foreign parties. Export controls act as a legal safeguard by complementing trade secret policies, especially for industries dealing with defense or high-tech information (and relate to #TradeRegulations and international enforcement).

**#LawEnforcement**—In this context, it encompasses government actions and investigations to combat trade secret theft. It includes the work of agencies (like the FBI or DOJ in the United States ) using statutes such as the #EEA to investigate and prosecute theft or economic espionage. Strong law enforcement cooperation, sometimes involving international agencies like #Interpol, is vital for addressing criminal trade secret cases that cross borders.

**#Interpol**—Interpol is an international policing organization that supports cross-border investigations into crimes, including intellectual property theft and trade secret misappropriation. Through Interpol's coordination, countries work together to track and apprehend individuals involved in foreign or #EconomicEspionage, reinforcing global enforcement efforts against trade secret theft.

## Related Legal Fields

These are adjacent legal domains that intersect with trade secret law. They affect its scope, enforcement, and strategic use within a broader intellectual property portfolio. Many trade secret issues arise at the intersection of these fields.

**#PatentLaw**—Protects inventions by granting exclusive rights in exchange for public disclosure of the invention. Unlike trade secrets (#TS), patents require full disclosure but then protect against independent development or reverse engineering by others. Patent law is a complementary form of #IP that must be weighed against trade secret protection; companies often face a strategic choice between patenting an invention or keeping it as a trade secret (the patent vs. trade secret decision).

**#CopyrightLaw**—Safeguards original works of authorship fixed in a tangible medium, such as software code, writings, or designs. It overlaps with trade secret protection when companies have confidential source code or algorithms: they may keep them secret or release them and rely on copyright. However, copyright does not protect underlying ideas or confidential know-how, so it cannot fully substitute for trade secret protection of things like formulas or processes.

**#TrademarkLaw**—Protects brand identifiers, like logos, names, and slogans. While largely unrelated to the substance of trade secrets, a strong trademark coupled with secret business methods or formulas (e.g., a famous brand plus a secret recipe) can strengthen a company's overall #CompetitiveAdvantage. Trade secret law might also protect proprietary branding strategies or product launch plans that are kept confidential before execution.

**#PropertyLaw**—Governs ownership rights in both tangible and intangible assets, including trade secrets. There is scholarly debate about whether trade secrets are true property rights or just contractual/privacy rights, but in practice they are treated as valuable #IntangibleAssets that can be bought, sold (licensed), or counted as assets of a company.

**#ContractLaw**—Is central to trade secrets because confidentiality agreements and related contracts are foundational protective tools. Enforcing #NDAs, invention assignment agreements, and #NonCompete clauses relies on contract law. Strong contract law allows companies to bind employees and partners to secrecy obligations, which directly supports the protection of #ConfidentialInfo.

**#EmploymentLaw**—Governs the workplace relationship and sets limits on what employers can require of employees. It affects the enforceability of #NonCompete agreements and the handling of confidentiality obligations in employment contracts. Employment law strikes a balance between employees' rights (to change jobs or use general skills) and the employer's interest in protecting #TS, and it provides remedies for breaches (often overlapping with trade secret misappropriation claims).

**#AntitrustLaw**—Antitrust (competition) law ensures fair competition in the marketplace. It can come into play if a company's trade secret enforcement is so aggressive that it stifles legitimate competition (for example, collusion through trade secret licensing or using #NonCompete agreements broadly). Antitrust law and #CompetitionLaw may also limit how competitors can jointly use information (to avoid market allocation or price-fixing masked as trade secret protection). Generally, antitrust issues are rare in trade secret cases, but they remind companies not to misuse trade secrets to violate competition laws.

**#CyberLaw**—Covers legal issues related to cybersecurity, hacking, and data breaches. With most trade secrets stored digitally, cyber law is critical: it establishes obligations and liability around protecting electronic trade secrets. It intersects with trade secret law when prosecuting hackers, determining corporate liability for #DataBreach incidents, and setting standards (like #PrivacyLaw or data security regulations) that companies must follow to protect their #TSProtection efforts.

**#PrivacyLaw**—Regulates the handling of personal and sensitive data (examples include the #GDPR in the EU and laws like CCPA in California). Privacy requirements often overlap with trade secret management, as companies must handle personal data (perhaps of customers or employees) within their information systems. In some cases, privacy laws can conflict with trade secret practices (e.g., an individual's right to their personal data versus a company's desire to keep records confidential), requiring careful compliance (#GDPRCompliance) to protect secrets without violating privacy rights.

**#WhiteCollarCrime**—Refers to financially motivated, nonviolent crime typically committed by business professionals. Trade secret theft and economic espionage fall into this category. Prosecuting trade secret theft under laws like the #EEA or fraud statutes is part of white collar crime enforcement. This highlights that misappropriation is not just a civil matter but can rise to serious criminal conduct with significant penalties.

**#CorporateLaw**—Involves the governance of business entities and fiduciary duties of directors/officers. It intersects with trade secrets in areas like #CorporateGovernance (ensuring company leadership protects key assets like #TS) and in transactions (board decisions about protecting or sharing secrets in deals). Also, if insiders misappropriate secrets, it could breach their fiduciary duty to the company, giving rise to corporate law claims alongside trade secret claims. Effective #TSManagement is often considered part of good corporate stewardship of intellectual assets.

**#CommercialLitigation**—The process of resolving business disputes in court, including trade secret misappropriation lawsuits. Many trade secret enforcement actions end up as commercial litigation, so understanding the procedures and strategies of commercial litigation (e.g., discovery, injunction practice, use of #EvidenceLaw) is important for enforcing #TS rights. This field also covers breach of contract cases (like broken NDAs), which frequently accompany trade secret claims.

**#TortLaw**—Provides civil remedies for wrongful acts causing harm. Trade secret misappropriation can be pleaded as a tort (e.g., as "unfair competition" or conversion in some jurisdictions, though the UTSA preempts many tort claims in the United States). Tort law principles also come into play with #UnfairCompetition practices and when seeking #Damages or #ExemplaryDamages for willful misconduct.

**#CompetitionLaw**—Competition law (another term for antitrust, especially in an international context) regulates market competition. In the trade secret arena, competition law might limit how companies share information (e.g., in joint ventures or standard-setting) or guard against companies' using trade secret claims to harass competitors. It is related to #AntitrustRisk and ensures that protecting secrets does not cross into anti-competitive territory.

**#EvidenceLaw**—Governs what evidence can be presented in legal proceedings. In trade secret litigation, courts must balance the need to prove a case with the need to keep the trade secrets themselves confidential. Evidence law questions (like when to allow in-camera review, protective orders, or sealed filings) are crucial in #TSLawsuit procedures. Proper handling of evidence (e.g., showing that information was secret and misappropriated) often determines success in trade secret cases.

**#AdminLaw**—Covers the regulations and procedures of government agencies. It can affect trade secrets in contexts like #ExportControl enforcement (agencies regulating technology exports) or when companies submit trade secret data to agencies (e.g., FDA or EPA filings) and rely on administrative protections against disclosure. Administrative processes (such as the ITC's Section 337 investigations for IP theft) also provide alternative forums for trade secret enforcement outside the court system.

**#BankruptcyLaw**—Addresses how assets are handled when a company becomes insolvent. Trade secrets, as #IntangibleAssets, are part of the debtor's estate. Bankruptcy law ensures trade secrets are valued and transferred properly (sometimes they may be sold to satisfy creditors, which requires maintaining secrecy during due diligence). It also raises questions about the assumption or rejection of NDAs and the continuation of confidentiality obligations if a business is sold out of bankruptcy.

# Business and Commercial Considerations

This category highlights how trade secrets factor into business strategies, transactions, and collaborative ventures. It covers the commercial use and valuation of trade secrets, and how companies share or protect these assets in deals and partnerships.

**#Licensing**—The commercial strategy of granting another party rights to use a trade secret under a contract, typically in exchange for fees or royalties. Proper licensing of trade secrets requires maintaining confidentiality (through strict #ConfidentialityAgreement terms and oversight) so the secret is not publicly disclosed. It can be a way to monetize #TS (e.g., licensing a proprietary manufacturing process to a partner), but it carries #AntitrustRisk if done between competitors and always requires trust and verification that the licensee upholds secrecy obligations (related to #TechTransfer and #JointVenture scenarios).

**#TechTransfer**—The controlled sharing of trade secrets or proprietary technology between entities, often through collaborative agreements, research partnerships, or joint development projects. This can occur via #Licensing deals, university–industry collaborations, or cross-border partnerships. Managing tech transfer involves ensuring the receiving party implements adequate protections and complies with any #ExportControl laws. It is closely related to #JointVenture arrangements and often necessitates detailed contracts defining permitted use of the shared know-how.

**#JointVenture**—A business arrangement where two or more companies collaborate (forming a new entity or a formal alliance) and may need to share their respective trade secrets or know-how to achieve a common goal. In a JV, careful legal and operational safeguards are required: each side should disclose only what is necessary (#NeedToKnowFailure must be avoided), and agreements must specify ownership and permitted use of any contributed #ConfidentialInfo. JVs tie into #TechTransfer (as a mechanism of sharing) and pose #ThirdPartyRisk if one partner mishandles the other's secrets.

**#MergersAcq**—Mergers and Acquisitions: Trade secrets often play a significant role in M&A transactions as valuable assets that can enhance the acquiring company's competitive position. This concept covers how trade secrets are handled during mergers, acquisitions, or divestitures—including their evaluation and pricing (#Valuation); disclosure to the acquirer under confidentiality during #DueDiligence; and post-transaction integration, where combining workforces and systems must be done without losing secrecy. #M&ARisk is a related concept focusing on the risk of leaks during these deal processes.

**#DueDiligence**—The process of assessing assets and risks before entering a business transaction such as an investment, partnership, or acquisition. In the context of trade secrets, due diligence involves evaluating the target's #TSProtection measures, identifying key trade secrets, and ensuring that any required disclosure of those secrets (to potential buyers, investors, etc.) is done under strict #NDA and data room security. Effective due diligence will mitigate #M&ARisk and inform proper #Valuation of the trade secret assets.

**#Valuation**—Determining the financial worth of trade secrets for purposes of transactions, litigation, or internal strategy. Companies perform valuation of trade secrets during #MergersAcq (to set a price or assess goodwill), when licensing technology, or when seeking damages in a #TSLawsuit (where a reasonable royalty or lost profits may be calculated). Accurate valuation reflects a trade secret's contribution to #CompetitiveAdvantage and may consider factors like development cost savings, future income streams, and risk of loss. It ties into treating trade secrets as #IntangibleAssets on the balance sheet.

**#OpenInnovation**—Refers to collaborative innovation initiatives where a company works with external parties (such as open-source communities, crowdsourcing platforms, or industry consortia) to develop new ideas. The challenge in open innovation is balancing collaboration with secrecy; participants share knowledge but must be careful not to reveal core #TS. Companies engaged in open innovation often delineate what information can be openly shared and what must remain internal. This concept intersects with #ThirdPartyRisk (external collaborators could leak info) and may require a shift from a strict #CultureOfSecrecy to a more nuanced approach that still protects key secrets.

**#Outsourcing**—Outsourcing involves hiring external firms or contractors to perform services or develop products, which can expose trade secrets if those external entities handle sensitive information. Protecting #TS during outsourcing requires robust contracts (#ConfidentialityAgreement clauses, clear IP ownership) and oversight of the vendor's security practices. This concept highlights the need to extend internal #SecurityPolicy and #TSProtection measures to third parties. It is closely related to #VendorRisk and #ThirdPartyRisk, since an outsourcer's weak security or its personnel could lead to misappropriation of the client company's secrets.

# Risks and Threats

This category identifies the dangers that can lead to the misappropriation or loss of trade secrets, including external threats, legal pitfalls, regulatory challenges, economic pressures, and technological vulnerabilities.

## External Risks

Risks arising from external actors or factors that may expose or compromise trade secrets.

**#EconomicEspionage**—Involves deliberate theft of trade secrets for financial or competitive gain, often orchestrated by businesses or state-sponsored actors targeting foreign companies. Such actions undermine a company's #CompetitiveAdvantage and are punishable under criminal laws like the #EEA (which specifically addresses espionage benefiting foreign entities).

**#IndustrialEspionage**—The covert collection of confidential information by competitors seeking a market edge. This can include spying on a competitor's facilities, infiltrating their workforce, or eavesdropping on communications. It frequently overlaps with economic espionage tactics and can encompass both #CorporateEspionage and #CyberThreats modes of operation.

**#CorporateEspionage**—Refers to espionage activities carried out by or against companies (as opposed to state actors) to illicitly obtain confidential business data. This threatens #TS by enabling competitors to acquire proprietary know-how or strategies. It impacts #CompetitiveAdvantage and often involves #ImproperMeans, such as bribing insiders or covert surveillance.

**#ForeignEspionage**—Involves the theft of trade secrets by state-sponsored agents or entities affiliated with foreign governments. The goal is often to bolster national industries or military capabilities using stolen technology. Such acts are a focus of the #EEA (which has provisions for foreign government-sponsored theft) and underscore the need for international cooperation and robust #LawEnforcement efforts.

**#CyberThreats**—Include digital attacks such as hacking, malware, ransomware, or phishing that target a company's confidential information systems. Modern trade secrets are frequently stored digitally, so cyberattacks can compromise #TSProtection measures and lead to massive #DataBreach incidents. Companies must counter cyber threats with strong #EndpointSecurity, network monitoring, and incident response plans.

**#DataBreach**—A data breach is the unauthorized access, acquisition, or disclosure of sensitive information, often through cyberattack or accidental exposure. If the compromised data includes trade secrets or #ConfidentialInfo, the breach can destroy the information's secrecy and value. Data breach incidents can result from insufficient security, #InsiderThreat, or external hacking, and they often trigger legal obligations to respond and possibly notify authorities (though companies try to avoid disclosing exact trade secrets publicly even when reporting breaches).

**#SupplyChainRisk**—Supply chain risk arises when third-party vendors, suppliers, or partners with access to a company's information fail to secure it properly. A weakness anywhere in the supply chain (e.g., a parts manufacturer or an IT services provider) can lead to trade secret leakage. This concept highlights that a company's #TS is only as secure as the weakest link among its external collaborators, tying into #ThirdPartyRisk and emphasizing the need for #SupplyChainSecurity practices.

**#ThirdPartyRisk**—Third-party risk is the possibility that external partners, contractors, or vendors may mishandle or inadvertently expose confidential data entrusted to them. When companies share #ConfidentialInfo with outside parties (for outsourcing, partnerships, cloud services, etc.), those parties' security lapses or internal threats become an indirect risk. Third-party risk underscores why contracts, due diligence, and ongoing oversight of partners are critical for protecting #TS outside the organization's walls.

**#OverrelianceOnNDAs**—The mistaken belief that nondisclosure agreements alone are sufficient to protect trade secrets. While #NDAs are essential legal tools, the risk is that a company might neglect technical and administrative #ReasonableMeasures (like access controls, encryption, and monitoring) based on the belief that paper agreements will prevent leaks. Overreliance on NDAs can give a false sense of security: if an NDA is breached, the damage may already be done unless other protections are in place.

**#CompetitorThreat**—Refers to the active efforts by rival companies to acquire a target company's confidential information in order to weaken that target's #CompetitiveAdvantage. Competitors might use #CorporateEspionage, #TalentPoaching, aggressive #ReverseEngineering, or other tactics that, if crossing legal lines, amount to misappropriation. This concept underscores that competition is not always fair and that companies must be vigilant about competitor-driven risks.

**#TalentPoaching**—The deliberate hiring away of a competitor's employees with the intent to gain access to their expertise or trade secret knowledge. While recruiting experienced talent is legal, doing so specifically to obtain confidential know-how can lead to inevitable disclosure of the former employer's #TS. This practice raises concerns under #EmployeeMobility: it tests the limits of what a new hire can use from memory versus what is protected, and it often triggers #NonCompete disputes or litigation if there is suspicion of trade secret theft.

**#WhistleblowerRisk**—The potential that an employee, in disclosing wrongdoing to authorities or the public, might inadvertently or intentionally reveal trade secrets. It blurs the line between legitimate reporting (protected by #Whistleblower laws) and trade secret misappropriation. Companies mitigate this risk by having internal compliance programs (so issues can be reported internally under confidentiality) and by narrowly tailoring secrecy policies so they do not unlawfully silence whistleblowing.

## Legal Risks

Risks arising from legal challenges, disputes, or weaknesses in a company's intellectual property strategy that could weaken trade secret protection.

**#LitigationRisk**—The potential for costly and damaging legal disputes over trade secret issues. This includes the risk of being sued for misappropriation (defense costs, injunctions stopping your product) or the need to sue another (which can be expensive and expose your secrets in court). High-profile #TSLawsuits can also damage a company's reputation or distract management. Effective #IPStrategy and clear agreements can reduce litigation risk, but if a dispute arises, skilled #CommercialLitigation management is needed.

**#WeakIPStrategy**—Refers to a company's choosing the wrong form of intellectual property protection or not adequately protecting an innovation at all. For example, patenting an invention that would have been better kept as a secret (thereby disclosing it to competitors), or vice versa, or failing to identify key trade secrets to protect. This misstep can leave valuable information exposed or unprotected, undermining overall #TS security. It is related to #PatentLaw vs. trade secret decisions and can be revealed during #DueDiligence or #EmploymentDisputes when gaps are discovered.

**#EmploymentDisputes**—Conflicts with current or former employees over trade secret issues. This can include claims that an employee stole secrets to benefit a new employer, wrongful termination suits after an employee is fired for suspected misappropriation, or battles over the scope of #NonCompete and non-solicitation agreements. Such disputes can result in trade secret litigation and affect #EmployeeMobility broadly within an industry (e.g., a well-known case might deter other employees from jumping ship with knowledge).

**#BreachOfContract**—This risk arises when confidentiality agreements, NDAs, or other contracts meant to protect trade secrets are violated. If an ex-employee or business partner breaks their promise and discloses a secret, the contract breach not only undermines #ConfidentialInfo security but also forces the company to seek remedies through litigation. This risk underlines the importance of enforcing #ContractLaw provisions and possibly obtaining #Injunctions quickly when a breach is discovered.

**#AntitrustRisk**—Antitrust risk (competition law risk) is the possibility that actions taken to protect or share trade secrets may run afoul of competition laws. For instance, if competitors secretly agree to share certain technical information only with each other (excluding others), it could be seen as collusion. Or overly broad #NonCompete agreements could attract antitrust scrutiny for suppressing competition. Companies must ensure their trade secret enforcement or collaboration practices do not inadvertently limit market competition, linking this risk to #CompetitionLaw compliance.

## Regulatory and Compliance Risks

Risks associated with the evolving regulatory landscape and the challenges of meeting legal disclosure or compliance requirements while protecting trade secrets.

**#DataProtectionLaws**—Data protection laws such as the EU's GDPR or California's CCPA impose strict requirements on how sensitive data (including certain business data) is handled, stored, and transferred. Compliance with these laws can complicate trade secret management: for example, responding to a regulatory inquiry or data subject access request could risk revealing #ConfidentialInfo. Failure to comply is its own risk (fines, penalties), so companies must reconcile data privacy obligations with maintaining #TS secrecy.

**#ExportControls**—Regulations limiting the transfer of sensitive technology or information across national borders. Noncompliance can result in legal penalties and also inadvertently expose trade secrets (e.g., if a company must apply for a license, it might need to describe the technology). Adhering to #ExportControl laws protects against unauthorized foreign access to trade secrets but can be complex and impact collaborative research or international hiring. It is a compliance risk that intersects with trade secret strategy, especially in high-tech and defense sectors.

**#CrossBorderIP**—Refers to the difficulties in protecting trade secrets across multiple jurisdictions. Different countries may have varying definitions of trade secrets or levels of enforcement, complicating a unified protection strategy. For instance, pursuing a misappropriator who flees to another country can be hard if that country's laws are weaker. This risk underscores the need for awareness of international frameworks (like #TRIPS and local laws such as #ChinaTradeSecrets) and, sometimes, for pursuing remedies like #Interpol notices or multinational litigation.

**#GDPRRisk**—Refers to the specific challenges posed by the EU's data protection regime (GDPR) to trade secret practices. For example, GDPR might require a company to divulge certain personal data it holds if an individual requests it, even if that data is part of an internal database a company considers secret. There is also a risk that stringent security and minimization rules affect how companies collect and store proprietary data. Balancing GDPR compliance with #ConfidentialInfo preservation is an ongoing compliance tightrope for global companies.

**#TradeSecretDisclosure**—The danger that a company's confidential information might be revealed during legal or regulatory processes. This can happen in litigation (through #EvidenceLaw requirements or discovery) or in government filings (e.g., required submissions to patent offices, courts, or agencies). If not managed with protective orders or confidentiality provisions, such disclosures can destroy #TS status. Companies mitigate this risk by seeking court orders to seal records, by limiting detail in public filings, and by aggressive legal strategies to avoid compelled disclosure of the "crown jewels."

## Economic Risks

Financial pressures and market dynamics that may lead to the loss or devaluation of trade secrets.

**#VendorRisk**—The potential for external suppliers or service providers to mishandle confidential data, thereby exposing trade secrets and compromising #TSProtection. It highlights that outsourcing or relying on third-party technology (like cloud services or consultants) can introduce vulnerabilities if those vendors do not have strong security. Contractual clauses and vendor audits are common mitigations, but this risk is ever-present in complex supply chains (see #SupplyChainRisk).

**#M&ARisk**—M&A risk arises during mergers, acquisitions, or due diligence when sensitive information must be shared with the other party. There is a risk a deal may fall through and the would-be buyer walks away with knowledge of the target's secrets or that during integration, employees from the acquiring company improperly access the acquired company's confidential info. Such scenarios can undermine a company's #IntangibleAssets value. Careful staging of disclosure (only as needed), use of clean teams, and strong legal remedies in deal contracts help reduce M&A-related trade secret risk.

**#EconomicDownturnRisk**—Refers to increased vulnerability of trade secrets during tough economic times. In recessions or budget-cutting phases, companies might reduce spending on security or personnel training, or they may lay off employees (who could leave with knowledge or be disgruntled). Financial strain can also lead some to be more susceptible to selling secrets. Maintaining #TSProtection as a priority during downturns is critical despite pressure to cut costs.

**#InvestorRisk**—The possibility that during fundraising rounds or investor meetings, a startup or company might inadvertently disclose trade secrets to potential investors or analysts, reducing its #CompetitiveAdvantage. While investors often sign confidentiality agreements, the more people who know a secret, the greater the risk of leaks. Additionally, once investors are on board, they receive reports and data that could contain secrets. Companies must strike a balance between transparency with investors and safeguarding key details.

## Technological Risks

Risks stemming from digital vulnerabilities and emerging technologies that could compromise trade secrets.

**#AITradeSecretTheft**—Refers to the risk that advanced artificial intelligence tools could be used to infer or extract confidential information from available data. For example, an AI might analyze outputs or patterns (from a product or code) to reconstruct the underlying secret algorithm. As AI grows more powerful, traditional #TS safeguards may be challenged, which will require new methods (like monitoring AI outputs or employing AI to detect anomalies) to protect secrets.

**#WeakEncryption**—A vulnerability where a company's data encryption is outdated or insufficient, allowing attackers to decipher stolen data. If trade secret files or communications are not properly encrypted, a breach could immediately expose their contents. Weak encryption undermines #ConfidentialInfo protection. This risk prompts organizations to follow strong cryptographic practices and to update encryption methods in anticipation of threats like #QuantumRisk (quantum computing attacks on encryption).

**#QuantumRisk**—Quantum risk is the threat that emerging quantum computing technology could break current encryption methods, putting digitally stored trade secrets at risk. Much of today's secure storage relies on encryption that quantum computers may eventually crack. This risk is driving interest in "post-quantum" cryptography. It also relates to #CyberLaw and national security policy, as governments and companies prepare for a future where quantum attackers might target secret data archives.

**#CloudSecurityRisk**—Arises when a company stores trade secrets in cloud services or remote servers that are not adequately secured or configured. While reputable cloud providers invest in security, misconfigurations (like leaving a storage bucket public) or breaches at the provider could expose secrets. This risk underscores the need for strong #TSProtection policies specifically for cloud usage: encryption of data at rest, careful identity and access management, and vetting cloud providers' security protocols.

**#ZeroTrustFailure**—Occurs when an organization's "zero trust" security model (which assumes no user or device is trustworthy by default) is not properly implemented, thus allowing unauthorized access to sensitive data. If zero trust principles fail (due to misconfiguration or user workarounds), sensitive #TS could be accessed by threat actors who penetrated one part of the network. This highlights that even modern security frameworks require continuous assessment. A zero trust approach, when working, can greatly strengthen #TSProtection, but failure in any link can open a door to attackers.

**#ShadowIT**—The use of unauthorized hardware, software, or cloud services within an organization, outside the official IT infrastructure. Employees might use personal apps or devices to handle work data for convenience. This practice bypasses official security controls and can lead to trade secret exposure (for example, an engineer using an unapproved file-sharing app might inadvertently leak a confidential design document). Shadow IT is a challenge for #SecurityPolicy enforcement and calls for employee training (#EmployeeTraining) to prevent unsanctioned tech use.

**#DeviceSecurity**—This risk involves threats like lost, stolen, or compromised devices (laptops, USB drives, smartphones) that contain trade secret information. If an employee's laptop with unencrypted confidential files is stolen, the trade secrets could be revealed. This risk is managed by #EndpointSecurity measures such as encryption, remote wipe capabilities, and strong authentication. It reminds organizations that physical loss of hardware can be as damaging as a cyber breach if not mitigated.

**#DeepFakeThreat**—Refers to the use of AI-generated audio or video impersonations to deceive individuals into disclosing confidential information. For example, a deepfake could mimic an executive's voice on a phone call to trick an employee into sharing a trade secret. This is a novel social-engineering risk that challenges traditional verification methods. Combating it requires updated policies (like multi-factor verification for sensitive requests) and awareness training, linking it to both #CyberThreats and human factor vulnerabilities.

## Internal Risks

This category focuses on risks originating within the organization due to employee behavior, management practices, or organizational culture that can lead to the inadvertent or deliberate loss of trade secrets.

**#InsiderThreat**—The risk that employees, contractors, or other trusted insiders will intentionally or unintentionally disclose confidential information. Insiders have legitimate access to #ConfidentialInfo, so their actions (from malicious theft to careless handling) can undermine trade secret protection. Effective mitigation includes monitoring, access controls ("need-to-know" principles), and fostering loyalty and awareness to reduce the likelihood of insiders turning into threats.

**#EmployeeNegligence**—Refers to inadvertent mistakes by staff—such as mishandling documents, using weak passwords, falling for phishing scams, or losing devices—that result in exposure of trade secrets. This highlights the human error component of security. Regular #EmployeeTraining, clear #SecurityPolicy, and technical safeguards (like requiring encryption on devices) are used to combat negligence-related leaks.

**#OnboardingRisk**—The danger that new hires may bring proprietary information from their former employer (which is not legally theirs to bring) or that they might mishandle their old employer's secrets within their new role. This can inadvertently compromise the new employer and violate the old employer's trade secret rights. Companies mitigate this risk by training new hires not to reveal others' secrets, using "clean room" designs for sensitive projects, and sometimes delaying start of assignments to avoid #InevitableDisclosure claims.

**#ExitInterviewRisk**—The possibility that departing employees may take or fail to return confidential information when they leave a company. If the offboarding process is lax—no check of devices, no reminders of obligations—an employee might walk out with trade secret files or simply rely on memory of sensitive information at a new job. Conducting thorough exit interviews and exit protocols (collecting devices, disabling access, reiterating #NDA obligations) is essential to maintain #TSProtection post-employment.

**#NeedToKnowFailure**—Occurs when confidential information is shared internally with individuals who do not require it for their work. If a company does not enforce need-to-know principles, then more employees than necessary will know a given trade secret, which will increase the odds of accidental or intentional leaks. Such failures weaken internal controls and can be exploited by insiders or through social engineering. Maintaining proper #AccessControl and compartmentalization of secrets helps prevent this risk.

**#CultureOfSecrecy**—Means fostering an environment where confidentiality is a priority and employees understand the importance of protecting information. A failure in this culture (i.e., a culture that does not emphasize secrecy) increases the likelihood of trade secret disclosures because employees may not take policies seriously or may share information casually. Conversely, a strong culture of secrecy supports all other measures by making security "everyone's responsibility." Balancing this with openness for innovation is important (too much secrecy can stifle collaboration), so leadership must promote prudent confidentiality.

## Operational Protections

This category outlines proactive internal measures and policies that organizations implement to secure their trade secrets against both internal and external threats. These are the best practices and tools for prevention.

**#TSProtection**—In practice, this encompasses the overall strategies, policies, and physical/digital safeguards an organization uses to secure confidential information and maintain its secrecy. It is an umbrella concept that includes legal agreements, technical security, employee training, and any other method deployed to prevent misappropriation or leaks of #TS.

**#TSManagement**—The systematic process of identifying, classifying, and maintaining trade secrets within an organization. This involves creating a registry or inventory of what the company considers its trade secrets, labeling and securing them appropriately, and regularly auditing these assets. Good #TSManagement ensures no important secret is overlooked and that all are adequately protected through #ReasonableMeasures.

**#TSPP**—Trade Secret Protection Program: A formal, comprehensive framework that a company establishes to safeguard its trade secrets. A #TSPP typically integrates multiple elements (asset inventory, risk assessment, employee policies, incident response plans) into one cohesive program. It often involves cross-department coordination (legal, IT, HR, physical security) and is reviewed and updated over time as new threats emerge.

**#ReasonableMeasures**—The practical, proportionate steps that a trade secret owner is expected to take to keep information secret. Laws like the UTSA/DTSA require owners to implement such measures for information to qualify as a trade secret. Examples include using #NDAs, restricting access on a need-to-know basis, encryption of files, facility security, #EmployeeTraining, and monitoring. What is "reasonable" may scale with the value of the secret; extremely valuable secrets might warrant very extensive measures (like the Coca-Cola vault example).

**#NDA**—Nondisclosure agreement: A legally binding contract in which one or more parties agree to keep specified information confidential and not disclose it to others. NDAs are foundational in protecting trade secrets when sharing information with employees, contractors, or business partners. A well-drafted #NDA defines the confidential information, the permitted uses, and the duration of secrecy. It provides a contractual basis to sue for #BreachOfContract if someone leaks a secret, and it often deters casual disclosures.

**#ConfidentialityAgreement**—A broad term for contracts that impose confidentiality obligations, of which #NDAs are a common example. It can also include clauses within larger contracts (like employment agreements, joint venture agreements, or service contracts) that require parties to keep shared information secret. These agreements both reinforce and complement trade secret protections by legally binding parties to secrecy. (In essence, this is synonymous with an NDA, but the term can encompass various forms such obligations take in different contracts.)

**#NonCompete**—An agreement that restricts an employee (or business seller, etc.) from working for competitors or starting a competing business for a specified period after leaving a company. The primary aim is to prevent the #InevitableDisclosure of trade secrets and sensitive know-how to competitors via employee mobility. Noncompetes must be reasonable in duration and scope to be enforceable, and their use is regulated or restricted in many jurisdictions for policy reasons. They are often used alongside NDAs to protect #TS, although their enforceability varies by state/country.

**#EmployeeTraining**—Involves, in the context of trade secret protection, educating staff about the company's confidentiality policies, its security procedures, and employees' personal obligations to protect sensitive information. Regular training sessions and reminders reduce #EmployeeNegligence by making employees aware of social engineering tricks (like phishing), proper document handling, and reporting protocols for suspected leaks. By instilling good practices, training supports a stronger #CultureOfSecrecy and helps every employee become a line of defense for #TSProtection.

**#SecurityPolicy**—Refers to the internal rules and procedures a company establishes to safeguard its information and systems. This includes written policies on topics like clean desk rules, document classification, password requirements, device use, remote access, incident response, and more. A robust security policy underpins trade secret protection by setting clear expectations and guidelines for behavior. It works hand-in-hand with technical measures and #EmployeeTraining, and it provides a framework to enforce discipline if someone violates security protocols (which could lead to an #InsiderThreat incident if not addressed).

**#EndpointSecurity**—Encompasses protective measures for end-user devices (computers, smartphones, tablets, USB drives) that store or access company data. For trade secrets, endpoint security means ensuring that devices are encrypted, require strong authentication, are kept updated against malware, and can be remotely wiped if lost. Since many breaches occur through lost or compromised devices (#DeviceSecurity issues), maintaining strict endpoint security is a critical part of #ReasonableMeasures to guard #ConfidentialInfo.

## Enforcement and Remedies

This category details the legal avenues and remedies available to trade secret owners when misappropriation occurs, including both civil and criminal actions.

**#Injunction**—A court order that requires a party to do or refrain from doing specific acts. In trade secret cases, injunctions are often used to stop further misappropriation or disclosure of secrets; for example, a court might bar a defendant from using the stolen secret or sharing it with others. Injunctions (especially temporary restraining orders or preliminary injunctions) are crucial early remedies to prevent ongoing harm and preserve the status quo while a case is litigated.

**#ExParteSeizure**—A unique remedy introduced by the #DTSA that allows a court to order the seizure of property (e.g., computers, documents) containing misappropriated trade secrets without prior notice to the defendant. It is used only in extraordinary circumstances where there is a high risk that the defendant would destroy or hide the evidence if warned. This remedy helps quickly secure the stolen trade secret material and is followed by a hearing shortly after. It is a powerful but sparingly used tool to prevent imminent threats.

**#Damages**—Refers to monetary compensation awarded to a trade secret owner for losses resulting from misappropriation. Under trade secret law, damages can include the actual loss suffered by the plaintiff (e.g., lost profits or costs incurred from the theft) and/or the unjust enrichment obtained by the defendant (profits the wrongdoer gained from using the secret). In some cases where calculating these is difficult, courts may impose a reasonable royalty for the unauthorized use of the secret. Damages aim to make the injured party whole.

**#ExemplaryDamages**—Also known as punitive damages, these are additional damages awarded to punish and deter particularly egregious behavior. Under the UTSA and the DTSA, if the misappropriation is found to be willful and malicious, courts may award up to double the amount of normal damages as exemplary damages. These are not meant to compensate the owner but to penalize the wrongdoer and send a message. Exemplary damages, along with possible #AttorneysFees, serve as a deterrent against intentional trade secret theft.

**#AttorneysFees**—The legal costs incurred by the parties. In trade secret cases, courts can order the losing party to pay the prevailing party's attorneys' fees, but typically only in scenarios of bad faith or willful/malicious misappropriation (under UTSA/DTSA provisions). This is to discourage frivolous claims or willful wrongdoing. The possibility of attorneys' fees recovery can influence the strategy of litigation (e.g., a company might be more willing to sue a willful thief, knowing they could recover legal costs).

**#CriminalTSTheft**—Refers to the prosecution of trade secret misappropriation under criminal laws (such as the #EEA in the United States or similar statutes elsewhere). Unlike civil #Litigation brought by the trade secret owner, criminal cases are brought by the government and can result in fines and imprisonment for the offenders. This emphasizes that stealing trade secrets is not just a civil wrong but can be a crime, especially if it involves foreign espionage (#ForeignEspionage) or large-scale theft.

**#Litigation**—The process of resolving disputes through the court system. In the context of trade secrets, litigation typically means a civil lawsuit filed by a trade secret owner against an alleged misappropriator (a #TSLawsuit). Litigation encompasses pleadings, discovery (where evidence is exchanged—often tricky when the evidence is a secret), motions, trial, and possibly appeals. It is a key enforcement mechanism when other measures (like negotiations or cease-and-desist letters) fail to stop misappropriation.

**#TSLawsuit**—Refers to a specific civil action initiated by a trade secret owner to seek legal redress for misappropriation. Such a lawsuit can be filed under state law (UTSA-based) or federal law (#DTSA), or both. In a #TSLawsuit, the plaintiff aims to prove that the information was a protectable trade secret and that the defendant misappropriated it, in the hope of obtaining remedies like #Injunctions, #Damages, or permanently halting the defendant's use of the secret. #TSLawsuits often involve complex evidence (technical data, forensic records of access) and may be filed in conjunction with other claims, like breach of contract.

**#StatuteOfLimitations**—The legally prescribed time period within which a trade secret claim must be filed. Under the DTSA and most versions of the UTSA, the statute of limitations is 3 years from when the misappropriation was discovered or reasonably should have been discovered. This rule encourages prompt action by trade secret owners once they learn of a theft. If a company waits too long and the statute expires, they lose the right to bring a lawsuit, regardless of the merits.

# Table of Cases

# Index